Maturin Murray Ballou

Due North

Or, Glimpses of Scandinavia and Russia

Maturin Murray Ballou

Due North

Or, Glimpses of Scandinavia and Russia

ISBN/EAN: 9783337164966

Printed in Europe, USA, Canada, Australia, Japan

Cover: Foto ©Andreas Hilbeck / pixelio.de

More available books at **www.hansebooks.com**

DUE NORTH

OR

GLIMPSES OF SCANDINAVIA AND RUSSIA

BY

MATURIN M. BALLOU

AUTHOR OF "EDGE-TOOLS OF SPEECH," "DUE SOUTH; OR, CUBA, PAST AND PRESENT," "GENIUS IN SUNSHINE AND SHADOW," ETC.

> Only that travelling is good which reveals to me the value of home, and enables me to enjoy it better. — THOREAU.

BOSTON
TICKNOR AND COMPANY
1887

University Press:
JOHN WILSON AND SON, CAMBRIDGE.

PREFACE.

ABOUT five years ago, the Author, having then just returned from circumnavigating the globe, was induced to record his experiences of the long journey, which were published in a volume entitled "Due West; or, Round the World in Ten Months." The public favor accorded to this work led, a couple of years later, to the issuing of a second volume of travels, upon the Author's return from the West Indies, entitled "Due South; or, Cuba, Past and Present." The popular success of both books and the flattering comments of the critics have caused the undersigned to believe that a certain portion of the public is pleased to see foreign lands and people through his eyes; and hence the publication of the volume now in hand. These pages describing the far North, from which the Author has just returned, — including Norway, Sweden, Russia, and Russian Poland,— seem naturally to suggest the title of "Due North." Without permitting prejudice to circumscribe judgment in treating of Russia, the effort has been to represent the condition of that country and its Polish province truthfully, and to draw only reasonable deductions. This special reference is made to the pages relating to the Tzar's government, as it will be found that the Author does not accord with the popularly expressed opinion upon this subject.

M. M. B.

Boston, March, 1887.

CONTENTS.

CHAPTER I.

Copenhagen. — First Stroll in a Strange City. — Danish Children. — Antiquity of Copenhagen. — English Arrogance. — The Baltic Sea. — Danish Possessions. — Descendants of the Vikings. — Covetous Germany. — The Denmark of To-day. — Thorwaldsen's Remarkable Museum. — The Ethnological Museum. — Educational Matters. — Eminent Natives. — Charitable Institutions. — Antique Churches. — Royal Palaces. — Historical Memories. — City Architecture. — Zoölogical Gardens 1-23

CHAPTER II.

Public Amusements in Copenhagen. — Danish Sovereigns. — The Fashionable Promenade. — Danish Women. — Palace of Rosenborg. — A Golconda of Gems. — A Poet's Monument. — A Famous Astronomer. — Our Lady's Church. — The King's Square. — The Curious Old Round Tower. — The Peasantry. — A Famous Deer Park. — Röskilde. — Elsinore. — Gypsies. — Kronborg Castle. — The Queen's Prison. — Hamlet and Ophelia's Grave. — A Danish Legend 24-40

CHAPTER III.

Gottenburg. — Ruins of Elfsborg. — Gustavus Adolphus. — A Wrecked Monument. — The Girdle-Duellists. — Emigration to America. — Public and Private Gardens. — A Kindly People. — The Götha Canal. — Falls of Trollhätta. — Dainty Wild-Flowers. — Water-Ways. — Stockholm and Lake Maelaren. — Prehistoric Tokens. — Iron Mines of Sweden. — Pleasing Episode with Children. — The Liquor Traffic Systematized. — A Great Practical Charity. — A Domestic Habit 41-56

CHAPTER IV.

Capital of Norway. — A Grand Fjord. — A Free and Independent State. — The Legal Code. — Royal Palace and Gardens. — Oscar's Hall. — The University. — Public Amusements. — The Ice Trade. — Ancient Viking Ships. — Heathen Tombs. — An Interesting Hostelry. — A Steam Kitchen. — Environs of Christiania. — Horses and their Treatment. — Harvest Time. — Women's Work. — The Sæter. — A Remarkable Lake. — Wild Birds. — Inland Travel. — Scandinavian Wild Flowers. — Lonely Habitations. — A Land of Alpine Heights . . . 57–85

CHAPTER V.

Ancient Capital of Norway. — Routes of Travel. — Rain! — Peasant Costumes. — Commerce of Bergen. — Shark's *vs.* Cod Liver Oil. — Ship-Building. — Public Edifices. — Quaint Shops. — Borgund Church. — Leprosy in Norway. — Sporting Country. — Inland Experiences. — Hay-Making. — Pine-Forest Experiences. — National Constitution. — People's Schools. — Girls' Industrial School. — Celebrated Citizens of Bergen. — Two Grand Norwegian Fjords. — Remarkable Glaciers 86–101

CHAPTER VI.

Ancient and Modern Trondhjem. — Runic Inscriptions. — A Famous Old Cathedral. — Local Characteristics. — Romantic Story of King Olaf. — Curious Local Productions. — An Island Prison. — Lafoss Falls. — Corn Magazines. — Land-owners. — Wood-cutters. — Forests. — A Tumble Overboard. — A Genuine Cockney. — Comparative Length of Days. — Characteristics of Boreal Regions. — Arctic Winter Fisheries. — The Ancient Town of Lund; the Oxford of Sweden. — Pagan Times 102–115

CHAPTER VII.

Along the Coast of Norway. — Education at the Far North. — An Interesting Character. — A Botanical Enthusiast. — Remarkable Mountain Tunnel. — A Hard Climb. — The Seven

CONTENTS. ix

Sisters. — Young England. — An Amateur Photographer. — Horseman's Island. — Ancient Town of Bodöe. — Arctic Flowers. — The Famous Maelström. — Illusions! — The Wonderful Lofoden Islands. — Grand and Unique Scenery. — Glaciers. — Nature's Architecture. — Mysterious Effects. — Attraction for Artists 116-135

CHAPTER VIII.

Birds of the Arctic Regions. — Effect of Continuous Daylight. — Town of Tromsöe. — The Aurora Borealis. — Love of Flowers. — The Growth of Trees. — Butterflies. — Home Flowers. — Trees. — Shooting Whales with Cannon. — Prehistoric Relics. — About Laplanders. — Eider Ducks. — A Norsk Wedding Present. — Gypsies of the North. — Pagan Rites. — The Use of the Reindeer. — Domestic Life of the Lapps. — Marriage Ceremony. — A Gypsy Queen. — Lapp Babies. — Graceful Acknowledgment 136-155

CHAPTER IX.

Experiences Sailing Northward. — Arctic Whaling. — The Feathered Tribe. — Caught in a Trap. — Domestic Animals. — The Marvellous Gulf Stream. — Town of Hammerfest. — Commerce. — Arctic Mosquitoes. — The Public Crier. — Norwegian Marriages. — Peculiar Bird Habits. — A Hint to Naturalists. — Bird Island. — A Lonely Habitation. — High Latitude. — Final Landing at the North Cape. — A Hard Climb. — View of the Wonderful Midnight Sun 156-168

CHAPTER X.

Journey Across Country. — Capital of Sweden. — Old and New. — Swedish History. — Local Attractions. — King Oscar II. — The Royal Palace. — The Westminster Abbey of Stockholm. — A Splendid Deer Park. — Public Amusements. — The Sabbath. — An Official Dude. — An Awkward Statue. — Swedish Nightingales. — Linnæus and Swedenborg. — Dalecarlia Girls. — A Remarkable Group in Bronze. — Rosedale Royal Cottage. — Ancient Oaks. — Upsala and its Surroundings. — Ancient Mounds at old Upsala. — Swedenborg's Study 169-192

CHAPTER XI.

The Northern Mediterranean. — Depth of the Sea. — Where Amber comes From. — A Thousand Isles. — City of Åbo. — Departed Glory. — Capital of Finland. — Local Scenes. — Russian Government. — Finland's Dependency. — Billingsgate. — A Woman Sailor in an Exigency. — Fortress of Sweaborg. — Fortifications of Cronstadt. — Russia's Great Naval Station. — The Emperor's Steam Yacht. — A Sail up the Neva. — St. Petersburg in the Distance. — First Russian Dinner 193–205

CHAPTER XII.

St. Petersburg. — Churches. — The Alexander Column. — Principal Street. — Cathedral of Peter and Paul. — Nevsky Monastery. — Russian Priesthood. — The Canals. — Public Library. — Cruelty of an Empress. — Religious Devotion of the People. — A Dangerous Locality. — Population. — The Neva and Lake Ladoga. — The Nicholas Bridge. — Winter Season. — Begging Nuns. — Nihilism. — Scandal Touching the Emperor. — The Fashionable Drive. — St. Isaac's Church. — Russian Bells. — Famous Equestrian Statue. — The Admiralty. — Architecture 206–240

CHAPTER XIII.

The Winter Palace. — The Hermitage and its Riches. — An Empress and her Fancies. — A Royal Retreat. — Russian Culture. — Public Library. — The Summer Garden. — Temperature of the City. — Choosing of the Brides. — Peter's Cottage. — Champ de Mars. — Academy of Fine Arts. — School of Mines. — Precious Stones. — The Imperial Home at Peterhoff. — Curious and Interesting Buildings. — Catherine's Oak. — Alexander III. at Parade. — Description of the Royal Family. — Horse-Racing. — The Empress's Companions 241–264

CHAPTER XIV.

Power of the Greek Church. — Freeing the Serfs. — Education Needed. — Mammoth Russia. — Religion and Superstition. — Memorial Structures. — Church Fasts. — Theatres and

Public Amusements. — Night Revels. — A Russian Bazaar. —
Children's Nurses in Costume. — The one Vehicle of Russia.
— Dress of the People. — Fire Brigade. — Red Tape. —
Personal Surveillance. — Passports. — Annoyances. — Spying
Upon Strangers. — The Author's Experience. — Censorship of
the Press 265–279

CHAPTER XV.

On the Road to Moscow. — Russian Peasantry. — Military Station Masters. — Peat Fuel for the War-Ships. — Farm Products. — Scenery. — Wild-Flowers. — City of Tver. — Inland Navigation. — The Great River Volga. — The Ancient Muscovite Capital. — Spires and Minarets. — A Russian Mecca. — Pictorial Signs. — The Kremlin. — The Royal Palace. — King of Bells. — Cathedral of St. Basil. — The Royal Treasury. — Church of Our Saviour. — Chinese City. — Rag Fair. — Manufactures 280–305

CHAPTER XVI.

Domestic Life in Moscow. — Oriental Seclusion of Women. — The Foundling Hospital. — A Christian Charity. — A Metropolitan Centre. — City Museum. — The University. — Tea-Drinking. — Pleasure Gardens. — Drosky Drivers. — Riding-School. — Theatres. — Universal Bribery. — Love of Country. — Russians as Linguists. — Sparrow Hill. — Petrofski Park. — Muscovite Gypsies. — Fast Life. — Intemperance. — A Famous Monastery. — City Highways. — Sacred Pigeons. — Beggars 306–332

CHAPTER XVII.

Nijni-Novgorod. — Hot Weather. — The River Volga. — Hundreds of Steamers. — Great Annual Fair. — Peculiar Character of the Trade. — Motley Collection of Humanity. — An Army of Beggars. — Rare and Precious Stones. — The Famous Brick Tea. — A Costly Beverage. — Sanitary Measures. — Disgraceful Dance Halls. — Fatal Beauty. — A Sad History. — Light-Fingered Gentry. — Convicts. — Facts about Siberia. — Local Customs. — Russian Punishment 333–352

CHAPTER XVIII.

On the Road to Poland. — Extensive Grain-Fields. — Polish Peasantry. — A Russian General. — No evidence of Oppression. — Warsaw and its Surroundings. — Mingled Squalor and Elegance. — Monuments of the City. — Polish Nobility. — Circassian Troops. — Polish Language. — The Jews of Warsaw. — Political Condition of Poland. — Public Parks. — The Famous Saxony Gardens. — Present Commercial Prosperity. — Local Sentiment. — Concerning Polish Ladies and Jewish Beauties 353-373

DUE NORTH;

OR,

GLIMPSES OF SCANDINAVIA AND RUSSIA.

CHAPTER I.

Copenhagen. — First Stroll in a Strange City. — Danish Children. — Antiquity of Copenhagen. — English Arrogance. — The Baltic Sea. — Danish Possessions. — Descendants of the Vikings. — Covetous Germany. — The Denmark of To-day. — Thorwaldsen's Remarkable Museum. — The Ethnological Museum. — Educational Matters. — Eminent Natives. — Charitable Institutions. — Antique Churches. — Royal Palaces. — Historical Memories. — City Architecture. — Zoölogical Gardens.

HAVING resolved upon a journey due north, twenty days of travel over familiar routes carried the author across the Atlantic and, by the way of Liverpool, London, Paris, and Hamburg, landed him in Copenhagen, the pleasant and thrifty capital of Denmark. As the following pages will be devoted to Scandinavia, Russia, and Russian Poland, this metropolis seems to be a proper locality at which to begin the northern journey with the reader.

It was already nearly midnight when the Hôtel D'Angleterre, fronting upon the Kongens Nytorv, was reached. So long a period of uninterrupted travel, night and day, rendered a few hours of quiet sleep something to be gratefully appreciated. Early the next morning the consciousness of being in a strange city, always so stimulating to the observant traveller, sent us forth with curious eyes upon the thoroughfares of the Danish capital before the average citizen was awake. The importunities of couriers and local guides, who are always on the watch for visitors, were at first sedulously ignored; for it would be foolish to rob one's self of the great pleasure of a preliminary stroll alone amid scenes and localities of which one is blissfully ignorant. A cicerone will come into the programme later on, and is a prime necessity at the proper time; but at the outset there is a keen gratification and novelty in verifying or contradicting preconceived ideas, by threading unattended a labyrinth of mysterious streets and blind alleys, leading one knows not where, and suddenly coming out upon some broad square or boulevard full of unexpected palaces and grand public monuments.

It was thus that we wandered into the old Market Square where Dietrick Slagheck, Archbishop of Lund and minister of Christian II., was burned alive. A slight stretch of the imagination made the place still to smell of roasted bishop. "Is this also the land of wooden shoes?" we asked ourself, as the rapid clatter of human feet upon the pavements recalled the familiar street-echoes of Antwerp. How eagerly the eye receives and retains each new impression under such circumstances! How sharp it is to search out peculiarities of dress, manners, architecture, modes of conveyance, the attractive display of merchandise in shop-windows, and even the expression upon the faces of men, women, and children! Children! if any one says the Danish children are not pretty, you may with safety contradict him. Their delicately rounded, fresh young faces are lit up by such bright, turquoise-colored, forget-me-not blue eyes as appeal to the heart at once. What a wholesome appetite followed upon this pioneer excursion, when we entered at breakfast on a new series of observations while satisfying the vigorous calls of hunger, each course proving a novelty, and every dish a fresh voyage of gastronomic discovery!

Copenhagen was a large commercial port many centuries ago, and has several times been partially destroyed by war and conflagration. It has some two hundred and fifty thousand inhabitants, and is about six miles in circumference. The site of the city is so low as to render it necessary to protect it from the waters of the Baltic by artificial embankments. Like Amsterdam and Venice, it may be said to possess "remarkable water-privileges." We were told that the citizens were making earnest remonstrance as to the inefficient drainage of the city, which is believed to be the prime cause of a somewhat extraordinary percentage of mortality. In past times it has more than once been visited by the plague, which so late as 1711 caused the death of over twenty-eight thousand of its inhabitants. It is only some thirty years since, that over five thousand persons died here of cholera in one season. Fevers of a typhoid character prevail annually, which are no doubt with good reason attributed to want of proper drainage. Notwithstanding Copenhagen is situated so nearly at tide level, modern engineering could easily perfect a system of drainage which would render it independent of this circumstance. The safe and spacious harbor is formed by the channel between the islands of Zeeland and Amager, where there is ample depth and room to answer the demands of a far more extended commerce than the city is ever likely to maintain. The houses are mostly of brick, some of the better class being built of Norwegian granite, while the newer portion of the town presents many examples of fine modern architecture. The streets are of good width and laid out with an eye to regularity, besides which there are sixteen spacious public squares. Taken as a whole, the first impression of the place and its surroundings is remarkably pleasing and attractive. As one approaches the city, the scene is enlivened by the many windmills in the environs, whose wide-spread arms are generally in motion, appearing like the broad wings of enormous birds hovering over the land and just preparing to alight. One is hardly surprised that Don Quixote should mistake them for palpable enemies, and charge upon them full tilt. Perhaps the earliest associations in its modern history which the stranger is likely to remember, as he looks about him in Copenhagen, is that of the dastardly attack upon the city, and the shelling of it for three consecutive days, by

the British fleet in 1807, during which uncalled for
and reckless onslaught an immense destruction of
human life and property was inflicted upon the place.
Over three hundred important buildings were laid in
ashes on that occasion, because Denmark refused permission for the domiciling of English troops upon her
soil, and declined, as she had a most unquestionable
right to do, to withdraw her connection with the neu-
tral powers. It was one of the most outrageous examples of English arrogance on record, — one which
even her own historians feel compelled to denounce
emphatically. No wonder the gallant Nelson expressed his deep regret at being sent to the Baltic on
such distasteful service. Copenhagen received the expressive name it bears (Merchant's Haven) on account
of its excellent harbor and general commercial advantages. As in the Mediterranean so in the Baltic, tidal
influence is felt only to a small degree, the difference
in the rise and fall of the water at this point being
scarcely more than one foot. It should be remembered,
however, that the level of the waters of the Baltic are
subject, like those of the Swiss lakes, to barometric
variations. Owing to the comparatively fresh character of this sea, its ports are ice-bound for a third of
each year, and in extreme seasons the whole expanse is
frozen across from the Denmark to the Swedish coast.
In 1658, Charles X. of Sweden marched his army
across the Belts, dictating to the Danes a treaty of
peace; and so late as 1809, a Russian army passed
from Finland to Sweden across the Gulf of Bothnia.

The possessions of Denmark upon the main-land are in our day quite circumscribed, consisting of Jutland only; but she has besides several islands far and near, of which Zeeland is the most populous, and contains the capital. As a State, she may be said to occupy a much larger space in history than upon the map of Europe. The surface of the island of Zeeland is uniformly low, in this respect resembling Holland, the highest point reaching an elevation of but five hundred and fifty feet. To be precise in the matter of her dominions, the colonial possessions of Denmark may be thus enumerated: Greenland, Iceland, the Faroe group of islands, between the Shetlands and Iceland; adding St. Croix, St. Thomas, and St. John in the West Indies. Greenland is nearly as large as Germany and France combined; but its inhabitants do not quite reach an aggregate of ten thousand. Iceland is about the size of our New England States, and has a population of seventy-five thousand. The Faroes contain ten thousand inhabitants, and the three West Indian islands united have a population of a little over forty thousand.

A slight sense of disappointment was realized at not finding more visible evidences of antiquity while visiting the several sections of the capital, particularly as it was remembered that a short time since, in 1880, the Danish monarchy reached the thousandth anniversary of its foundation under Gorm the Old, whose reign bridges over the interval between mere legend and the dawn of recorded history. Gorm is supposed to have been a direct descendant of the famous Viking, Regnar Lodbrog, who was a daring and imperious ruler of the early Northmen. The common origin of the three Baltic nationalities which constitute Scandinavia is clearly apparent to the traveller who has visited Denmark, Sweden, and Norway, or to any one who has even an ordinary knowledge of their history. The race has been steadily modified, generation after generation, in its more vivid characteristics, by the progressive force of civilization. These Northmen are no longer the haughty and reckless warriors who revelled in wine drunk from the skulls of their enemies, and who deemed death only respectable when encountered upon the battle-field. Clearer intelligence and culture have substituted the duties of peaceful citizens for those of marauders, and the enterprises of civilized life for the exaggerated romance of chivalry. Reading and writing, which were looked upon among them as allied to the black art a few centuries ago, are now the universal accomplishment of all classes, and nowhere on the globe will the traveller find a people more cheerful, intelligent, frank, and hospitable than in the three kingdoms of the far North.

Though the Danes are physically rather small, resembling in this respect the Japanese, still they spring, as we have seen, from a brave and warlike race, and have never been subjugated by any other people. On the contrary, in the olden time they conquered England, dismembered France, and subjugated

Norway and Sweden. The time has been when the Danes boasted the largest and most efficient navy in the world, and their realm still justly bears the title of "Queen of the Baltic." As to seamanship, they are universally acknowledged to be among the best sailors who navigate the ocean. That Germany covets Denmark is more than hinted at. The author heard a loud-talking naval gentleman, of German nationality, coolly express the opinion that Denmark as an independent kingdom had nearly reached the close of its existence. This was on board the German mail-steamer, while crossing a branch of the Baltic between the ports of Kiel and Korsoer. Whether this individual reflected the ambitious purposes of the present German government, or only echoed a popular sentiment of his nation, the reader is left to judge. Were Bismarck to attempt, upon any subterfuge, to absorb Denmark, it is reasonable to suppose that other European powers would have something to say upon the subject; but that the map of Europe, as now constructed, is destined to undergo radical changes in the near future cannot be doubted.

The Denmark of to-day, typified by Copenhagen its capital, is a great centre of science and of art, quite as much so as are Munich or Dresden. It is surprising that so few travellers, comparatively, resort thither. For the study of ethnological subjects, there is no country which affords greater facilities, or which is more interesting to scientists generally. The spirit of Thorwaldsen here permeates everything; and in making his native city his heir, he also bequeathed to her an appreciation of art, which her eminent scientists have ably supplemented in their several departments of knowledge. To visit the unique Thorwaldsen Museum alone would repay a journey to Copenhagen, and no visitor to this Venice of the North should fail thoroughly to explore its riches. It is in the very centre of the city, situated close to the Palace of Christiansborg, and was erected in 1845 from the great sculptor's own design, based on the Egyptian order of architecture. It is two stories in height, and quadrangular in form,— the lower story containing sculpture only; the upper, both statuary and pictures. The external aspect of the structure is certainly not pleasing, but within, " where the marble statues breathe in rows," may be seen collected together and appropriately arranged six hundred of the great master's works, exhibiting the splendid and it is believed, as regards this department of art, unequalled result of one man's genius and industry. With galleries and vestibules the Museum contains over forty apartments, ample space being afforded for the best display of each figure and each group. The ceilings are elaborately and very beautifully decorated with emblematical designs by the best Danish artists. This enduring monument to art is also Thorwaldsen's appropriate mausoleum, being fashioned externally after an Etruscan tomb, and decorated in fresco with scenes illustrative of the sculptor's life. These crude and unprotected frescos, however, have become quite dim, and are being gradually effaced by exposure to the elements. So far as any artistic effect is concerned, we are honestly forced to say that the sooner they disappear the better. The interior of the Museum is peculiar in its combined effect,—a little depressing, we thought, being painted and finished in the sombre Pompeian style. It contains only Thorwaldsen's works and a few pictures which he brought with him when he removed hither from Rome, where so many years of his artistic life were passed. We have here presented to us the busts, models, sketches, and forms in clay, plaster, or marble, which represent all his works. Thorwaldsen's favorite motto was: "The artist belongs to his work, not the work to the artist," — a conscientious devotion which seems to invest everything which came from his hand. His body lies buried in the centre of the open court about which the building is constructed, without any designating stone, the ground being slightly raised above the surrounding pavement, and appropriately covered with a bed of growing ivy. A sense of stillness and solemnity seems to permeate the atmosphere as one pauses beside this lowly but expressive mound.

Among the portrait-statues which linger in the memory are many historic and familiar characters, such as Copernicus, Byron, Goethe, Hans Andersen, Humboldt, Schiller, Horace Vernet, Christian IV., the favorite monarch of the Danes, and many more. We have said that the general effect of these artistic halls was a little depressing; still, this was not the influence of the great sculptor's creations, for they are full of the joyous, elevating, and noble characteristics of humanity. Thorwaldsen revelled in the representation of tenderness, of youth, beauty, and childhood. Nothing of the repulsive or terrible ever came from his hand. The sculptor's regal fancy found expression most fully, perhaps, in the *relievi* which are gathered here, illustrating the delightful legends of the Greek mythology. He gives us here in exquisite marble his original conceptions of what others have depicted with the pen and the brush. No one can wonder at the universal homage accorded by his countrymen to the memory of the greatest of modern sculptors. The bust of Luther is seen in the main hall in an unfinished condition, just as the sculptor left it, and upon which, indeed, he is said to have worked the day before his death. It depicts a rude, coarse face, but one full of energy and power. In the Hall of Christ, as it is called, is the celebrated group of our Lord and the Twelve Disciples, the original of which is in the Cathedral. The impressive effect of this remarkable group is universally conceded; no one can stand before it unaffected by its grand and solemn beauty. Thorwaldsen's household furniture, writing-desk, books, pictures, and relics are here disposed as they were found in his home on the day of his death, — among which a clock, made by him when he was but twelve years of age, will interest the visitor.

A large proportion of the many persons whom we met in the Museum were Danes, whose respectability and admirable behavior impressed us most favorably, — a conviction which was daily corroborated upon the public streets, where there was none of the grossness observable which is so glaring among the middle and lower classes of more southern cities. There are no mendicants upon the thoroughfares; order and cleanliness reign everywhere, reminding one of Holland and the Hague. The young trees and delicate flowers in the public gardens require no special protection, and one looks in vain for anything like rowdyism in the crowded thoroughfares. Though the Danes are free consumers of malt liquors, not a case of intoxication met the author's eye while he remained in Copenhagen.

The Ethnological Museum of the city, better known as the Museum of Northern Antiquities, is generally considered to be the most remarkable institution of its class in Europe. Students in this department of science come from all parts of the civilized world to seek knowledge from its countless treasures. One is here enabled to follow the progress of our race from its primitive stages to its highest civilization. The national government liberally aids all purposes akin to science and art; consequently this Museum is a favored object of the State, being also liberally endowed by private munificence. Each of the three distinctive periods of Stone, Bronze, and Iron forms an elaborate division in the spacious halls of the institution.

MUSEUM OF NORTHERN ANTIQUITIES. 13

In classifying the objects, care has been taken not only to divide the three great periods named, but also in each of these divisions those belonging to the beginning and the end of the period are chronologically placed, as fast as such nice distinctions can be wrought out by careful, scientific study and comparison. Here the visitor gazes with absorbing interest upon the tangible evidences of a race that inhabited this earth probably thousands of years before it was broken into islands and continents. Their one token, these rude, but expressive stone implements, are found equally distributed from the Arctic Circle to the Equator, from Canada to Brazil, from England to Japan. Scientists whose culture and intelligence entitle their opinion to respect, place the Stone Age as here illustrated at least twenty thousand years before the birth of Christ. How absorbing is the interest attaching to these relics which ages have consecrated! No matter what our preconceived notions may be, science only deals with irrefutable facts. The periods delineated may be thus expressed: first the Flint period, which comes down to fifteen hundred years before Christ; followed by the Bronze, which includes the next twelve or thirteen hundred years; then the Iron, which comes down far into the Christian era. What is termed the Mediæval brings us to 1536, since which time there is no occasion for classification. No wonder the antiquarian becomes so absorbed in the study of the past. "The earliest and the longest has still the mastery over us," says George Eliot. Progress is daily making in the correct reading of these comprehensive data, and those who may come after us will be born to a great wealth of antiquity. Other countries may learn much from the admirable management of this Museum in the matter of improving the educational advantages which it affords. Professors of eminence daily accompany the groups of visitors, clearly explaining the purport and the historical relations of the many interesting objects. These persons are not merely intelligent employees, but they are also trained scientists; and, above all, they are enthusiastic in freely imparting the knowledge which inspires them. Such impromptu lectures are both original and impressive. Indeed, to go through the Ethnological Museum of Copenhagen understandingly is a liberal education. It should be added that the zeal and affability of these able officials is as freely and cheerfully extended to the humblest citizen as to distinguished strangers. One returns again and again with a sort of fascination to these indisputable evidences of history relating to periods of which there is no written record. If they are partially defective in their consecutive teachings, they are most impressive in the actual knowledge which they convey. Without giving us a list of sovereigns or positive dates, they afford collectively a clearer knowledge of the religion, culture, and domestic life of the people of their several periods than a Gibbon or a Bancroft could depict with their glowing pages.

The Danes are a cultured people, much more so, indeed, than the average classes of the continental

States. The large number of book-stores was a noticeable feature of the capital, as well as the excellent character of the books which were offered for sale. These were in German, French, and English, the literature of the latter being especially well represented. Copenhagen has more daily and weekly newspapers, magazines, and current news publications than Edinburgh or Dublin, or most of the provincial cities of Great Britain. It may be doubted if even in this country, outside of New England, we have many districts more liberally supplied with free library accommodations, or with educational facilities for youth, than are the populous portions of Zeeland and Jutland. Even small country villages have their book-clubs and dramatic clubs. A very general taste for the drama prevails. Indeed, Denmark has a national drama of its own, which exercises a notable influence upon its people. This Government was the first in Europe to furnish the means of education to the people at large on a liberal scale, to establish schoolhouses in every parish, and to provide suitable dwellings and incomes for the teachers. The incipient steps towards this object began as far back as the time of Christian II., more than three centuries ago, while most of the European States were grovelling in ignorance. Copenhagen has two public libraries, — the Royal, containing over six hundred thousand books; and the University, which has between two hundred and fifty and three hundred thousand volumes, not to speak in detail of a particularly choice collection of manuscripts.

These under reasonable restrictions are free to all, citizen or foreigner. The National University is of the first class, and supports a well organized lecture-system, like that of the Sorbonne in Paris, and which is also free to all, women having the same facilities afforded them as those enjoyed by the sterner sex. This institution, we were assured, is conducted upon the most modern educational system. It was founded in 1478, and at the present writing has between twelve and fifteen hundred students, instructed by about fifty able professors.

Though Denmark is a small kingdom, containing scarcely three millions of people, yet it has produced many eminent men of science, of art, and of literature. The names of Hans Christian Andersen, of Rasmus Rask the philologist, of Oersted the discoverer of electro-magnetism, of Forchhammer the mineralogist, and Eschricht the physiologist, will occur to the reader's mind in this connection. It is a country of legend and romance, of historic and prehistoric monuments, besides being the very father-land of fairy tales. The Vikings of old have left their footprints all over the country in barrows and tumuli. It is not, therefore, surprising that the cultured portion of the community are stimulated to antiquarian research. The masses are clearly a pleasure-loving people, easily amused and contented, troubling themselves very little about religious matters; the arts, poetry, and the drama being much more reverenced than the church. The accepted and almost universal doctrine is that of

CHARITABLE INSTITUTIONS. 17

Lutheranism. One meets comparatively few intelligent persons who cannot speak English, while many speak French and German also. The Danish language is a modified form of the old Gothic, which prevailed in the earliest historic ages.

Copenhagen is liberally supplied with free hospitals and charitable institutions, but except the Communal Hospital, the buildings devoted to these purposes have no architectural merit. A child's home was pointed out to us designed for the children of the poor, whose parents are unable to take care of them during their working hours. Before going out to a day's labor, a mother can place her child in this temporary home, where it will be properly cared for and fed until she returns for it. "Is any charge made for this service?" we asked. "Certainly," replied our informant, himself an official of importance; and he named a sum equal to about five cents of our money as the price per day for the care of each infant. "If it were entirely gratuitous," he added, " it would not be nearly so well appreciated, and would lead to imposition. The payment of this trifling sum enhances the estimate of the privilege far beyond its cost." The institution could not be sustained by such limited charges however; its real support is by the local government. Another institution was visited, designed for the sick and poor, where they can be properly nursed when temporarily ill, yet not sufficiently so to seek admission to a regular hospital. There have been as many as eight thousand patients admitted within a twelve-month to this establishment. There are also homes for old men and old women, intended for indigent persons who are too old to work. From the latter "home" there was observed driving upon the Lange Linie, beside the sea, a large open wagon full of dames who were enjoying a healthful outing. As the vehicle passed us, the driver was pointing out to his charges the distant view of Sweden, across the intervening Sound. The Royal Theatre or Opera House, situated on the King's Square, was to us a surprise, — it is so similar, at first sight, to the more elaborate and costly Opera House in the Place de l'Opéra in Paris, and as it antedates that elegant structure, it would certainly seem to have suggested some of its best lines. The Danish theatre will accommodate seventeen hundred persons, and is usually well filled, the royal box being seldom empty. The corridors are remarkable for spaciousness, and form a popular promenade for both sexes during the intervals between the acts. This furnishes an agreeable social break to the often long-protracted performances. On one side of the theatre facing the Square is a hideous bronze statue of Adam Oehlenschlaeger, the Danish lyric author; and on the opposite side is another representing Ludwig von Holberg, the Norwegian dramatist. This latter, in an artistic sense, is still more objectionable than the first named. The ballet as represented here is unique, being mostly designed to illustrate the early history of Scandinavia.

On one of the main thoroughfares leading from the Square already named, the triple domes of a Russian church dazzle the eye with their bright gilded surface and long hanging chains, depending from cross and crescent of the same metal, the whole reflecting the sun's rays with the force of a Venetian mirror. The interior, however, is plain, though rich in white marble, here and there carved in lattice pattern to form balustrades and dädos. Near by this church is the residence of the Russian Minister. On this same street, called the Bredgade, is the Frederick's Church, begun as long ago as 1749, after a grand design, and not yet finished. It is half surrounded to-day by a broad high staging, upon which groups of mechanics were seen busily at work, as has been the case for so many generations. This is known as the Marble Church, and is surmounted by a grand if not graceful dome of immense proportions. The English residents of the city are building an Episcopal church on the Esplanade, the local government having given the ground for this purpose. The corner-stone was laid by the Prince of Wales in 1885, with a grand ceremony, at which the Emperor and Empress of Russia assisted, with all the Danish royal family. It is the first English church erected in the country. On the Amaliegade, which runs parallel with the Bredgade and which is the next street to it, are four spacious palaces, which form a square, in the centre of which stands a bronze statue of Frederick V. These palaces are the town residence of the present royal family, one being also devoted to the business of the Foreign Office. The Amaliegade ends at the Lange Linie, where the Esplanade begins.

The spire of the large city Exchange is very curious, being formed of the twisted tails of three marvellous dragons, their bulging heads resting on the four corners of the tower,—altogether forming the most ridiculous attempt at architectural ornamentation we have yet chanced to behold. The building thus surmounted dates back to 1624, forming a memento of the reign of Christian IV. The Church of our Saviour has also a remarkable spire, with a winding staircase outside leading to the pinnacle. The bell which surmounts this lofty spire, and upon which stands a colossal figure of our Saviour, is said to be large enough to contain twelve persons at a time; but without climbing to the summit, the local guide's assurance that there were just three hundred and ninety three steps between base and top was unhesitatingly accredited. This church was consecrated in 1696. A peculiarity of its steeple is the fact that the spiral stairs wind upwards in the opposite direction from that which is usual. This was undoubtedly an accident on the part of the mechanics. Christian IV. detected the awkwardness and pointed it out to the architect, who, singular to say, had not before realized a circumstance which is now so obvious. His consequent chagrin was so great as nearly if not quite to render him insane. He ascended the spire on the day when the work was completed, and ended his life by throwing himself from the summit. Such was the entertaining legend rehearsed with great volubility to us by our local guide, who was evidently annoyed at our smile of incredulity.

The Christiansborg Palace, which was the Louvre of Copenhagen, contained many fine paintings by the old masters, including choice examples by Tintoretto, Nicholas Poussin, Raphael, Rubens, Salvator Rosa, Vandyke, Rembrandt, and others. The building was partially burned in 1884, — a fate reserved it would seem for all public structures in this country, a similar fortune having befallen this same palace seventeen or eighteen years ago. It still remains in ruins, and the pictures and other works of art, which were saved, have not yet found a fitting repository. Not even fire has purged this now ruined palace of its many tragic histories, its closeted skeletons, and its sorrowful memories. It was here that Caroline Matilda was made the reigning queen, and here a court mad with dissipation held its careless revels. From this place the dethroned queen went forth to prison at Elsinore, and her reputed lover (Struensee) was led to the scaffold. There was poetical justice in the retributive conduct of the son of the unfortunate queen, one of whose earliest acts upon assuming the reins of government was to confine the odious queen-mother Juliana in the same fortress which had formed the prison of Caroline Matilda. Though the Christiansborg Palace is now in partial ruins, its outer walls and façade are still standing nearly complete, quite enough so to show that architecturally it was hugely ugly. When it was intact its vast courts contained the chambers of Parliament, as well as those devoted to the suites forming the home of the royal family, and spacious art galleries.

In strolling about the town one comes now and then upon very quaint old sections, where low red-tiled roofs and houses, with gable ends towards the street, break the monotony. The new quarters of Copenhagen, however, are built up with fine blocks of houses, mostly in the Grecian style of architecture, — palatial residences, with façades perhaps a little too generally decorated by pilasters and floral wreaths, alternating with nymphs and cupids. The two-story horse-cars convey one in about fifteen minutes over a long, level, tree-shaded avenue from the centre of the city to Fredericksborg Castle in the environs. It is a palace erected by Frederick IV. as a summer residence for himself and court, but though capacious and finely located, it is void of all aspect of architectural grandeur. As a portion of the grounds commands a fine view of the city, the castle is generally visited by strangers. The spacious building is at present used for a military educational school. The park which surrounds Fredericksborg Castle is the great charm of the locality, being ornamented in all parts by immemorial trees, deep sylvan shades, purling streams, graceful lakes, and inviting greensward. It forms the daily resort of picnic parties from the close streets of the town near at hand, who come hither on summer afternoons in such numbers as to tax the full capacity of the tramway. At the entrance to the park stands a bronze statue of Frederick IV., which presents so strong a likeness to Lamartine, in form and feature, as instantly to recall the French orator and poet. Adjoining the extensive grounds of the castle is the Zoölogical Garden, which appears to occupy about ten acres of well-wooded and highly cultivated territory, ornamented with choice flower-beds, small lakes for aquatic birds, and a large brook running through the midst of the grounds. There is here an admirable collection of animals. The author's visit chanced upon a Saturday afternoon, when a bevy of primary-school children, composed of boys and girls under twelve years, was being conducted from section to section by their teachers, while the nature of each animal was lucidly explained to them. No advantage for educational purposes seems to be forgotten or neglected in Denmark.

CHAPTER II.

Public Amusements in Copenhagen. — Danish Sovereigns. — The Fashionable Promenade. — Danish Women. — Palace of Rosenborg. — A Golconda of Gems. — A Poet's Monument. — A Famous Astronomer. — Our Lady's Church. — The King's Square. — The Curious Old Round Tower. — The Peasantry. — A Famous Deer Park. — Röskilde. — Elsinore. — Gypsies. — Kronborg Castle. — The Queen's Prison. — Hamlet and Ophelia's Grave. — A Danish Legend.

COPENHAGEN is not without its ballets, theatres, Alhambras, Walhallas, and *cafés chantants*. The principal out-door resort of this character is the Tivoli Gardens, laid out in the Moorish style, where the citizens, representing all classes,— the cultured, the artisan, and the peasant,— assemble and mingle together in a free-and-easy way. Here they enjoy the long summer evenings, which indeed at this season of the year do not seem like evenings at all, since they are nearly as light as the day. Whatever may be said in advocacy of these public assemblies, enjoyed amid the trees, flowers, soft air, and artistic surroundings, there seems to a casual visitor to be too much freedom permitted between the sexes for entire respectability, and yet nothing actually repulsive was observable. In Berlin or Vienna these popular resorts would be designated as beer gardens; here they are called tea-gardens. The Tivoli has a fine ballet troup among its attractions, and employs two orchestras of forty instrumental performers each, stationed in different parts of the spacious gardens. The price of admission to these illuminated grounds is merely nominal. Some of the wealthiest families as well as the humbler bring their children with them, as is the custom of those who frequent the beer gardens of Munich and Dresden. As a popular place of varied and attractive amusements the Tivoli of Copenhagen has hardly its equal in Europe.

Just across the harbor is the spacious and fertile island of Amager, some twenty square miles in extent, which serves as the kitchen or vegetable garden of the capital. It was first occupied by a colony of Flemings who were brought hither in 1516 by Charles II., for the purpose of teaching his subjects how to cultivate vegetables and flowers. The descendants of these foreigners still retain traces of their origin, remaining quite distinctive in their costume and personality. These peasants, or at least those who daily come to market, must be well off in a pecuniary sense, judging by their gold and silver ornaments and fanciful dresses.

Tramways render all parts of the city and environs accessible, the double-decked cars enabling them to carry a large number of passengers. Broad streets and convenient sidewalks invite the promenaders along the open squares, which are frequently lined with umbrageous trees and embellished with monuments. The fashionable drive and promenade is the Lange Linie (that is, the "Long Line"), bordering the Sound and forming a complete circle. It reminded one of the Chiaja of Naples, though there is no semi-tropical vegetation to carry out the similitude. It was pleasant to meet here the members of the royal family, including the Queen and Prince Royal. The two servants upon the box in scarlet livery were the only distinctive tokens of royalty observable, and there were no other attendants. Her Majesty and the Prince were both prompt to recognize and salute us as a stranger. The present king, Christian IX., it will be remembered, was crowned in 1863, and is now in his sixty-fifth year. Being in poor health, during our visit he was absent at Wiesbaden, partaking of its mineral waters. It must be admitted that the past sovereigns of Denmark have not always been so deserving of popular respect as have the people of the country generally. The late king was by no means a shining light of morality. He was married three times, divorcing his first queen; the second divorced him, and the royal roué ended by marrying his mistress, who was a fashionable milliner. He first created her a countess, but he could not make a lady of her, even in outward appearance, and she remained to the last a social monstrosity to the court. She was fat, vulgar-looking, snub-nosed, bourgeoise, and ruled the King in all things. She was totally ignored by decent society in the capital, and became so obnoxious that she nearly provoked open rebellion. However, the fortunate death of the King finally ended this condition of affairs; and as he left no children by any of his wives, the crown descended to his cousin the present King, who, it is pleasant to record, has not failed to dignify the throne.

The ladies walk or drive very generally in the afternoon upon the Lange Linie, and are certainly attractive with their fair complexions, light golden hair, and smiling blue eyes. They have both sunny faces and sunny hearts, emphasized by the merriest tones of ringing laughter that ever saluted the ear. They are lovable, but not beautiful, excelling in ordinary accomplishments, such as music and dancing; "but above all," said a resident American to us, "they are naturally of domestic habits, and care nothing for politics or so-called woman's rights, except the right to make home happy." The well-to-do portion of the community very generally live in "flats," after the French and modern American style. Some large and elegant buildings of this character were observed in course of construction at the extreme end of the Bredgade. There is no very poor or squalid district in the town, and one looks in vain for such wretched hovels as disfigure so many European cities.

The Palace of Rosenborg with its superb gardens, noble avenues of chestnut trees, and graceful shrubbery is situated near the present centre of the city. It was once a royal residence, having been built by Christian IV. as a dwelling-place, whither he might retire at will from the noise and interruptions of the capital. At the time of its erection in 1604 it was outside the walls, a radius which the modern city has long since outgrown. The room in which the King died in 1648 is shown to visitors, and recalled to us the small apartment in which Philip II. died at the Escurial, near Madrid. Among the few paintings upon the walls of this apartment is one representing the King upon his death-bed, as he lay in his last long sleep. The palace is now devoted to a chronological collection of the belongings of the Danish kings, spacious apartments being devoted to souvenirs of each, decorated in the style of the period and containing a portion of the original furniture from the several royal residences, as well as the family portraits, gala-costumes, jewelry, plate, and weapons. Altogether it is a collection of priceless value and of remarkable historic interest, covering a period of about four hundred and fifty years. One is forcibly reminded of the Green Vaults of Dresden while passing through the many sections of Rosenborg Castle. The extraordinary and valuable collection within its walls has, it is believed, no superior in point of interest in all Europe. The founder of this museum was Frederick III., the son and successor of Christian IV. Some of the cabinets and other articles of furniture in the various halls and rooms are marvellous works of art, inlaid with ivory and mother-of-pearl, representing birds, flowers, landscapes, and domestic scenes with all the finished effect of oil paintings by a master-hand. In the cabinets and tables secret drawers are exposed to view by the touching of hidden springs. While some tables are formed of solid silver, as are also other articles of domestic use, still others are composed of both gold and silver. Many of the royal regalias are profusely inlaid with diamonds, sapphires, emeralds, rubies, and other precious stones,— forming an aggregated value too large for us to venture an estimate. The toilet sets were numerous, and had belonged to the several queens, each embracing eight or ten finely wrought pieces made of solid gold, superbly inlaid with precious stones. Among these costly sets was observed the jewelled casket of Queen Sophia Amalie, wife of Frederick III., a relic of great interest, inlaid with scores of large diamonds. The costly and very beautiful bridal dresses of several royal personages are here exhibited, all being carefully and chronologically arranged, so that the intelligent visitor clearly reads veritable history amid this array of domestic treasures.

It is difficult to designate the order of architecture to which the Rosenborg Palace belongs, though it is clearly enough in the showy renaissance of the seventeenth century. It is attributed to the famous architect Inigo Jones. In the spacious grounds is a fine monument erected to the memory of Hans Christian Andersen, the Danish poet and author, whose popular tales are the delight not only of all Scandinavian children, but of those of larger growth, being full of acute observation and profound views under a simple and familiar guise. At the foot of this statue, as we passed by, there stood a group of young children, to whom one evidently their teacher was explaining its purport. A school of gardening is also established here, with extensive conservatories and hot-houses.

These grounds are called the Kindergarten of the city, being so universally the resort of infancy and childhood during the long summer days, but are officially known as Kongen's Have (King's Garden).

Close to the Rosenborg Palace is the Astronomical Observatory, in the grounds of which is a monument to the astronomer Tycho Brahe, who died in 1610. This monument was unveiled on the 8th day of August, 1876, just three hundred years after the founding of Brahe's famous observatory on the Island of Hveen, where he discovered on the 1st of November, 1572, the Cassiopeia, which is best known as Tycho Brahe's star. "Only Venus at her brightest surpasses this new star," wrote the enthusiastic astronomer. Science, however, has since shown that it was no new star, but one that shines with great lustre for a few months once in a period of three hundred years. One sunny afternoon the author took a trip up the Sound to Hveen, familiarly known as Tycho Brahe's Island, and which was presented to Tycho by the King of Denmark. The foundation in ruins is all that remains of the famous castle which the somewhat vain astronomer built here, and to which he gave the name of Uraniborg ("Castle of the Heavens."). This man was a strange compound of science and superstition; he was a poet of no ordinary power, and was courted by many of the eminent men of his day. James VI. of Scotland was at times his guest at Hveen. He was well connected, but mortally offended his relatives by marrying an humble peasant girl of Amager.

The most interesting Christian temple in the capital is that of Our Lady's Church, being also the oldest and best endowed. It was founded early in the twelfth century, and is in the Greco-Roman style; but its greatest attraction is the possession of some of Thorwaldsen's finest sculpture. The sad-fated Caroline Matilda was married with great ceremony in this church, in 1766, to her cousin Christian VII. Outside of the church are two statues in bronze,— one of David by Jerichau, and one of Moses by Bissen. The King's Square already spoken of is situated very near the actual centre of the city, whence radiates a dozen more or less of the principal streets, of which the Bredgade (Broad Street) is one. In the middle of this area there is a statue of Christian V. surrounded by grotesque, allegorical figures. The material of the statue is lead, the whole forming a colossal caricature upon art, entirely unworthy of its present situation. There is a friendly collection of tall shrubbery clustered about the leaden statue, forming a partial screen. The spacious square, or circus as it would be called in London, or piazza in Rome, is bordered by several public buildings, mingled with tall narrow dwellings, characterized by fantastic gables and long sloping roofs full of little dormer windows. The Royal Theatre, the Academy of Arts, Count Moltke's picture gallery, and some hotels centre here.

The Round Tower of Copenhagen has been pronounced one of the most remarkable buildings in the world. It is certainly very peculiar, designed as a sort of annex to the Church of the Holy Trinity. Formerly it served as an astronomical observatory; and it is an observatory still, since it affords one of the best and most comprehensive views that can be had of the low-lying capital. The tower consists of two hollow cylinders, and between them a spiral, gradually-inclined foot-way leads from base to summit, somewhat similar to the grand Campanile in the piazza of St. Mark, Venice. It is quite safe for a horse and vehicle to ascend; indeed, this performance is said to have been achieved by the Empress Catherine, and it is also recorded that Peter the Great accomplished the same feat on horseback in 1707. From the top of the Round Tower the red-tiled roofs of the city lie spread out beneath the eye of the visitor, mingled with green parks, open squares, tall slim steeples, broad canals, public buildings, long boulevards, palaces, and gardens. To this aspect is added the multitude of shipping lying along the piers and grouped in the harbor, backed by a view of the open sea. The Swedish coast across the Baltic is represented by a low range of coast-line losing itself upon the distant horizon. Turning the eyes inland, there are seen thick groves of dark woods and richly cultivated fields, sprinkled here and there by the half-awkward but picturesque and wide-armed wind-mills in lazy motion. The bird's-eye view obtained of Copenhagen and surroundings from this eyrie is one to be long and vividly remembered.

The environs within eight or ten miles of the city are rather sparsely inhabited, though there are many delightful villas to be seen here and there. Everything is scrupulously neat; human and animal life appears at its best. The whole of the island, from one end to the other, is interspersed with thrifty farms, and no dwellings, barns, or other farm buildings are so humble but that the walls are kept of snowy brightness with whitewash, while all are surrounded by well-kept shrubbery, birches, and flower-plats. The peasant girls seen at work in large numbers in the field are smiling, ruddy, and stout; the men are of low stature, but hale and hearty. We were informed that the nominal increase of the population is so small as to be hardly recognizable, being but about one per cent per annum, and — singular fact — that suicide is more prevalent in Denmark than in any other portion of Europe. Emigration from this country is far less in proportion than from Norway and Sweden, but yet amounts to a respectable aggregate annually. Some of the birch and linden woods not far from the city form beautiful and picturesque groves, particularly in the suburb north of the capital, where the Prince Imperial has a large château, situated amid rich woodland glades. Though the spruce and pine are so abundant in Norway and Sweden just across the narrow Sound, no conifer will grow in Denmark. Tea-gardens abound in these environs, the citizens knowing no greater pleasure than to resort thither to enjoy their tea or supper in the open air. The short summer season is more than tropical in the haste it imparts to vegetation, making up for its brevity by its intensity. Were this not the case, the crops would hardly reach maturity in Scandinavia.

There is what is called the Dyrehave, or Deer Park, a couple of miles beyond the Prince's château, where the people of Copenhagen annually enjoy a midsummer revel lasting some weeks, perhaps a little too fast and free, if the truth be told, where even Nijnii-Novgorod is exceeded in lasciviousness. A fair of some days' continuance is held in the park, which reaches its climax on St. John's Eve, when its well-arranged precincts, groves, cafés, shooting galleries, flower-booths and verdant vistas make a rare picture of gayety and sportive life. A large herd of the picturesque animals after whom the park is named, roam at will over the more secluded portions. Among them two noble white stags were observed, the first we had ever chanced to see. The park is reached by a pleasant drive over an excellent road, or by steam tramway cars any hour in the day.

Twenty miles northwest of the city are situated the village and the royal palace of Fredericksborg, one of the noblest of all the royal residences of the kings of Denmark. It stands about midway between the capital and Elsinore. The original building was begun under Frederick II., grandfather of Charles I. of England, and completed in 1608 by his son and successor Christian IV. The palace occupies three small islands in the middle of Lake Hilleröd, which is also the name of the neighboring market-town, the islands being connected therewith by a bridge. The building is four stories in height, composed of red sandstone, elaborately ornamented with sculpture, the whole surmounted by tall towers and a steeple containing a chime of bells. It has been pronounced a dream of architectural beauty, quite unequalled elsewhere in Denmark.

It is not the author's purpose to take the reader far away from Copenhagen, or at least from the shores of the Sound, as the plan of the present volume is so comprehensive in other directions as to circumscribe the space which can properly be devoted to Denmark.

On the peninsula, as well as in Zeeland, the land is generally undulating. There being as we have said no mountains or considerable elevations, consequently no waterfalls or rapids are to be met with; the rivers are smooth and the lakes mirror-like. The soil is sandy, often marshy, but produces good crops of grain and affords fine pasturage. The green fields were sprinkled far and near on the line of the railroad from Korsoer to Copenhagen with grazing cattle, sheep, and horses, forming a pleasing rural picture under a clear azure sky. The produce of the dairy is the great staple of Denmark. On this route one passes through the village of Leedoye, where there was once a grand Pagan temple and place of sacrifice, exceeded in importance in Scandinavia only by that at Upsala. Close at hand is Röskilde, so historically interesting, — though save its grand cathedral, dating from the twelfth or thirteenth century, it has little left to show that for five hundred years it was the capital of Denmark, even down to 1448. Here is to be seen the black marble sarcophagus of the renowned Queen Margaret of Scandinavia, surmounted by her recumbent effigy; also a mortuary chapel of Christian IV. and Frederick V. Other queens and monarchs are here interred, from the time of Harold to Frederick VII. The whole forms an exceedingly interesting monument of mediæval days.

Upon this line of road there are occasional districts so well wooded as to be called forests; but that word does not signify the same in Zeeland as it does in America. There are still to be seen occasional groups of gypsy vagrants in the inland districts, but are rarely to be found in the cities. Not many years ago they were here in great numbers, but are now gradually disappearing. One group was observed whose members presented all the peculiar characteristics of their Asiatic origin. They are dark-skinned, with raven-black hair and black piercing eyes, presenting a picture of indolence and sensuousness. The young women were mostly handsome, even in their dirt, rags, and cheap jewelry.

The ramparts and fortifications generally which formerly surrounded Copenhagen on the seaside have nearly all been demolished, the ground being now turned into fine garden-walks planted with umbrageous trees and bright-hued flowers, adding greatly to the beauty of the Danish capital. The last unimproved portion of these now defunct fortifications is being levelled and brought into ornamental condition.

The former moats have assumed the shape of tiny lakes, upon which swans are seen at all hours; and where death-dealing cannon were planted, lindens, rose-bushes, peonies, heliotrope, and tall white lilies now bloom and flourish. The outer-island defences have in the mean time been greatly strengthened and the more modern weapons of warfare adopted, so that Copenhagen is even better prepared for self-defence than ever before.

No finer scenery is to be found in Europe than is presented by the country lying between Copenhagen and Elsinore, composed of a succession of forests, lawns, villas, cottages, and gardens for a distance of twenty-five miles. Elsinore is a small seaport, looking rather deserted, bleak, and silent, with less than ten thousand inhabitants. From out of the uniformity of its red brick buildings there looms up but one noticeable public edifice; namely, the Town Hall, with a square, flanked by an octagonal tower built of brick and red granite. The charm of the place is its remarkable situation, commanding an admirable view of the Baltic with Sweden in the distance, while the Sound which divides the two shores is always dotted in summer with myriads of steamers and sailing vessels. The author counted over eighty marine craft at one view, glancing between "the blue above and the blue below." The position of Elsinore recalls that of Gibraltar and the Dardanelles as surely as its name recalls Hamlet and Shakspeare. North of the town, on the extreme point of the land, stands the famous castle of Kronborg, with its three tall towers, the central one overtopping the others by forty or fifty feet. The tower upon the most seaward corner is now devoted to the purpose of a lighthouse. The castle is about three centuries old, having been built by Frederick II. for the purpose of commanding the entrance to the Sound, and of enforcing the marine tolls which were exacted from all foreign nations for a period of two or three centuries. Kronborg contains a small collection of oil paintings, nearly all of which are by Danish artists. A portrait of Rubens's daughter by the hand of the great master himself was observed. There is also an ideal portrait of considerable merit entitled Hamlet, by Abildgaard. But to the author, as he strolled from one spacious apartment to another, there came forcibly the sad memory of the young and lovely Caroline Matilda, Queen of Denmark and sister of George III. It was here that she was confined, upon a preposterous charge of infidelity to her husband, — that royal lunatic! — instituted by the malignity of the Queen Dowager, who wished to secure the succession to her son. After a trying period of imprisonment in this castle, the ill-fated Matilda was permitted, through the influence of her royal brother to retire to Zell, in Hanover, where she died of a broken heart at the age of twenty-three. During her misfortune she wrote that memorable line on the window of Fredericksborg Castle, with a diamond ring, —

"Lord keep me innocent: make others great."

One has only to study for a moment the serene and beautiful face of the Queen, as exhibited in Rosenborg Palace, to feel entire confidence in her innocence.

If you come to Elsinore the guide will show you what is called Hamlet's grave, located in a small grove of trees, where some cunning hands long ago erected a rude mound of stones. Shakspeare, who had a royal way of committing anachronisms, made Hamlet live in this place after the introduction of gunpowder, whereas, if any such person ever did exist, it was centuries earlier and hundreds of miles farther north upon the mainland, in what is now Jutland. However, that is unimportant. Do not leave Elsinore without visiting Ophelia's fatal brook! To be sure it is not large enough for a duck to swim in, but a little stretch of the imagination will overcome all local discrepancies.

Far back in Danish legendary story, a time when history fades into fable, it is said there was a Hamlet in northern Denmark, but it was long before the birth of Christ. His father was not a king, but a famous pirate chief who governed Jutland in conjunction with his brother. Hamlet's father married the daughter of a Danish king, the issue being Hamlet. His uncle, according to the ancient story, did murder Hamlet's father and afterwards married his mother; and this was the basis of Shakspeare's grand production.

The great, gloomy-looking castle of Kronborg, which has stood sentinel here for three centuries, would require two thousand men and more to defend it in time of war, but modern gunnery has rendered it, for all offensive purposes, of no account. The Sound, which at Copenhagen is about twenty miles wide, here narrows to two, the old fort of Helsingborg on the Swedish coast being in full view. Thus the passage here forms the natural gate to the Baltic. There are delightful drives in the environs of Elsinore presenting land and sea views of exquisite loveliness, the water-side bristling with reefs, rocks, and lighthouses, while that of the land is picturesque with villas, groves, and cultivated meads.

CHAPTER III.

Gottenburg. — Ruins of Elfsborg. — Gustavus Adolphus. — A Wrecked Monument. — The Girdle-Duellists. — Emigration to America. — Public and Private Gardens. — A Kindly People. — The Götha Canal. — Falls of Trollhätta. — Dainty Wild-Flowers. — Waterways. — Stockholm and Lake Maelaren. — Prehistoric Tokens. — Iron Mines of Sweden. — Pleasing Episode with Children. — The Liquor Traffic Systematized. — A Great Practical Charity. — A Domestic Habit.

ONE day's sail due north from Copenhagen through the Sound and the Cattegat — Strait of Catti — brings us to Gottenburg, the metropolis of southwestern Sweden. The Strait, which is about a hundred miles in width, is nearly twice as long, and contains many diminutive islands. Gottenburg is situated on the Götha River, about five miles from its mouth. In passing up this water-way the old fortification of Elfsborg was observed, now dismantled and deserted, though it once did good service in the war with the Danes. Cannon-balls are still to be seen half embedded in the crumbling stonewalls, — missiles which were fired from the enemy's ships. Though Gottenburg is less populous, it is commercially almost as important as Stockholm the capital, and it is appropriately called the Liverpool of Scandinavia. The town, with its eighty thousand inhabitants, has a wide-awake aspect, especially in the neighborhood of the river, where the numerous well-stocked timber-yards along the wharves show that product to be a great staple of the local trade. One is agreeably prepossessed upon landing here by a certain aspect of neatness and cleanliness observable on all sides. Indeed, few foreign towns produce so favorable a first impression. The business centre is the Gustaf-Adolf-Torg, in which is situated the Börs, or Exchange, decidedly the finest building architecturally in the city. In the centre of the Torg is a bronze statue of Gustavus Adolphus, the founder of the town, and which, as a work of art, is extremely creditable to the designer, Fogelberg. The history of the statue is somewhat curious. It seems that the first one designed for this public square was wrecked at sea while on its passage from Hamburg to Gottenburg, but was rescued by a party of sailors off Heligoland, who claimed so extraordinary a sum as salvage that the Gottenburgers refused to pay it, and ordered of the sculptor a second one to replace that which had been saved from the sea. In due time the second statue was furnished and set up in the Torg, Nov. 5, 1855, on the two hundred and twenty-third anniversary of the death of Gustavus. The extortionate seamen who held the first statue were finally glad to sell it to other parties for a comparatively small sum, representing its bare metallic value. It now stands in the Domshide of Bremen.

The deep, broad watercourse which runs through the centre of the city to the harbor is the beginning of the famous Götha Canal, which joins fjord, river, locks, and lakes together all the way to Stockholm, directly across southern Sweden, thus connecting the North Sea and the Baltic. The two cities are also joined by railroad, the distance between them being over three hundred miles. The rural parts of the country through which the canal passes are not unlike many inland sections of New England, presenting pleasant views of thrifty farms and well-cultivated lands. There are some sharp hills and abrupt valleys to be encountered, which are often characterized by grand waterfalls, wild-foaming rivers, and surging rapids.

Though there is no striking similarity between the two cities, one is yet reminded of Amsterdam by Gottenburg, aided perhaps by the memory that it was originally founded by Gustavus Adolphus, in 1619, and that Dutch settlers were among its first inhabitants. The descendants of such people are pretty sure to retain an ancestral atmosphere about them which is more or less distinctive. The place is divided into an upper and lower town, the latter being a plain cut up into canals, and the former spread picturesquely over the adjoining hills. The town is made up of two or three principal boulevards, very broad, and intersecting one another at right angles, with a canal in their centres, these waterways being embanked by substantial granite borders, which are interspersed at convenient distances with granite steps connecting the street with the water. The spacious harbor admits of vessels drawing seventeen feet of water.

Gottenburg is built mostly of brick, which are brought either from Denmark or Holland; and yet the whole peninsula of Scandinavia abounds in stone. Large blocks of dwelling-houses were observed in course of construction which were of four or five stories, and quite elegant in design. The citizens feel a just pride in a well-endowed College, a large Public Library, an Exchange, two Orphan Asylums, a flourishing Society of Arts and Sciences, a large Theatre, and two spacious public parks. In front of the theatre is an admirable reproduction of Molin, the Swedish sculptor's famous group of two figures representing "the girdle-duellists," the original of which stands in front of the National Museum at Stockholm. This popular and vigorous composition is reproduced in plaster and terra-cotta, and offered for sale in all the cities of the North, being particularly numerous in the art stores of Copenhagen. It depicts one of the ancient Scandinavian duels, wherein the combatants, stripped to the skin, were bound together by their united leather belts, and thus confined, fought out their battle with their knives, the result proving nearly always fatal to both. Previous to engaging in the conflict, each of the contestants drove the blade of his knife as deep into a thick pine-board as he could do with one stroke of his arm. All the rest of the blade was then blunted and bound securely with cord, leaving only the inch, more or less, exposed which had been buried in the wood. If the weapons had not been thus partially protected, the first blow might have proved fatal, whereas these ancient belt-duels were designed to exemplify strength and endurance. The splendid pose and fine muscular development of the two figures, represented at the height of their struggle, have justly given its author lasting fame. This group has been declared to hold the same place in modern sculpture that Meissonier's picture of "The Quarrel," the original of which is the property of Queen Victoria, holds in modern painting.

Gottenburg is not without its cathedral and numerous fine churches, but especially it has excellent common schools of the several grades, primary, middle, and high. It will be remembered that education is compulsory throughout Sweden. English is regularly taught in her schools and very generally spoken by the educated classes. In conversation with the common people, it was discovered that the goal of their ambition was to emigrate to America. The departures for this country, though not excessive, are yet steady both from this port and Stockholm, aggregating in some years forty thousand from Sweden and Norway combined, now and then a group of Finns going to make up the number. Money among the lower classes is almost as scarce as it is in Ireland; but those who have emigrated, and have been successful, liberally remit money wherewith to enable family and friends to join them in America.

The Public Gardens of Gottenburg are beautifully arranged, and are kept in exquisite condition,— one large division being designated as the Botanical Gardens, and abundantly supplied with exotics, especially from tropical regions. Blooming hawthorn, white and pink lilacs, and a great variety of beautiful trees challenge admiration on entering these grounds. Among many familiar flowers a species of dwarf lobelia of azure blue and the Alpine forget-me-not, with pale-blue flowers and yellow eyes, were particularly observable, mingled with pansies in a confused variety of mammoth proportions. The golden-leaved verbena and a large, tall, pearly-white tiger-flower were both abundant, the latter speckled with ruby-colored spots. The horse-chestnut trees were in great variety and the largest we had ever seen. There were many grand old oaks and fine Lombardy poplars in stately ranks, as upright as soldiers at a review. Inland excursions showed the pine and the fir to be the prevailing trees, the birch becoming more abundant farther north. Fully one third of the country, as we were assured, is covered with woods, some of which seemed almost endless in extent. The immediate environs of Gottenburg are very attractive, well wooded, and adorned with picturesque cottages and some large villas. Among others which we visited was that of Oscar Dickson, famous for his interest in Arctic expeditions. No private gardens in England or America are more admirably kept, and the grape-houses we have never seen surpassed in the varieties or perfection of the fruit. The low-lands were found occasionally bright with the golden petals of the marsh-marigold, which fairly blazed under the direct rays of the sun. There is a saying here, that when it blooms the cuckoo comes and the roach spawns. A fine old bit of mouldering, ivy-grown ruins in the shape of a Martello tower, situated upon rising ground and overlooking the entrance to the inland waters, is sure to attract the traveller's admiring eye.

The kindness of the common people and their pleasant manners are most captivating, being characterized by quiet self-possession and thoughtfulness for a stranger's well-being. In more than one instance a casual inquiry was not only promptly responded to, but we were taken pleasantly in hand, and other welcome though unsought guidance and information were voluntarily offered. Education is far more general and culture is of a higher grade in Sweden than is common with the people of Southern Europe, while music seems to be as universal an accomplishment here as it is in Italy. The population is frugal, honest, self-helping, and in many respects resembles that of Switzerland.

The system of inland communication by means of the Götha Canal is one of the most remarkable ever achieved by man, when the obstacles which have been overcome and the advantages accomplished are taken into consideration. Steam-vessels, limited to one hundred and six feet in length on account of the size of the locks, are carried regularly hundreds of miles by it across and over the highlands of southern Sweden from sea to sea. The reader can easily realize what a triumph of engineering skill it is when he sees a well-freighted steamboat climb a mountain side, float through lock after lock, and after reaching the apex of the hilly country, descend with equal facility towards the coast and sea-level. Steamboats and sailing vessels navigating the canal rise, in all, three hundred and eighty feet above the level of the Baltic during the passage across the country. At the little town of Berg the locks are sixteen in number, and form a gigantic staircase, by means of which vessels are raised at this point one hundred and twenty feet. Here, as well as at the famous Falls of Trollhätta, the traveller can leave the steamer for three or four hours, walking on in advance, and thus obtaining some charming views of inland scenery. No intelligent person can fail to appreciate the grandeur of the remarkable falls just mentioned, with their pine-clad, precipitous banks and wild tumult of waters, partially screened by a white foam-cloud reaching far heavenward.

If possible, it is well to tarry for a day at Trollhätta, visiting the various points of interest about the famous rapids, and watching the many steamboats and other vessels which pass so mysteriously through the ponderous locks, ascending and descending the elevations with mathematical regularity and speed. The valley through which the railroad passes, often parallel with the canal, on the way from

THE FALLS OF TROLLHÄTTA. 49

Gottenburg to Trollhätta, is one of the most fertile in Sweden, and when we saw it was rich with ripening grains. The falls are accessible from Gottenburg by rail in about two hours' travel, or by canal leaving the city early in the morning and returning in the evening, giving the visitor six or eight hours' time at the falls. Trollhätta presents one of the great curiosities of Sweden, to visit which tourists come from all parts of Europe. It is true that the hoarse music of these falls is mingled with the din of sawmills, foundries, and smithies, — but one need not specially regard them. A little poetical latitude adds zest to imagination, and we see the beauties and marvels which we come prepared to see. The falls consist of a series of tremendous rapids extending over a distance of about two hundred yards; and producing an uproar almost equal to the ceaseless oratorio of Niagara. The rapids are intersected by two or three rocky but well-wooded islands, on either side of which the angry waters rush with a wild, resistless power, tossed by the many sub-currents. The whole array of rapids forms a succession of falls of which the first is called Gullöfallet, where on both sides of an inaccessible little island the waters make a leap of twenty-six feet in height, the rebound creating a constant cloud of feathery spray. Then follows the highest of the falls, the Toppöfallet, of forty-four feet in height, likewise divided by a cliff into two parts, against which the frantic waters chafe angrily. The next fall measures less than ten feet in height, followed a little way down the rapids by what is called the Flottbergström, — all together making a fall of foaming eddies and whirls equal to about one hundred and twelve feet. While near to these roaring waters amid the general chaos, conversation is impossible. As at all extensive falls, rainbows constantly hang over and about the wild surging waters reflected in the gauze-clouds of transparent mist.

While strolling through the wood-paths and over the rocky ways which line this sleepless disorder of the waters, the grounds in many places were seen to be gorgeously decked with flowers of Nature's planting, — many-colored, sunshine-loving things. Among those more particularly abundant was the pretty violet-purple flower of the butterwort, each circle of pale-yellow leaves, with the stalk rising from the centre crowned with its peculiar bloom. "Beautiful objects of the wild-bee's love." But for the glutinous exudation one would be tempted to gather them by handfuls. The town of Trollhätta is a village of three thousand inhabitants, and contains a graceful little Gothic church. The people are mostly manufacturers, who manage to utilize profitably a portion of the enormous water-power afforded by the falls. The word Trollhätta, we were told, signifies "the home of the water-witches." The local legends with which the traveller is freely regaled by the guides would fill a good-sized volume in print, but we feel disinclined to inflict them second-hand and wholesale upon the patient reader.

SWEDISH LAKES.

The Götha Canal, as before intimated, utilizes and connects several of the great lakes of southern Sweden, the principal ones in Scandinavia being located in this region. Lake Wener, which receives the waters of eighty rivers large and small, has an area of twenty-four hundred square miles, being nearly ten times as large as the famous Lake of Geneva. Lakes Wetter and Maelaren are the next in importance, either of which is fully twice the size of the Swiss lake just named. The canal proper — that is, the portion which has been artificially constructed — is ten feet deep, fifty wide at the bottom, and ninety at the surface. Two hundred and seventy miles of the route traversed by the vessels navigating the canal between Gottenburg and Stockholm are through lakes and rivers, all of which are remarkable for their clear spring-like character and the picturesqueness of their surroundings. Stockholm is situated on the Maclaren lake, where it finds an outlet into the Baltic. This large body of water is studded all over with islands of every form and size, on some of which are quaint old castles, mysterious ruins, and thick woods, haunted only by those rovers of the sky, the eagle and the hawk. Others are ornamented by charming villas, surrounded by fine landscape gardening, with graceful groves of drooping willows and birch-trees. Some contain only fishermen's huts, while here and there clusters of their small cottages form an humble village. The marine shells which are found in the bottom of some of the inland lakes of both Norway and Sweden show that the land which forms their bed was once covered by the sea. This is clearly apparent in Lake Wener and Lake Wetter, which are situated nearly three hundred feet above the present ocean level. The first-named body of water is some eighty miles long by a width of thirty. The latter is as long, but averages only ten miles in width. Complete skeletons of whales have been found far inland, at considerable elevations, during the present century. The oldest shell-banks discovered by scientists in Scandinavia are situated five hundred feet above the present level of the ocean. How significant are these deposits of a prehistoric period!.

Sweden has comparatively few mountains, but many ranges of hills. Norway monopolizes almost entirely the mountain system of the great northern peninsula; but the valuable large forests of pine, fir, and birch which cover so much of the country are common to both. Though iron is found in large deposits in Norway, it is still more abundant in Sweden, where it is chiefly of the magnetic and hæmatite character, yielding when properly smelted the best ore for the manufacture of steel. It is believed that there is sufficient malleable and ductile iron in the soil of Sweden to supply the whole world with this necessary article for a thousand years to come. Mount Gellivare, which is over eighteen hundred feet in height, is said to be almost wholly formed of an ore containing fully eighty per cent of the best quality of merchantable iron; so that a dearth of this mineral is certainly not imminent.

But let us not wander too far from our course due north. Nor are we yet quite ready to depart from Gottenburg. While strolling alone through its broad and pleasant avenues, the writer met a couple of girls of about eleven and twelve years respectively. They were evidently sisters, and they looked so bright and so pleasantly into the stranger's face that he addressed them in the few native words at his command. That we were a foreigner was at once realized, and the eldest asked from whence we came. So much could be understood, and happily the name America was plain enough to them. It acted like a charm upon them, lighting up their soft blue eyes and wreathing their lips with smiles, while it also elicited their confidence. Each put a tiny hand within our own, and thus escorted we passed along until the nearest confectioner's shop was reached. Here we met upon terms where pantomime was quite sufficiently expressive, and we were soon engaged in partaking gleefully of bon-bons, cakes, and cream. What a merry half hour we three passed together, and how rapidly the time flew! Was real pleasure ever more cheaply purchased than at the moderate price demanded by the shop-keeper, who placed a little packet of sweets in each of the children's hands as we parted? On passing out upon the avenue we came full upon a person who was all astonishment and courtesy combined. It was René, our Danish courier. "I did not think, sir," he said, "that you knew any one in Gottenburg." "You were right, René," was the reply, "but these little fairies took

possession of us, and we have had a delightful half
hour together." Then both of the children began to
speak to him at the same time, and he to reply to
them. It was soon made apparent why they should so
have affiliated with and trusted a stranger. They
understood. that the writer was from America, where
in the State of Pennsylvania they had a well-beloved
brother. It seemed to the dear little blondes that
we must have come as it were direct from him. On
parting, a kiss was pressed upon the innocent lips
of each of the children, while tremulous tears were
only too obvious in the sweet, sympathetic eyes of
the elder.

We were told of a rather curious system which orig-
inated here of controlling the liquor traffic, and which
has long been in successful operation.

It appears that a certain number of shops only are
licensed for the sale of pure, unadulterated spirits,
wine, and beer within the town, and none others are
permitted to engage in the business. These licensed
establishments are all in the hands of an incorporated
company, whose members are content to take five per
cent per annum upon their invested capital, handing
over the surplus to the town treasury, the sum thus
received being appropriated towards reducing the regular tax-rates imposed upon the citizens. The mana-
gers of these shops where liquor is sold have fixed
salaries, not at all contingent upon the profits realized
from the business, and therefore they have no inducement to urge customers to drink. We saw scarcely

any indications of intemperance here, and were assured by an intelligent resident that there had been much less drunkenness since this system had been adopted twelve years ago. As will be readily conceived, there is now a smaller number of dram-shops opened to tempt the weak. It is only too true that the " means to do ill deeds makes ill deeds done."

There is here also a system in operation designed to supply workingmen and persons of humble means with permanent dwelling-houses, — with homes which they may own. Comfortable brick houses are erected with all reasonable accommodations, and a title is made out to the would-be owner, he paying for the same by a small monthly instalment, until finally he owns the establishment. This being a philanthropic object, no profit above actual cost is designed to be realized by the promoters. The moral effect of the plan is excellent, leading to a sense of responsibility and economy among a class which is only too prone to expend its earnings for drink, or to fritter them away without realizing an equivalent.

It was found that the people in their domestic establishments had an odd way of prefacing their family meals; namely, partaking of raw salted salmon, smoked herring, chipped beef, and pickles of various kinds, which they washed down with one or two wine-glasses of strong spirit. It seemed to be an obvious inconsistency of purpose. This ceremony takes place at a side-table just before sitting down to the regular meal, be it breakfast, luncheon, or dinner.

This custom was noticed afterwards at various places in Scandinavia as well as in Russia, the practice in the latter country being universal in hotels and private houses; but it seemed obvious to us that it was only an excuse for dram-drinking as an appetizer. Bad habits are easily acquired, and soon make slaves of their incautious victims. More than one person admitted to us in Russia that without this preliminary tipple, dinner to them would have no relish.

CHAPTER IV.

Capital of Norway. — A Grand Fjord. — A Free and Independent State. — The Legal Code. — Royal Palace and Gardens. — Oscar's Hall. — The University. — Public Amusements. — The Ice Trade. — Ancient Viking Ships. — Heathen Tombs. — An Interesting Hostelry. — A Steam Kitchen. — Environs of Christiania. — Horses and their Treatment. — Harvest Time. — Women's Work. — The Sæter. — A Remarkable Lake. — Wild Birds. — Inland Travel. — Scandinavian Wild Flowers. — Lonely Habitations. — A Land of Alpine Heights.

IN approaching the capital of Norway by sea from Gottenburg, the Christiania fjord is ascended for a distance of seventy miles to its head, bordered on either side nearly the whole way by finely-wooded hills, and its surface dotted by emerald isles reflected in the deep mirror-like waters. It must be understood that a fjord is not a sound, nor is it a thoroughfare in the full sense of that word; it is a *cul de sac*. This of Christiania at its *débouchure* is just fifteen miles in width, and like many other Norwegian fjords is much deeper than the sea beyond its mouth. The entrance is marked by a powerful and lofty lighthouse on the island of Færder. The ancient citadel of Akershus, built upon a bold and rocky promontory some six hundred years ago, commands the approach to the city. In this curious old fortification are kept the regalia and national records, the tree-adorned ramparts serving as a pleasant promenade for the public. One is often reminded while sailing upon Norwegian fjords of the Swiss lake-scenery. This leading to the capital is not unlike Lake Geneva in the vicinity of Vevay and Chillon, except that it is bolder in its immediate shores and is also broader and deeper than Lake Leman. The city, which is built upon a gradual slope facing the south, is seen to good advantage from the harbor. No more appropriate spot could have been selected for the national capital by Christian IV., who founded it, and after whom it is named, than the head of this beautiful elongated bay. An ancient town named Oslo occupied the site in the middle of the eleventh century. It is the seat of the Storthing, or Parliament; and the King, whose permanent residence is at Stockholm, is expected to reside here, attended by the court, at least three months of the year. With its immediate suburbs, the population of the city is a hundred and twenty-five thousand. It should be remembered that Norway is a free and independent State, though it is under the crown of Sweden, and that the people are thoroughly democratic, having abolished all titles of nobility by enactment of the Storthing (Great Court) so early as 1821, at which time a law was also passed forbidding the King to create a new nobility. Nevertheless, the thought occurs to us here that these Northmen, who overran and conquered the British Isles, founded the very nobility there which is the present boast and pride of England. We find some problems solved in Norway which have created political strife elsewhere. Though its Church is identical with the State, unlimited toleration exists. There is also a perfect system of political representation, and while justice is open to one and all, litigation is sedulously discouraged. The meetings of the Storthing are quite independent of the King, not even requiring a writ of assemblage from him. Thus it will be seen that though nominally under despotic rule, Norway is really self-governed.

The legal code of Norway is well worthy of study, both on account of its antiquity and its admirable provisions. The old sea-kings, or free-booters as we have been accustomed to consider them, had a more advanced and civilized code than any of the people whose shores they devastated. Before the year 885 the power of the law was established over all persons of all ranks, while in the other countries of Europe the independent jurisdiction of the feudal lords defied the law until centuries later. Before the eleventh century the Scandinavian law provided for equal justice to all, established a system of weights and measures, also one for the maintenance of roads and bridges, and for the protection of women and animals,— subjects which no other European code at that time embraced. These laws were collected into one code by Magnus VII. about the year 1260. They were revised by Christian IV. in 1604, and in 1687 the present system was drawn up. So simple and compact is it that the whole is contained in a pocket volume, which is in the possession of every Norwegian family. Each law occupies but a single paragraph, and all is simple and intelligible. Speaking of these early law-makers (as well as law-breakers!) Carlyle says: "In the old Sea-Kings, what an indomitable energy! Silent, with closed lips, as I fancy them, unconscious that they were specially brave; defying the wild ocean with its monsters, and all men and things; progenitors of our Blakes and Nelsons!"

The Royal Palace of Christiania is pleasantly situated on an elevated site, the highest ground in fact within the city, surrounded by an open park containing miniature lakes, canals, and groves of charming trees. The park is called the Royal Gardens, which are always open to the public. Fronting the palace is an admirable equestrian statue in bronze of the citizen King Bernadotte, who ascended the throne of Sweden under the name of Carl Johan XIV., and it bears his consistent motto: "The people's love is my reward." The palace is a large plain edifice of brick, quadrangular in shape and painted a dull ugly yellow, with a simple portico. It was erected within the last fifty years, and looks externally like a huge cotton-factory. The Queen's apartments are on the ground floor and are very beautifully furnished, especially the White Saloon, so called. Above these are the King's apartments, embracing the usual variety of state halls, audience chambers, reception rooms and the like, plainly and appropriately furnished. The palace contains some of Tidemand's best pictures. There is also a royal villa called Oscar's Hall, situated in the immediate environs on the peninsula of Ladegaardsöen, less than three miles from the city proper. It is a Gothic structure amid the woods, eighty feet above the level of the waters of the harbor which it overlooks. Oscar Hall, with its one castellated tower, is scarcely more than a shooting-box in size, though it is dignified with the name of palace. The grounds are wild and irregular, covered mostly with a fine growth of trees, mingled with which the mountain ash was conspicuous with its clusters of berries in royal scarlet. The air was full of the fragrance of the lily-of-the-valley, which lovely little flower grows here after its own sweet will in rank profusion. There are a few choice paintings in the Hall, especially some admirable panels by Tidemand representing scenes in Norwegian peasant life, and called "The Age of Man from the cradle to the grave." There are also, we feel constrained to say, some very poor pictures on the walls of Oscar's Hall. In the garden near the villa were many familiar flowers in a thrifty condition, such as lilacs, white and scarlet honeysuckles, sweet peas, yellow tiger-lilies and peonies, besides some curious specimens of cacti and a wonderfully fragrant bed of low-growing mignonette. It was singular to see flowers and fruits which with us have each their special season, here hastening into bloom and ripeness all together.

The streets of the city are quite broad, most of them running at right angles with each other. The houses are generally of brick, stuccoed, though there are some of stone, and all have the effect of stone structures. There was once a richly endowed cathedral here, where James I. of England was married to Anne of Denmark in 1589, but it was destroyed by fire, which element has completely devastated the place at different periods, so that the present aspect is one of a substantial modern character. The old wooden houses have almost entirely disappeared. The present cathedral is in the shape of a Greek cross, but it is of no special interest. Over the altar is a painting by a German artist representing our Saviour in the Garden of Gethsemane, a work of much more than ordinary merit. The inhabitants of Christiania are almost exclusively Protestants.

The University founded by Frederick VI. in 1811 is a plain but massive structure, the front ornamented with Corinthian pillars of polished red granite. It accommodates at the present writing some nine hundred students, the tuition being free to all native applicants suitably prepared; it contains also a noble library of over two hundred thousand volumes, besides many manuscripts of inestimable value. The library is freely open even to strangers under very simple restrictions. The University also contains an extensive Museum of Zoölogy and Geology, which in the departments of the bronze and iron periods excels even the admirable one at Copenhagen. Christiania has a Naval, a Military, and an Art school, a Lunatic Asylum, an Astronomical Observatory, and various charitable institutions; nor should we forget to mention its admirably conducted Botanical Garden situated about a mile from the town, containing among other interesting varieties a very finely-arranged collection of Alpine plants from Spitzbergen and Iceland. The town has its Casino, Tivoli, or whatever we please to call it; the good citizens here have named it the Klinkenberg. It is a place of out-door amusement for old and young, where grown up children ride wooden-horses and participate in childish games with apparently as much zest as the little ones. Here we found peep-shows, pistol-galleries, Russian slides, a small theatre, and cafés where were dispensed beer, music, and Swedish punch,—this last very sweet and very intoxicating! The acrobat, with his two small boys in silver-spangles and flesh-colored tights, was present and especially active, besides the conventional individual who eats tow and blows fire from his mouth. On the occasion of our visit the last named individual came to grief, and burned his nether lip severely.

The commerce of Christiania is increasing annually. Over two thousand vessels were entered at its custom house during the year 1885. There are regular lines of steamers established between here and London, Hull, Glasgow, Copenhagen, and other ports, which transact a large amount of business in the freight department, with a considerable incidental passenger trade. The harbor is frozen over at least three months of the year, though that of Hammerfest, situated a thousand miles farther north on the coast of Norway, is never closed by ice, owing to the genial influence of the Gulf Stream, — an agent so potent as to modify the temperature of the entire coast of Scandinavia on its western border. Wenham Lake Ice, which was originally and for some years shipped from Massachusetts to England, now comes direct from the Christiania fjord! An English company has long owned a lake near Dröbak, which yields them an ample supply of ice annually. The London ice-carts still bear the name of " Wenham Lake," but the ice comes from Norway. We were told that the quantity shipped for use in England increases yearly as ice grows to be more and more of a domestic necessity.

The Storthing's Hus is quite a handsome and imposing building, of original design in the Romanesque and Byzantine style, facing the Carl Johannes Square, the largest open area in the city. It was finished and occupied in 1866. The Market Place is adorned with a marble statue of Christian IV. Another fine square is the Eidsvolds Plads, planted with choice trees and carpeted with intensely bright greensward. The chief street is the Carl Johannes Gade, a broad boulevard extending from the railroad station to the King's Palace, half way between which stands the imposing structure of the University. Opposite this edifice is the Public Garden, where an out-door concert is given during the summer evenings by a military band. In a large wooden building behind the University is kept that great unrivalled curiosity, the Viking ship, a souvenir of more than nine hundred years ago. The blue clay of the district where it was exhumed in 1880, a few miles south from Christiania at Gokstad, has preserved it nearly intact. The men who built the graceful lines of this now crumbling vessel, "in some remote and dateless day," knew quite as much of the principles of marine architecture as do our modern shipwrights of to-day. This interesting relic, doubtless the oldest ship in the world, once served the Vikings, its masters, as a war-craft. It is eighty feet long by sixteen wide, and is about six feet deep from gunwale to keel. Seventy shields, spears, and other war equipments recovered with the hull show that it was designed for that number of fighting men. A curious thrill is felt by one while regarding these ancient weapons and armor, accompanied by a wish that they might speak and reveal their long-hidden story. In such vessels as this the dauntless Northmen made voyages to every country in Europe, and as is confidently believed they crossed the Atlantic, discovering North America centuries before the name of Columbus was known. Ignoring the halo of romance and chivalry which the poets have thrown about the valiant Vikings and their followers, one thing we are compelled to admit: they were superb marine architects. Ten centuries of progressive civilization have served to produce none better. Some of the arts and sciences may and do exhibit great progress in excellence, but shipbuilding is not among them. We build bigger but not better vessels. This ancient galley of oak, in the beauty of its lines, its adaptability for speed, and its general sea-worthiness, cannot be surpassed by our best naval constructors to-day. An American naval officer who chanced to be present with the author, declared that there were points about this exhumed vessel which indicated retrogression rather than progress on the part of modern builders of sea-going craft. The bent timbers on the inside are of natural growth, the sheathing boards are an inch and a half in thickness, firmly riveted, the iron bolts clinched on either end. Near the gunwales the bolts are of oak. The planking slightly overlaps, being bevelled for the purpose; that is, the hull is what we technically call clinker-built, and would probably draw about four feet of water in a sea-going trim. The bow and stern are of the same pointed shape, and rise a considerable distance above the waist, giving the vessel what sailors term a deep sheer inboard.

The burial of this ship so many centuries ago was simply in accordance with the custom of those days. When any great sea-king perished, he was enclosed in the cabin of his galley, and either sunk in the ocean or buried with his vessel and all of its war-like appointments upon the nearest suitable spot of land. In this instance, as has been intimated, weapons of war were buried with the deceased, just as our Indian tribes of western America do to this day. Tombs dating much farther back than the period when this sepulchral ship was buried have been opened in both Norway and Sweden, showing that the dead were sometimes burned and sometimes buried in coffins. The cinerary urns were usually found to have been either of terra-cotta or of bronze, — seldom, however, of the latter material. In these tombs trinkets and weapons were also discovered, with the skeletons of horses and other domestic animals. To the period of these burials belong the earliest Runic inscriptions, differing materially from those which were in use a few centuries later. One may believe much or little of the extravagant stories handed down by tradition concerning these ancient Scandinavians, but certainly we have tangible evidence in these tombs that some of the legends are literally true. We are told that when a chieftain died in battle, not only were his war-horse, his gold and silver plate, and his money placed upon his funeral pyre, but that a guard of honor from among his followers slew themselves, that he might enter the sacred halls of Odin properly attended. The more elevated the chief the larger was the number who must sacrifice themselves as his escort to the land of bliss. So infinite was the reliance of the Heathen horde in their strange faith, that, far from considering their fate to be a hard one, they adopted its extremest requirements with songs of joy!

A general aspect of good order, thrift, industry, and prosperity prevails at Christiania. The simplicity of dress and the gentle manners, especially among the female portion of the community, were marked features. No stranger can fail to notice the low, sympathetic tones in which the women always speak; but though decorous and worthy, it must be admitted that the Norwegian ladies are not handsome. The people resort to the ramparts of the old castle as a promenade, with its grateful shade of lime-trees, and they also throng the pleasant Central Park near the Royal Palace. One sees here none of the rush and fever of living which so wearies the observer in many of the southern cities of Europe, — notably in Paris, London, and Vienna. The common people evince more solidity of character with less of the frivolities, and yet without any of the frosty chill of Puritanism. They may be said to be a trifle slow and phlegmatic, but by no means stupid. The most careless schoolboy when addressed by a stranger in the street instantly removes his hat, and so remains until he has fully responded to the inquiry made of him, showing thus the instinctive politeness which seems to permeate all classes in Norway.

The long-established Hotel Victoria is an interesting hostelry and museum combined, at least so far as ornithology is concerned. Its stuffed varieties of native birds disposed in natural positions here and there about the establishment, would prove the envy of any collector in this department of natural history. The house is built about a spacious court, which is partly occupied by a broad and lofty marquee or tent, under which the *table d'hôte* is served. Orange-trees and tropical plants are gracefully disposed, and creeping vines give a sylvan appearance to the court. The whole area is overlooked by an open and spacious

A STEAM KITCHEN. 69

balcony, where a band of musicians during the season dispense enlivening music. Tame sparrows and other birds hop about one's feet during each meal, even alighting upon the chairs and tables to share tid-bits with the guests. The whole formed a consistent purpose well carried out, and was entirely unlike any hotel whose hospitality we have shared. There are three or four excellent public houses besides the Victoria, including the Grand Hotel and the Scandinavia, the last two quite centrally located. We made our temporary home at the Grand, a spacious and comfortable establishment.

There is an original institution of a charitable nature in the capital, called a Steam Kitchen, where food is cooked upon a large scale, and entirely by steam. This large establishment, situated on the Torv Gade, was built especially for the purpose of benefiting the industrious poor of the city. Here two or three thousand persons are daily provided with good wholesome dinners at a minimum charge, calculated to cover the actual cost. While hundreds of persons carry away food to their families, larger numbers dine at the neat tables provided in the establishment for that purpose. The inference drawn from a casual observation of the system was, that no possible benevolence of a practical character could be better conceived or more judiciously administered. It seemed to be the consummation of a great charity, robbed of all objectionable features. None appeared to feel humiliated in availing themselves of its advantages, since all the supposed cost of the provisions was charged and paid for.

Upon visiting a new city in any part of the world, the writer has learned more of its people, their national characteristics and all local matters worth knowing, by mingling with the throng, watching their every-day habits and conventionalities, observing and analyzing the stream of life pouring through its great thoroughfares, reading the expression upon human faces, and by regarding now and again chance domestic scenes, than from all the grand cathedrals, art galleries, show palaces, and guide-books combined. Years of travel fatigue one with the latter, but never with Nature in her varying moods, with the peculiarities of races, or with the manners and customs of every-day life as characterizing each new locality and country. The delight in natural objects grows by experience in every cultivated and receptive mind. The rugged architecture of lofty mountains, tumbling waterfalls, noble rivers, glowing sunsets, broad land and sea views, each has a special, never-tiring, and impressive individuality. While enjoying a bird's-eye view of Christiania from the height of Egeberg, a well-wooded hill four hundred feet in height in the southern suburb, it was difficult to believe one's self in Icelandic Scandinavia, — the precise latitude of the Shetland Islands. A drowsy hum like the drone of bees seemed to float up from the busy city below. The beautiful fjord with its graceful promontories, its picturesque and leafy isles, might be Lake Maggiore or Como, so

placid and calm is its pale-blue surface. Turning the
eyes inland, one sees clustered in lovely combination
fields of ripening grain, gardens, lawns, cottages, and
handsome villas, like a scene upon the sunny shores
of the Mediterranean near the foot-hills of the Maritime Alps. An abundance of deciduous trees enliven
the scene, — plane, sycamore, ash, and elm in luxuriant foliage. Warmer skies during the summer period
are not to be found in Italy, nor elsewhere outside of
Egypt. As we stood upon the height of Egeberg that
delicious sunny afternoon, there hung over and about
the Norwegian capital a soft golden haze such as
lingers in August above the Venetian lagoons.

The houses in the vicinity of Christiania are generally surrounded by well-cultivated gardens embellished with choice fruit and ornamental trees. An
unmistakable aspect of refinement was obvious about
these homesteads, and one would fain have known
somewhat of the residents of such attractive domiciles.
The traveller who passes so few days in each new city,
and those occupied mostly in observations of a different
character, can hardly pretend to express an opinion
of the resident social life and domestic associations;
but we were credibly informed that there was no
dearth of circles composed of intelligent, polished,
and wealthy individuals in Bergen, Gottenburg, or
Christiania. Evidences of the truth of this are certainly obvious to the most casual observer. Here,
and afterwards still farther north, a tree new to us
was found, called the Hägg (*Prunus Padus*), so

abundantly clothed in snow-white blossoms as to entirely hide its leaves of green. It generally stood in the yards of dwelling-houses as a floral ornament, and reminded one of a New England apple-tree in full bloom. The blossoms emitted very little decided perfume, but the luxuriant growth and the pure white flower were very beautiful. A dainty bit of color now and again, caused by the single-leafed dog-rose, recalled the inland roads of far-off Massachusetts, where mingled blackberry and raspberry bushes and wild roses so often line the quiet paths. The immediate environs of the capital are characterized by fine picturesque elevations, the land rising gradually on all sides until it becomes quite Alpine. The forest road leading towards Rynkan Falls was fragrant with the soft, soothing odor of pines and firs, mingled with that of blue, pink, and yellow flowers, blossoms whose local names only served to puzzle us,—" wee, modest, crimson-tipped flowers." The giant larkspur, lilies-of-the-valley, and some orchids were familiar, and greeted the senses like old friends. The juniper bushes were luxuriant, and there were plenty of bilberries and wild strawberries in bloom. These last berries when ripe, as we afterwards found them farther north, are a revelation to the palate, being quite small, but of exquisite flavor, recalling the tiny wood-strawberries of New England, which were of such exquisite flavor and dainty aroma before we cultivated them into monstrosities. The summer is so short here as to give the fruits and flowers barely time to blossom, ripen, and fade, or the husbandman a chance to gather his harvest. Vegetation is wonderfully rapid in its growth, the sunshine being so nearly constant during the ten weeks which intervene between seed-time and harvest. Barley grows here two and a half inches and peas three inches in twenty-four hours, for several consecutive days. It is an interesting fact that if the barley-seed be brought from a warmer climate it requires to become acclimated, and does not yield a good crop until after two or three seasons. The flowers of the torrid and temperate zones as a rule close their eye-lids like human beings, and sleep a third or half of the twenty-four hours; but in Arctic regions life to these lovely children of Nature is one long sunny period, and sleep comes only with death and decay. It was also observed that the flowers here assume more vivid colors and emit more fragrance during their brief lives than in the south. The long delightful period of twilight during the summer season is seen here in all its perfection, full of suggestiveness and roseate loveliness, which no pen can satisfactorily describe. There is no dew to be encountered and avoided, no dampness. All is crystal clearness and transparency, " gilding pale streams with heavenly alchemy."

Nothing can be pleasanter or more exhilarating than driving over the Norwegian roads among the dark pine forests or by the side of dashing torrents and swift-gliding, seething rivers. The roads are kept in perfect condition upon all of the regular post-routes, and one rolls over them in the native carriole nearly as smoothly as though navigating a lake in a well-manned boat. The little horses, almost universally of a dun-color and having their manes cropped short, are wiry and full of life and courage, dashing down the hills at a seemingly reckless pace, which carries the vehicle half way up the next rising ground by the mere impetus of the descent. It was particularly gratifying to observe the physical condition of the horses both inland and in the streets of Christiania, all being in good flesh. Not a lame or poor animal was to be found among them, either in hack, dray, or country-produce cart. They are mostly pony-shaped, rather short in the legs, few standing over fourteen hands, and generally even less; but yet they are strong, tough, and round in form. It was pleasing to observe the drivers, who seemed also to be the owners, of these animals. When they came from the house or establishment where their business called them, they would often take some appetizing trifle from their pockets, — a small apple, a lump of sugar, or bit of bread, — and tender it to the waiting horse, who was evidently on the look-out for such a favor. The good fellowship established between the animal and his master was complete, and both worked the more effectively together. No observant person can fail to see what docility and intelligence kindness to any domestic animal is sure to elicit, while brutality and harshness induce only reluctant and inefficient service. If the whip is used at all upon these faithful animals it must be very uncommon, since a watchfulness in regard to the matter did not discover a single instance. When a driver has occasion to stop before a house and leave his horse, he takes one turn of the rein about the animal's near fore-foot and secures the long end loosely to the shaft. Custom has taught the horses that this process ties them to the spot, and they do not attempt to move away under any circumstances. Insects during the brief but intense heat of summer are very troublesome to animals exposed to their bite, and so the Norwegian horses are all wisely permitted to wear long tails as a partial defence against flies and gnats. The price at which they are valued is very moderate. A nicely-matched pair, quite sound, young, and well broken for pleasure driving, can be purchased for three hundred dollars or less.

Between Christiania and Stockholm the railroad follows almost a straight line due east across southern Norway and Sweden through a country dotted over with little hamlets of a dozen houses more or less, occupied by thrifty farmers. The people are of a social, kindly disposition, but to be known among them as an American insures instant service, together with unlimited hospitality. Nearly every family has one or more representatives living in the United States, and the very name of America is regarded by them with tenderness. A large percentage of the young people look forward to the time when they shall eventually make it their permanent home.

Emigration is neither promoted nor discouraged by the Government. Norway seems generally to be more fertile than Sweden. True, she has her numerous mountains, but between them are far-reaching and beautiful valleys, while the sister country with less elevations has a soil of rather a sandy nature, much less productive. But intelligent farming overcomes heavy drawbacks; and there are large tracts of land in Sweden that are rendered quite remunerative through the adoption of modern methods of cultivation. Immediately about the railroad stations on all the Scandinavian railroads there are fine gardens, often ornamented with fountains, bird-houses, blooming flowers, and miniature cascades. Some of the combinations of floral colors into graceful figures showed the hand of experienced gardeners. Most of these station-houses, all of which are constructed of wood, are extremely picturesque, built in châlet style, rather over-ornamented by fancy carvings and high colors, yet well adapted in the main for their special purpose. The Government owns and operates three quarters of all the railroads in either country, and will doubtless ere long, as we were assured, control the entire system.

In the rural districts women are very generally employed upon out-of-door work, as they are in Germany and Italy, and there is quite a preponderance of the sex in both Norway and Sweden. It was the haying and harvesting season when the author passed over the principal routes, and the fields showed four times as many women as men engaged in mowing, reaping, loading heavy carts, and getting in the harvest generally. What would our New England farmers think to see a woman swing a scythe all day in the haying season, cutting as broad and true a swath as a man can do, and apparently with as little fatigue! Labor is very poorly paid; forty cents per day is considered liberal wages for a man except in the cities, where a small increase is realized upon this amount. The houses all through Norway outside of the towns are built of logs, well-matched and smoothly finished, laid horizontally one upon another, like our frontier cabins in the far West. Each farm, besides the home acres, has also connected with it what is termed a "sæter," being a tract of mountain pasture, where a portion of the young members of the family (usually the girls only) pass the nine or ten weeks of summer engaged in cheese-making, the cattle being kept on the hills for that period. Here a very rude hut with but two apartments serves for the girls, and a rough shed for the cattle at night. The outer apartment of the hut contains a stove, a table, and a coarse bed, forming the living-room, while the inner one is improved for the dairy. The available soil about the home farm in the valley must raise hay and grain for the long winter's use. After being milked in the morning, at the sæter, the cows, goats, and sheep go directly to their allotted feeding ground, perhaps more than a mile away, and at the evening hour they by themselves as surely return to be milked. The only inducement for such regularity on the part of the intelligent creatures, so far as we could understand, was a few handfuls of salt which was given them nightly, and of which they seemed to be very fond. Great exertion is made by the girls in the mountains to excel one another as to the aggregate production of cheese for the season, much pride being felt also in the quality of the article. The sturdy figures and healthy blooming faces of these girls, "with cheeks like apples which the sun has ruddied," showed what physical charms the bracing mountain air and a simple manner of life in these regions is capable of producing.

Norway has been appropriately called the country of mountains and fjords, of cascades and lakes. Among the largest of the latter is Lake Mjösen, which is about sixty miles long and has an average width of twelve. It is certainly a very remarkable body of water. It receives into its bosom one important river, the Lougen, after it has run a course of nearly a hundred and fifty miles. At its southern extremity is the port of Eidsvold, and at the northern is Lillehammer. These are situated in the direct route between Christiania and Tröndhjem. But the most singular fact attached to the lake is that it measures over fifteen hundred feet in depth, while its surface is four hundred feet above the level of the ocean. Its bottom is known to be nearly a thousand feet below that of the North Sea, which would seem to show that it must be the mouth of some long-extinct volcano. Neither glacial action nor any other physical agent known to us can have dug an abrupt hole eight or ten hundred feet deep; and yet there are also some dry valleys in Norway whose bottoms are considerably below that of the sea. The river Mesna tumbles boisterously into the lake close to Lillehammer. A walk beside its thickly-wooded banks brings to view many beautiful cascades and waterfalls, some of which are worthier of a visit than many of the more famous falls of Scandinavia. On all the important inland routes not furnished with railroad or steamboat transit Government supports a system of postal service, whereby one can easily travel in almost any desired direction. On such excursions the keen air and free exercise are apt to endow the traveller with an excellent appetite, which Norwegian fare is not quite calculated to assuage. However, the milk is almost always good, and eggs are generally to be had. Even hard black bread will yield to a hammer, after which it can be soaked in milk and thus rendered eatable. One does not come hither in search of delicate and appetizing food, but rather to stand face to face with Nature in her wildest and most rugged moods. The pleasures of the table are better sought in the big capitals of southern Europe or America, where "rich food and heavy groans go together."

As to the fauna of Norway, the reindeer, the bear, the wolf, the fox, and the lynx about complete the list of indigenous animals. The ubiquitous crow abounds; and fine specimens of the golden eagle, that dignified monarch of the upper regions, may occasionally be seen sailing through the air from cliff to cliff, across the fjords and valleys. At certain seasons of the year this bird proves destructive to domestic fowls and young lambs. But we escaped in Norway the almost inevitable legend of a young child having been carried off by an eagle to its nearly inaccessible nest; that story is still monopolized by Switzerland. For some reason not quite understood by the author, the mischievous magpie is here held as half sacred. That is to say, the country people have a superstition that any injury inflicted upon these birds entails misfortune upon him who causes it; and yet the Government offers a premium for their destruction. Magpies appear to be as much of a nuisance in Norway as crows are in India or Ceylon, and to be quite as unmolested by the people generally. What are called the wild birds of Scandinavia are in fact remarkably tame, and they embrace a large variety. As the traveller proceeds through the country, he will observe sheaves of unthrashed grain elevated upon poles beside the farmhouses and barns, which are designed to furnish the feathered visitors with food. These sheaves are regularly renewed all through the winter season; otherwise the birds would starve. The confiding little creatures know their friends, and often enter the houses for protection from the severity of the weather. Neither man, woman, nor child would think of disturbing them, for they are considered as bringing good luck to the premises which they visit. The bounty paid for the destruction of bears and wolves in 1885 showed that nearly two hundred of each species of these animals were killed by the hunters. Bears are believed to be gradually decreasing, but wolves are still very numerous in the northerly regions and the thickly-wooded middle districts. In extreme seasons, when pressed by hunger, they prove destructive to the reindeer herds of the Lapps in spite of every ordinary precaution, and even in the summer season farmers never leave their sheep unguarded when they are pastured away from the homestead.

In journeying from the capital to Tröndhjem (where the steamer is taken for the North Cape) by the way of Lillehammer, one crosses the Dovrefjeld, or mountain plateau; but a more popular route is by rail from city to city. This fjeld lies a little above the sixty-second parallel of latitude, and is about one third of the distance from the southern to the northern extreme of the country, which reaches from the fifty-eighth to the seventy-first parallel. The famous elevation called the Sneehaettan — " Snow Hat " — forms a part of this Alpine range, and is one of the loftiest in Norway, falling little short of eight thousand feet in altitude. To be exact, it ranks sixth among the Scandinavian mountains. It should be remembered that one eighth of the country lies within the region of perpetual snow, and that these lofty and nearly inaccessible heights are robed in a constant garb of bridal whiteness. No other part of Europe or any inhabited portion of the globe has such enormous glaciers or snowfields, unless possibly some portions of Alaska. Here in Norway are glaciers which cover from four to five hundred square miles, descending from plateaus three and four thousand feet in height down to very near sea-level, as in the instance of the mammoth Svartisen glacier, which is visited by all travellers to the North Cape. Arctic and Alpine flowers abound in the region of the Dovrefjeld, — and glacial flowers are abundant, though not so much so as in the more frequently visited snow regions of Switzerland. As the ice and snow recede in the early summer, the plants spring up with magic promptness, so that within a few yards the same species are seen in successive stages of growth, spring and summer flowers blooming side by side in rather forced companionship. The blue gentians are extremely lovely, and are among the first to appear after the mantle of snow is lifted from the awaking earth. The most remarkable and abundant of the spring flowers however is the *linnæa borealis*, thus appropriately named after the great Swedish botanist and naturalist. It is a long, low-creeping plant bearing a pink blossom, and is in full bloom early in July, luxuriating all over the Scandinavian peninsula. Harebells nodding upon their delicate stems, primroses, snowdrops, and small blue pansies are also common. In the southern districts roses of various species thrive in glorious profusion in the open air annually during the short genial period, and also as domestic favorites during the long night of winter, adorning and perfuming the living-rooms of the people of every class in town and country.

Though the highest point in Norway or Sweden is only about eighty-five hundred feet above sea-level, an elevation which is reached only by the Jotunfjeld, or Giant Mountain, still no highlands in Europe surpass those of Scandinavia in terrific and savage grandeur, "rocked-ribbed and ancient as the sun." Mont Blanc is fully one third higher than this Giant Mountain, but being less abrupt is hardly so striking and effective in aspect. The grand elevations of Norway are intersected by deep dark gorges and fearful chasms, roaring with impetuous torrents and enormous waterfalls, and affording an abundance of such scenes as would have inspired the pencil of Salvator Rosa. The mountain system here does not form a continuous range, but consists of a succession of plateaus like the Dovrefjeld, and of detached mountains rising from elevated bases. The length of this series of peculiar elevations — mountains and plateaus — is that of the entire peninsula, from the North Cape to Christiansand on the Skager Rack, some twelve hundred miles, having an average width of about two hundred miles, — which gives to the mountains of Norway and Sweden an area larger than the Alps, the Apennines, and the Pyrenees combined, while the lakes, waterfalls, and cascades far surpass those of the rest of Europe. There is no other country where so large a portion is covered with august mountains as in Norway. It includes an area of about one hundred and twenty-three thousand square miles; and it has been said by those most familiar with its topography, that could it be flattened out it would make as large a division of the earth as would any of the four principal continents. The ratio of arable land to the entire area of Norway is not more than one to ten, and were it not that the support of the people at large comes mainly from the sea, the country could not sustain one quarter of even its present sparse population. Undismayed by the preponderance of rocks, cliffs, and chasms, the people utilize every available rod of land. Here and there are seen wire ropes extending from the low lands to the mountain sides, the upper ends of which are lost to sight, and which are used for sliding down bundles of compressed hay after it has been cut, made, and packed in places whither only men accustomed to scale precipices could possibly climb. The aspect of such regions is severe and desolate in the extreme, even when viewed beneath the cheering smiles of a summer sun. What then must be their appearance during the long, trying winter of these hyperborean regions? In snug corners, sheltered by friendly rocks and cliffs from the prevailing winds, are seen little clusters of cabins inhabited by a few lowly people who live in seeming content, and who rear families amid almost incredible deprivations and climatic disadvantages, causing one to wonder at their hardihood and endurance. It is not uncommon to see along the west coast of Norway, among the islands and upon the main-land, farm-houses surrounded by a few low buildings of the rudest character, perched among rocks away up on some lofty green terrace, so high indeed as to make them seem scarcely larger than an eagle's nest. To anybody but a mountaineer these spots are positively inaccessible, and every article of subsistence, except what is raised upon the few acres of available earth surrounding the house, must be carried up thither upon men's backs, for not even a mule could climb to these regions. A few goats and sheep must constitute the entire animal stock which such a spot can boast, with perhaps a few domestic fowls. These dwellings have been constructed of logs cut in some of the sheltered gulches near at hand and drawn to the spot with infinite labor, one by one. It would seem that such persistent and energetic industry applied in more inviting neighborhoods would have insured better results. What must life be passed in such an isolated, exposed place, in a climate where the ground is covered with snow for nine months of each year! Some few of these eyries have bridle-paths leading up to them which are barely passable; and yet such are thought by the occupants to be especially favored.

CHAPTER V.

Ancient Capital of Norway. — Routes of Travel. — Rain ! — Peasant Costumes. — Commerce of Bergen. — Shark's *vs.* Cod Liver Oil. — Ship-Building. — Public Edifices. — Quaint Shops. — Borgund Church. — Leprosy in Norway. — Sporting Country. — Inland Experiences. — Hay-Making. — Pine-Forest Experiences. — National Constitution. — People's Schools. — Girls' Industrial School. — Celebrated Citizens of Bergen. — Two Grand Norwegian Fjords. — Remarkable Glaciers.

BERGEN is situated some two hundred miles northwest of Christiania, and may be reached from thence by a carriole journey across the country over excellent roads, or by steamboat doubling the Naze. The latter route, though three times as far, is often adopted by travellers as being less expensive and troublesome. Still another and perhaps the most common route taken by tourists is that by way of Lake Mjösen, Gjöveg, the Fillefjeld and Laerdalsören, on the Sognefjord. This is called the Valders route, and affords by far the greatest variety of scenery. It involves railroad, steamer, and carriole modes of conveyance, and in all covers a distance of at least three hundred and fifty miles. It will be remembered that Bergen was the capital of Norway when it was under Danish rule, and was long afterwards the commercial rival of Christiania. Indeed, its shipping interests we were informed still exceed those of the capital, the verity of which statement one is inclined to question. The period of its greatest prosperity was in the Middle Ages and during the century when the great Hanseatic League flourished, at which time there was a numerous German colony resident here. The town appears very ancient, and naturally so, as it dates back to the eleventh century. Many of the dwellings are quaint with sharp-peaked roofs and gable-ends toward the streets. The boats which ply in the harbor and throng the wharves differ but little from the style of those used by the Norse pirates a thousand years ago, and who congregated in force about these very shores. The oldest part of the city lies on the eastern side of the harbor where the fortress of Bergenhuus and the double-towered Maria Kirke are situated. The inhabitants are not amphibious, but they certainly ought to be, since it rains here five days out of every seven. Some one has aptly called it the fatherland of drizzle, " where the hooded clouds, like friars, tell their beads in drops of rain." The first and foremost business of the place, therefore, is dealing in umbrellas and water-proof clothing. We did not observe any special crest as indicating the corporate arms of the city, but if such a design exists, it should be surmounted by a full-length figure of Jupiter Pluvius. We were assured that the rain-fall here averages six feet annually. There is a tradition of sunny days having occurred in Bergen, but much patience and long waiting are necessary to verify it. Still there is plenty of life and business activity in the broad clean streets, and more especially in and about the wharves and shipping.

One sees here more of the traditional Norwegian costumes than are to be met with either at Gottenburg or Christiania. Some of the old men who came from the inland villages were particularly noticeable, forming vivid and artistic groups, with their long snowy hair flowing freely about face and neck in the most patriarchal fashion. They wore red-worsted caps, open shirt-collars, knee-breeches, and jackets and vests decked with a profusion of silver buttons, like a Basque postilion. The women wear black jackets, bright-red bodices and scarlet petticoats, with white linen aprons. On the street called the Strandgade many Norse costumes mingle together like colors in a kaleidoscope. Our guide pointed out one group, which was perhaps more strongly individualized than the rest, as coming from the Tellemark district. Various nationalities were also represented, not forgetting the despised and much persecuted Jews, who are nearly as unpopular in Scandinavia as they are in Germany and Russia. The Strandgade is the longest thoroughfare in the city, and runs parallel with the harbor. By turning to the left after reaching the customhouse and passing up the rising ground, one reaches the Observatory, from whence a fine view of Bergen and its environs is obtained. The dusky red-tiled roofs crowded together, the square wooden towers of the churches mingled with the public gardens dressed in warmest verdure, form altogether a quaint and impressive picture. The town rises from the bay nearly in the form of a crescent, nestling at the feet of the surrounding hills on the west coast of Norway, between those two broad and famous arms of the sea, the Sognefjord and the Hardangerfjord. The first named indents the coast to a distance of one hundred and six miles, the latter seventy miles, — the first being north, and the last south of Bergen. The excellent situation of the harbor and its direct steam communication with European ports give this ancient city an extensive commerce in proportion to the number of inhabitants, who do not aggregate more than forty thousand. A large portion of the town is built upon a promontory, and between it and the main-land on its north side is the harbor, which is rarely frozen over owing to the influence of the Gulf Stream, while the harbor of St. Petersburg, in about the same latitude, is annually closed by ice for at least three months.

The staple commodity of Bergen is dried fish, mostly cod, supplemented by large quantities of cod-liver oil, lumber, and wood for fuel. It may not be generally known that a considerable portion of what is denominated cod-liver oil is produced from sharks' livers, which in fact are believed to be characterized by the same medicinal qualities as are those of the cod. At any rate, with this object sharks are sought for along the upper coast of Norway in the region of the Lofodens, and their livers are employed as described. An average-sized shark, we were told, will yield thirty gallons of good merchantable oil, but the article could not obtain a market except under the popular name of cod-liver oil. Catching the sharks is not an employment entirely devoid of danger, as they are often found to be large and very powerful, measuring from twenty-five to thirty feet in length. The shark like the whale, when it is struck with the harpoon, must at first be given plenty of line or it will drag down the boat in its rapid descent to deep water. Sometimes the struggle to capture the fish is a long and serious one, as it must thoroughly exhaust itself before it will yield. When finally drawn to the side of the boat, a heavy well-directed blow upon the nose completely stuns the creature, and the capture is then complete. The diminution in the number of sharks upon the coast has led to a large natural increase in the number of herring, the catching of which forms a special and profitable branch of Norwegian industry.

It is here at Bergen that the cargoes of fish caught on the coast at the far North and within the Arctic Circle are packed and reshipped to European ports. Lobsters are trapped in immense quantities just off the coast, whence the London market is mostly supplied. We were told that over two millions of this product were annually exported to Great Britain. They are shipped alive to England, where owing to some attributed excellence they are specially favored above those coming from any other locality. The Fish Market is the great business centre of Bergen, situated at the end of the Torv, at a small pier called Triangelen. The fish intended for local domestic use are kept alive in large tubs of water near the shore, and when desired by the purchaser are scooped out with a net, killed by a sharp blow upon the head, and sold by weight, the price being ridiculously low. Owing to its topographical character and location, Bergen will never become a railroad centre; its principal trade will remain in connection with the sea alone. Ship-building is carried on here to a considerable extent. We saw one iron steamer which was constructed and equipped in this harbor; and a finely finished craft she was, of over a thousand tons burden. There are some fine public squares, a People's Park, wherein a military band plays twice a week, half-a-dozen churches, a commodious Theatre, a Royal Palace, a Musical Institute, a Public Library, and a Museum; but there is scarcely a trace of architectural beauty in all Norway with the exception of the cathedral at Tröndhjem, which is formed of a mixture of orders, the Norman predominating. The Church of St. Mary is only interesting for its antiquity, dating as it does from the twelfth century. Its curious and grotesque façade bears the date of 1118.

A glance at the map will show the reader that Norway is broadest where a line drawn eastward from Bergen would divide it, giving a width of a little over two hundred and eighty miles, while the length of her territory is four times as great. The Gottenburg liquor-system, as it is called, has long been adopted in this city, and seems to operate as advantageously here as in the place of its origin. Nevertheless, the people are what we call in America hard drinkers, though little absolute drunkenness was observable. The quaint little shops of the town, which are slightly raised above the level of the street, have another and rather inferior class of stores under them, accessible by descending steps from the thoroughfare. This division of trade, by arranging a series of basement stores, is so common here as to form a feature of the town; and the same is observable in Copenhagen, where many jewelry, art, and choice retail stores are located in the basement of the houses, with an establishment devoted to some other line of trade above them. The shops in Bergen are well filled with odd antique articles, mostly of domestic use, such as old plate, drinking-cups, spoons, and silver goblets bearing the marks of age and the date of two or three centuries past. A little experience is apt to create considerable doubt in the minds of inquiring travellers as to the genuineness of these articles, which, like those found in the odd curio shops of Japan, are very largely manufactured to order in this blessed year of our Lord, however they may be dated.

The native jewelry is curious and some of it quite pretty, not for personal wear, but as a souvenir. Evidences of thrift and prosperity impress the stranger on every side, while extremes in the social condition of the people do not appear to exist. They are neither very rich nor very poor. There are no mendicants or idlers to be seen; all persons appear to have some legitimate occupation. One looks about in vain for any sign of the thirty-two churches and half-score of convents which history tells us once made of the place a noted religious centre and a Mecca for devotional pilgrims. The Cathedral of St. Olaf is venerable, dating from 1248; but except its antiquity it presents nothing of special interest to the stranger. There are numerous handsome villas in the immediate environs, where some very creditable landscape gardening is to be seen, while the surrounding fields are clothed in emerald vegetation. Some new villas were observed in course of erection, but as we continued our stroll the sterile and rocky hills which form the background to the picture of Bergen were soon reached. A favorite walk in the suburbs is to the Svartediket, a lake which supplies the city with water, pure and excellent. At Tjosanger, not far away, is one of the ancient wooden churches of the country, almost identical with the more noted one at Borgund. This queer old structure at the last named place now belongs to the Antiquarian Society of Christiania, and is very curious with its numerous gables, shingle-covered roofs, and walls surmounted with dragons' heads. It is strangely sombre, with its dark and windowless interior, but is the best preserved church of its kind in all Norway, dating as it does from the twelfth century. But we were speaking of the immediate environs of Bergen. About a mile outside of the city there is a leper hospital, devoted solely to the unfortunate victims of this terrible disease. Notwithstanding the persistent and scientific effort which has been made by the Government, still it seems extremely difficult to eradicate this dreaded pest from the country. The too free use of fish as a food is thought by many to be a promoting cause of leprosy. Those who are affected by it are not permitted to marry if the disease has once declared itself; so that as a hereditary affliction it is very properly kept in check. There are three hospitals set aside in the country for the exclusive treatment of those thus afflicted; one is at Molde, one at Trondhjem, and the other we have mentioned at Bergen. Physicians say that the disease is slowly decreasing in the number of its victims, and the patients now domiciled in the three districts amount to but fifteen hundred, equally divided among them. One mitigating feature of this loathsome affliction is the fact that it is not considered to be contagious; but those who inherit it can never escape its fatality.

The country lying between Bergen and Christiania, and indeed nearly every part of Norway, presents great attractions to the angler, who must, however, go prepared to rough it; but if he be a true lover of the sport, this will enhance rather than detract from the pleasure. The country is sparsely inhabited, and affords only the rudest accommodations for the wandering pedestrian who does not confine himself to the regular post-routes. The innumerable lakes, rivers, and streams swarm with delicious fish,— trout, grayling, and salmon being the most abundant species of the finny tribe. Many Englishmen come hither annually, attracted solely by this sport. The disciples of the rod who know these regions do not forget to bring with them ample protection against mosquitoes; for these tiny creatures are in wonderful abundance during the summer season, dividing the mastership with that other Norwegian pest, the flea, who is here the acknowledged giant of his tribe. Hotel accommodations even in Bergen are nothing to boast of. Every foreigner is supposed to be craving for salmon and reindeer meat, raw, smoked, pickled, or cooked.

A drive of a few leagues inland upon the charming roads in any direction will fill the stranger with delight, and afford characteristic pictures of great beauty. The farmers hang their cut grass upon frames of wood to dry, as we do clothes on washing-day. These frames are arranged in the mowing-fields in rows of a hundred feet in length, and are about five feet high. The effect in the haying season is quite striking and novel to the stranger. The agricultural tools used upon the farms are of the most primitive character; the ploughs are single-handed, and as awkward as the rude implement in use to-day in Egypt. The country houses are low, the roofs often covered with soil, and not infrequently rendered attractive with blooming heather and little blue-and-pink blossoms planted by Nature's hand, — the hieroglyphics in which she writes her impromptu poetry. In the meadows between the hills are sprinkled harebells as blue as the azure veins on a lovely face; while here and there patches of great red clover-heads are seen nodding heavily with their wealth of golden sweets. Farther away in solitary glens white anemones delight the eye, in company with ferns of tropical variety of form and color. The blossoms of the multebær, almost identical with that of the strawberry, are also abundant. The humidity of the atmosphere of the west coast, and especially in the latitude of Bergen, favors floral development. All through Scandinavia one meets these bright mosaics of the soil with a sense of surprise, they are so delicate, so frail, creations of such short life, yet lovely beyond compare, born upon the very verge of eternal frost. How Nature enters into our hearts and confides her amorous scents through winsome flowers! In these rambles afield one meets occasionally a peasant, who bows low, removing his hat as the stranger passes. Without showing the servility of the common people of Japan, they yet exhibit all their native courtesy. Now and again the road passes through reaches of pine forest, still and aromatic, the soil carpeted with soft yellow fir-needles, where if one pauses to listen there comes a low, undefined murmur of vegetable and insect life, like the sound that greets the ear when applied to an empty sea-shell. Some wood-paths were found sprinkled with dog-violets and saxifrage, fragrant as Gan Eden; others were daintily fringed with purple heart's-ease, captivating in their sylvan loveliness. Of song-birds there were none; and one could not but hunger for their delicious notes amid such suggestive surroundings.

THE NORWEGIAN CONSTITUTION. 97

English is very generally spoken by the merchants of Bergen, and may almost be said to constitute its commercial tongue. It is taught in all the "people's schools" as they are called, of which there are twenty supported by the town. In conversing with the citizens, they appear to be of more than average intelligence and liberal in opinions save for a few local prejudices. A Norwegian does not waste much love upon Sweden or its people. There is no bitterness expressed, but the two kingdoms united in one are still in a certain sense natural rivals. They are only combined to sustain their mutual political interests as it regards other nations. They have a saying at Bergen: "We love the English, and drink tea; the Swedes love the French, and drink coffee." Still, it is so clearly for their national interest to remain united that there is no fear of their seriously falling out. The Norwegian constitution is perhaps as near an approach to a perfect democracy as can possibly be achieved under a constitutional monarchy. This constitution is of her own making. She has "home rule" in its fullest sense, with her own Parliament and ministers in all departments except that of foreign affairs. She has even her own excise, and her own taxation direct and indirect. She contributes five, and Sweden twelve, seventeenths of the support of the royal family. She furnishes her proper quota of soldiers and sailors for the army and navy. In short, she makes her own laws and appoints her own officials to enforce them. No Swede holds any political office in Norway. The constitution was proclaimed on the 4th of November, 1814. The whole of the legislative and part of the executive power of the realm is invested in the Storthing, which is an emanation from and the representative of the sovereign people. So limited is the power of the King that he can make no appointment to public office in Norway, and over the laws passed by the Storthing he has but a limited veto. That is to say, he may veto a bill; but the passage of it a second time, though it may be by only a bare majority, places it beyond his prerogative.

There are a few Moravians settled in various parts of the country, but they are nowhere sufficiently numerous to establish organized congregations. The doctrine of Luther seems to be almost universally accepted, and appears to answer all the spiritual wants of the people.

Strangers visit with more than passing interest the admirable free industrial school for girls which flourishes and does its grand work faithfully at Bergen. Here female children from eight to sixteen years of age are taught practically the domestic industries under circumstances robbed of every onerous regulation, and are to be seen daily in cheerful groups at work upon all sorts of garments, supervised by competent teachers of their own sex. Such a well-conducted and practical institution cannot but challenge the admiration of even comparatively indifferent persons. Possessed of all these prudential and educational appreciations, it is not surprising that Bergen has sent forth some eminent representatives in science, art, and literature. Among them the most familiar are perhaps Ole Bull, the famous musician; Ludwig Holberg, the accomplished traveller; Johann Welhaven, the Norse poet; and J. C. C. Dahl, the justly celebrated painter.

We spoke of Bergen as situated on the west coast of Norway, between two of the most remarkable fjords in the country. The Hardanger richly repays a visit. The beauty, grandeur, and variety of its scenery is hardly surpassed in Scandinavia, which is so famous in these respects in all its parts. It is easily accessible from Bergen, as during the summer steamers sail thither three times a week, making the entire tour of the fjord. In many respects it resembles the Sognefjord. Though it is forty miles less in extent, it is yet the largest fjord in superficial measurement of any on the coast. Both are enclosed by rocky, precipitous, and lofty mountains, ranging from three to four thousand feet in height, characterized by snow-clad tops of virgin white, mingled with which are many extensive glaciers. The Sognefjord is more especially important as a water-way extending from the sea over a hundred miles inland, and averaging over four miles in width, having in parts the remarkable depth of four thousand feet. At its upper extremity is situated the largest glacier in Europe. In the Hardangerfjord there are many pleasant and thrifty hamlets near the water's edge, while broad fields of grain, thickly growing woods, and acres of highly cultivated soil show a spirit of successful industry seconded by the kindly aid of Nature. Wherever an opportunity occurs, the greensward springs up in such vivid color as to seem tropical, all the more intensified by its close proximity to the region of ceaseless frost. The traveller who is familiar with the Lake of Lucerne will be constantly reminded of that beautiful piece of land-locked water while sailing up either of these remarkable, grand, and interesting arms of the North Sea. So lofty are the mountains, and so abruptly do they rise out of the water at certain points, that while sailing near the shore within their deep shadow the darkness of night seems to encompass the vessel. If one has not time to go farther north in Norway, a visit to and careful inspection of these two extensive fjords will give a very good idea of the peculiarities of the entire coast. The grand fjords north of this point are none of them more extensive, but some of the mountain scenery is bolder and many of the elevations greater; the glaciers also come down nearer to the coast-line and to the sea.

Let no one who tarries for a few days at Bergen fail to make an excursion to the Folgefonden, or Hardanger glaciers. Of course an experienced guide is necessary, as fatal accidents sometimes occur here, particularly after a fresh fall of snow which covers up the huge clefts in the ice. These glaciers extend about forty miles in length by fifteen or twenty in width, here and there intersected by enormous chasms. Hunters and adventurous climbers have many times disappeared down these abysses, never again to be seen or heard from. Bears and reindeer have also fallen into and perished in these clefts. Persons who explore these glaciers wear spiked shoes as a necessary precaution, and to aid them in creeping along the slippery, rubbled surface of the ice. With a proper guide and reasonable care, however, there is little danger to be apprehended, or at least no more than is encountered by climbers among the Swiss Alps. These glaciers, as we have shown, are not confined to the mountain regions and elevated plateaus, but extend gradually downward in their lower portions very near to the shore, where vegetation in strong contrast thrives close to their borders. Farther northward the glacial effects are bolder and more numerous; but these accessible from Bergen are by no means to be neglected by travellers who would study understandingly this remarkable phase of Arctic and Alpine regions.

CHAPTER VI.

Ancient and Modern Trondhjem. — Runic Inscriptions. — A Famous Old Cathedral. — Local Characteristics. — Romantic Story of King Olaf. — Curious Local Productions. — An Island Prison. — Lafoss Falls. — Corn Magazines. — Land-owners. — Wood-cutters. — Forests. — A Tumble Overboard. — A Genuine Cockney. — Comparative Length of Days. — Characteristics of Boreal Regions. — Arctic Winter Fisheries. — The Ancient Cathedral Town of Lund ; the Oxford of Sweden. — Pagan Times.

TRONDHJEM is situated on a fjord of the same name occupying a peninsula formed by the river Nid, and is surrounded by beautiful and picturesque scenery. A delightful view of the town and its environs may be had from the old fort of Kristiansten. Here resided the kings of Norway in the olden time. It is now a thriving but small city, the seat of a bishopric, and contains a Royal Academy of Sciences, a Museum embracing some remarkable examples of ancient weapons besides well-preserved armor, and there is here also a good Public Library. The Cathedral of St. Olaf is quite famous, being the finest Gothic edifice in all Scandinavia, and the only local object of special interest to the traveller. In the eleventh and twelfth centuries it was the burial-place of the kings of Norway. It is built in its modern form of a soft gray stone which was quarried near the town, but the older walls and foundation date back many centuries, it being the restoration of a much more ancient church which was partially destroyed by fire in the year 1719. For many centuries carving in stone and wood has been a specialty in Scandinavia. The old Runic inscriptions are all carved in stone. Some of these works going back seven or eight hundred years, are of the most quaint and curious character. In this old cathedral there is a fine display of carvings in the way of bosses and capitals. Some of the Swedish churches exhibit similar specimens of rude art, which are of great interest to antiquarians. The Trondhjem cathedral contains a copy of Thorwaldsen's Christ, the original of which is in the Frue Kirke at Copenhagen. This colossal figure seen in the dim light of the cathedral eloquently expresses its inscription: "Come unto me all ye that labor and are heavy laden, and I will give you rest." Many of the tombs in the cemetery adjoining the cathedral were observed to be decked with flowers so fresh as to indicate frequent renewals, and yet many years had intervened since the date borne by the stone slabs above the dead who were thus gracefully remembered. The Scandinavians, like the Turks, make the graves of the departed a pleasant resort for leisure hours. The services performed in the old cathedral were those of the English Church on the occasion of our visit, which was on a Sunday; but the attendance was so small as to be remarked upon, not fifty persons being present, though there is quite a colony of English residents here.

After Christiania and Bergen Trondhjem is the next largest town in Norway, having fully twenty-five thousand inhabitants and enjoying quite an active commerce, as its shipping indicated. The thoroughfares are broad and cheerful, and are liberally and tastefully adorned with a fine growth of trees. The Kongensgade (King's Street), two hundred feet in width, runs from end to end of the city, and with the Munkegade, divides it like a cross. The latter street intersects the great market-place, which is in the centre of the town. The principal shops are found on the Strandgade. The houses, rarely over two stories in height, are painted white and roofed with red tiles, like scarlet caps upon light-haired men. The façades are full of windows, which in turn are crowded with growing and blooming plants. The irregularity of the cobble-stones used as pavements for the streets renders pedestrianism very uncomfortable, and riding in a vehicle even more so. The Arsenal on the left bank of the Nid was once the palace home of the ancient kings, and the royal throne is still exhibited to the curious visitor, preserved in an unused portion of the structure. Those familiar with Scandinavian history will remember that Trondhjem was founded about a thousand years ago by King Olaf Trygvason, upon the site of a much older city named Nidaros. There is certainly nothing visible to indicate its great antiquity. The adventurous life of King Olaf, which recurs to us in this connection, may be outlined in a few words, and is more romantic than that of any other ruler of Norway known to us. Born a prince, he barely escaped assassination at the hands of the usurper of his rights, by fleeing from the country in charge of his mother. They were captured by pirates, separated and sold into slavery. Then followed a period of deprivation and hardship; but at a comparatively early age Olaf was opportunely discovered and ransomed by a relative who had never ceased to seek for the missing youth. He soon after became a distinguished sea-king, of that class which we call pirates in our day. His career in this field of adventure is represented to have been one of daring and reckless hardihood, characterized by merciless aggression and great success. Finally Olaf married an Irish princess, embraced Christianity, and fought his way to the throne of Norway, assuming the crown in the year of our Lord 991. From this time he became a zealous missionary, propagating his faith by the sword; and like all other religious zealots he was guilty of outrageous acts of cruelty, proving the axiom that "the worst of madmen is a saint run mad." Seven years subsequent to the last named date he destroyed the Pagan temple of Thor and Odin at Trondhjem, with all its venerated idols. Upon the site of this temple he built a Christian church, making the city his seat of government; and so it remained the capital down to the time of the union with Denmark. Olaf was slain in battle while fighting for his throne, and was canonized by the church, his shrine at Trondhjem being for centuries a Mecca for pious pilgrims from all parts of Europe. In such veneration were the memory and services of this converted pirate held by a certain class of religionists, that churches were erected in his name at Constantinople and elsewhere. His body lies buried in the present cathedral; and, remarkable to relate, it was found to be incorrupt so late as 1541, according to reliable historical record, at which time the tomb underwent an official examination induced by some State question of importance. It was in this cathedral that Bernadotte was crowned King of Norway, in 1818; Oscar I., in 1844; Charles XV., in 1860; and Oscar II., the present sovereign of the two Kingdoms, in 1873.

In some of the fancy-goods shops on the Strandgade one can purchase silver ornaments of native design and workmanship, quite as original and peculiar as those produced at Trichinopoly in middle India, or at Genoa in Italy. Choice furs, such as delicate and well-cured skins of sable and fox, can be had here at reasonable rates, made up in the form of simple mantles and robes. It was observed that upon entering a shop here the customer invariably removes his hat out of respect to the store-keeper, whether man or woman, and remains thus uncovered while perfecting his purchase. Courtesy is a cheap though potent commodity, and wholesome lessons may often be acquired in unexpected places. One curious local production was observed in the form of eider-down rugs, capes, cloaks, and the like, which were also seen at Christiania. One very fine specimen was in the form of a cloak designed for ladies' wear, but which seemed to be rather an expensive luxury at the price asked, which was a thousand dollars.

A short walk from the town brings one to Hlade, where stands the famous, or rather infamous, Jarl Hakon's castle, and from whence he ruled over the country round about with an iron hand in the olden time. He was a savage Heathen, believing in and practising human sacrifices, evidences of which are pointed out to the curious visitor. About a mile from the town, in the fjord, is the island of Munkholm, once the site of a Benedictine monastery, as its name indicates, and which was erected in 1028. The base of one of the towers, mouldering and moss-grown, now only remains. Victor Hugo graphically describes this island in his "Han d'Islande." Here the famous minister of Christian V., Griffenfeldt, was confined for many weary years. His crime was absolutely nothing, his incarceration for this long period being purely the result of political intrigue. When he was finally brought to the scaffold for execution, a messenger interrupted the headsman at the last moment, and announced a pardon from the King. "The pardon," said the worn out sufferer, "is severer than the penalty!"

A walk or drive of three or four miles up the beautiful valley of the Nid carries one to the Lafoss Falls, upper and lower, situated about a mile from each other; and though classed among the ordinary waterfalls of Norway, they are superior to anything of the sort in Switzerland. The upper fall is nearly a hundred feet high, with a width of five hundred feet; the lower one is eighty feet in height and about one third as wide as the other. The falls of the Rhine at Schaffhausen may be compared to them; but these Scandinavian falls are more remarkable in size, as well as more perpendicular. They are annually visited by large numbers of tourists from Europe and America, and have, like all such strong demonstrations of Nature, an individuality quite impressive. The salmon-fishing in this neighborhood is said to be the best in the country. The topographical formation of Norway precludes the extensive building of railroads, but three thousand square miles of the kingdom are covered with lakes which greatly facilitate inland communication. Lake Mjösen, already spoken of, and Randsfjord are respectively sixty and forty-five miles long. The hundreds of fjords which indent the west coast form another system of waterways, the four largest being the Hardangerfjord, Sognefjord, Porsanger, and Christiania. The population concentrates on and about these natural means of communication, and thus all are more or less utilized. About the shores of the Trondhjemfjord are to be seen delightful green fields and thrifty farms, vegetation advancing as if by magic under the continuous heat of the ardent sun. The latitude here is 64° 65'. The mean annual temperature is set down in the local statistics at 42° Fahrenheit, which it will be found by comparison corresponds with the winter temperature on the southern coast of England.

We were here told of a system of storage for grain, long established, but which was quite new to us, and which as a local expedient appears to possess considerable merit. It seems that there are what is called Corn Magazines organized in various districts, to which farmers may send a portion of their surplus produce, and whence also they may be supplied with loans of grain when required. The depositors receive at the rate of twelve and a half per cent increase upon their deposit of grain for twelve months, and the borrowers replace the quantities advanced to them at the expiration of the same period, paying an interest of twenty-five per cent in kind. The difference in the amount of interest on the grain received and that loaned pays the necessary expenses of storage and of sustaining the system. As the sole object is the mutual benefit of all concerned, no profit above actual expenses is demanded or considered to be desirable. The necessity for these magazines is owing to the precarious character of the crops, — a peculiarity of which is that there may be an abundance in one locality, and a partial or even total failure of the crop in another, though they may be separated by only a few miles from each other. These granaries are fostered by the Government.

As one travels northward, it is found that farming as a permanent occupation gradually and naturally ceases. The populace, gathered about the fjords in small villages, devote their time to fishing, trading in skins, reindeer-meat, and the like. In middle and southern Norway, where farming is the principal occupation of the people, at the death of the head of the family the land belonging to the deceased is equally divided among the surviving children. No estates are entailed in this country. The division of real property tends to foster a spirit of independence and self-respect which will be looked for in vain among those nations where the land is in the possession of the few. It is a remarkable fact that the number of landed proprietors in Norway, in proportion to the aggregate of the population, is greater than in any other country in Europe. Reliable statistics show that there is here one estate for every twenty-two persons; while in Scotland, for instance, there is but one for each seven hundred! The Scandinavian farmer is neither poor nor rich; he raises from his own soil nearly all the necessities of life, even including the family clothing, — exchanging a small portion of his surplus for such articles as he requires, but which are not of home product. The average farms in Norway consist of from sixty to seventy-five acres each, though some are much larger. This does not include a certain portion of mountain pasturage, only available in summer, but which is attached to every farm located in the valleys, known (as already described) as the sæter.

The mountain scenery of the northern part of the country, especially near the coast, is not excelled in its bold and rugged character in any part of the world. Norway is here very sparsely inhabited, — a few huts, as we have shown, being occasionally perched upon elevations which seem to be accessible to eagles and reptiles only, where footways or narrow paths are built upon piles across gaping ravines, or are formed of timber suspended by chains securely fastened to the rocks. The inhabitants of these desolate regions find occupation and procure a precarious living by cutting wood for fuel, which they transport upon their backs, or by the production of charcoal. In the more accessible places they cut timber for building purposes, which they float down the seething rapids and tortuous rivers to the villages and cities. Occasionally these people kill a bear or trap a wolf, from which sources they realize both food and a small government bounty in money. The fir, the pine, and the white birch abound, the first growing at an elevation of twenty-five hundred feet above the level of the sea. Now and again the eye is arrested by the gracefully-disposed mountain-ash, heavy with clusters of red berries; and often intermingled with the undergrowth, the pale dog-rose is seen growing far beyond the reach of human hands. In Sweden there are immense forests of firs hundreds of miles in extent, where the aspen and mountain-ash also abound. The oak is rare, but is found well developed in some of the southern districts of both Norway and Sweden. Wood is almost universally used for family fuel, as well as for manufacturing purposes, though some considerable quantities of peat are realized from the bogs in some of the southern districts, which is also consumed in domestic use.

The usual route of those who seek to gain a view of the "midnight sun,"— that is, of witnessing the phenomenon of the sun passing round the horizon without sinking beneath it,— is to depart from Trondhjem by sea for the North Cape, skirting the iron-bound coast for a distance of about seven hundred miles. This was the route taken by the author, and over which he will ask the reader to accompany him. As the steamer was just casting off her shore-lines and getting underway, a passenger who seemed to have been accidentally detained came running down the pier to get on board, in doing which he missed his proper footing and fell into the water alongside. He was promptly relieved from his somewhat perilous position, but in a decidedly dripping condition. After descending to his cabin for a short time he appeared in more presentable shape, wearing a plaid travelling suit which was rather "loud" in the size of the diagonal figures. He wore a single eye-glass, stuck after the English fashion before his right eye, depending from which was a thin gold chain. His principal occupation seemed to be the manipulation of that eye-glass, shaking it out of place by a vigorous jerk of the head, and replacing it again incessantly. The fellow was an unmistakable cockney, and a more verdant specimen it would be difficult to conceive of. His great simplicity as exhibited at times was almost beyond belief. He appeared to be travelling alone, but though evidently near his majority he was scarcely fit to do so. His ideas of geography, or indeed of whither we were sailing, seemed to be ludicrously involved. A Yankee schoolboy of ten years would have proved to be a veritable Solomon compared with our cockney fellow-passenger.

As we sail northward, the rapid lengthening of the days becomes more and more obvious. At Lund, in the extreme south of Sweden, the longest day experienced is seventeen hours and a half; at Stockholm, two hundred miles farther north, the longest day of the year is eighteen hours and a half; at Bergen, in Norway, three hundred miles north of Lund, the longest day is nineteen hours; and at Trondhjem, five hundred miles north of Lund, the longest day is twenty-one hours. Above this point of latitude to the North Cape there is virtually no night at all during the brief summer season, as the sun is visible, or nearly so, for the whole twenty-four hours. From early in May until about the first of August, north of Trondhjem, the stars take a vacation, or at least they are not visible, while the moon is so pale as to give no light, the Great Bear puts by his seven lustres, and the diamond belt of Orion is unseen. But the heavenly lamps revive by the first of September, and after a short period are supplemented by the marvellous and beautiful radiations of the Aurora Borealis. Winter now sets in, the sun disappears entirely from sight, and night reigns supreme, the heavens shining only with subdued light. Were it not for the brilliancy of the Auroral light, the fishermen could hardly pursue their winter vocation, that being the harvest-time with them, and midnight is considered to be the best period of the twenty-four hours for successful fishing in these frosty regions. In and about the Lofoden Islands alone five thousand boats are thus regularly employed at the height of the season, giving occupation to from twenty to twenty-five thousand men. These people are mostly Scandinavians, properly so designated; but other countries also contribute their quota to swell the number, many coming especially from northern Russia and northern Finland east of the Bothnian Gulf.

Though Lund is not in the direct route over which we propose to take the reader, still having mentioned this ancient and most interesting locality, a few words in relation to it will not be out of place. To-day it has a population of some twelve or fifteen thousand only, but according to popular tradition it was once a city of two hundred thousand inhabitants, and was a famous and flourishing capital two thousand years ago, long before the birth of Christ. Its former churches and monasteries have crumbled to dust, the grounds and neighborhood being now only remarkable for the beautiful trees which have sprung up and covered the wrinkles that ruthless time has scored upon the face of the earth. The Lund of our day is a sleepy, dreamy old town, called by some the Oxford of Sweden, because of the acknowledged excellence of its University. The number of students attached thereto we could not learn, but we saw them in goodly numbers, living in separate lodgings about the town and only coming together at the period of recitations and public lectures. The system of instruction here is unique; enough was learned to satisfy one of that, but the details were not clearly defined.

Lund has also its cathedral, a noble Norman structure dedicated to Saint Lawrence, and which is all things considered one of the finest in Sweden, though it is a little grotesque by reason of the marvellous giants and impossible dwarfs sculptured upon the pillars of the interior. It was founded in the eleventh century, and has been more than once fully renovated. The town is of easy access. One has only to cross the Sound from Copenhagen, and it is richly worth visiting. It was a "holy" city in Pagan times, containing in those days temples to Odin and Thor, and was especially remarkable for the ceremonies which took place there connected with the worship of these Heathen deities, accompanied by human sacrifice.

CHAPTER VII.

Along the Coast of Norway. — Education at the Far North. — An Interesting Character. — A Botanical Enthusiast. — Remarkable Mountain Tunnel. — A Hard Climb. — The Seven Sisters. — Young England. — An Amateur Photographer. — Horseman's Island. — Ancient Town of Bodöe. — Arctic Flowers. — The Famous Maelström. — Illusions ! — The Wonderful Lofoden Islands. — Grand and Unique Scenery. — Glaciers. — Nature's Architecture. — Mysterious Effects. — Attraction for Artists.

THE coast of Norway from the most southerly part which is known as the Naze, to the North Cape which is its extreme point in that direction, is bordered by innumerable rocky islands, and also by deep fjords winding inland from ten to fifty miles each among masses of rock forming lofty, perpendicular walls, often towering a thousand feet and more in height. The traveller is reminded by the aspect of these fjords of the striking scenery of the Saguenay River in North America. The turbulent waves of the North Atlantic and Arctic Oceans hurled against the coast by the western gales for many thousands of years, have steadily worn into the land, and thus formed these remarkable fjords; or perhaps after they were begun by volcanic action, the wearing of the water has gradually brought about their present condition. The coast of Sweden, on the other hand, is formed by the

Baltic Sea and the Gulf of Bothnia, both of which are inland waters; and though there are many islands on the Swedish coast, there are no fjords worthy of mention. Notwithstanding that the extreme length of Norway from north to south is hardly twelve hundred miles, yet so numerous and extensive are these peculiar arms of the sea that its coast-line is estimated to measure over three thousand miles,— which gives to these deep indentures of the west coast a length of eighteen hundred miles. The entire peninsula known under the general name of Scandinavia is composed of Norway, Sweden, and a small portion of the Russian possessions in the northeast. This division of country supports a population of little less than seven millions, and contains in round numbers three hundred thousand square miles. To geologists it is especially interesting to know that the mountains of this section of the globe are almost wholly of primitive rocks, presenting as near as possible the same form as when they were first solidified. They are rarely overlaid with more recent formations, but stand forth as tangible evidence of the great antiquity of this region.

In her course northward the steamer winds in and out among the many islands and fjords, touching occasionally at small settlements on the main-land to discharge light freight, and to land or take on board an occasional passenger. The few persons who came from the little clusters of houses, which are not sufficient in number to be called a village, were found to be of more than ordinary intelligence, neat and clean in their appearance; and, much to our surprise, they often spoke English. We were told that even in these sparsely inhabited regions, education is provided for by what is termed the "ambulatory system;" that is, one able teacher instructs the youth of three or four neighboring districts, accommodating the convenience of all by suitable variations of time and place in holding school-sessions.

Among the passengers who came on board our steamer at Trondhjem as we were starting for the north was one whose personal peculiarities had attracted some attention. He was a man of fifty years or more, with iron-gray hair, and a tall, slim figure. He wore a long gray surtout, a flat, flabby cloth cap, with a broad, straight leather visor, beneath which were shaggy grizzly brows, so heavy indeed as to throw his eyes into shadow, deep as a well. His wrinkled face, long and narrow, was supplemented by a double chin as full of folds as his cap. This man glanced about him occasionally, with large blue eyes of such marked intelligence as to indicate the possession of plenty of brains. Fastened across his shoulder there depended upon his left side a long round tin box painted green. He seemed quite wrapped up in his own thought, and addressed no one. He had just seated himself in one corner of the deck, apparently for a nap, when we rounded to at a landing, on the second day of the voyage northward. Among those who came on board from this place were two or three peasant women destined for the next station, with whom was a young girl who held in her hand a tiny bouquet of simple cut flowers. The drowsy figure of the old German, for that was his nationality, suddenly became animated, and he was seen hastening towards the girl, and extending a piece of silver, which was quickly exchanged for the cluster of flowers. A moment later he had assumed his former position, and with his tin box open before him was arranging his floral prize. His profession was no longer a mystery. He was a botanist,— a botanist *con amore*. Meeting him upon this ground, he was found to be a most delightful talker and a devout disciple of Linnæus. He was so eloquent upon the properties of flowers,— their disposition, their genealogy, their connubial ties, the fragrance of their breath, their length of life,— that he might have been talking of humanity rather than of the denizens of Flora's kingdom. Every bit of fern was treasured; every leaf, every pale blossom possessed feeling, consciousness of care, interesting habits, and spoke a familiar language to him. It was delightful to hear him discuss their properties with such enthusiasm, so tenderly and lovingly. It is to the faithful researches of such simple and sincere devotees of science that we are indebted for our knowledge of Nature's daintiest secrets. Among the flowers brought on board by the young girl was a deep blue orchis. "See," said the narrow-chested, thin-voiced old man, "this is the *Orchis maculata*, the Virgin's and Devil's hand, with one prong of the root dark and crooked, while the other is straight and white. Behold! I place it in this basin of water; the white hand floats upon the surface, the black hand sinks!" The old man gazed in silence for a moment; then added: "It is the emblem of good triumphing over evil."

How gentle and benignant the nature that dwelt within the rough exterior of this enthusiast!

The course of the northern-bound steamers takes them by the celebrated island of Torghatten, which is pierced entirely through by a remarkable natural tunnel. The opening on the precipitous side occurs about half way up between the sea-level and the apex. The island rises gradually from the water at first, but soon becomes abrupt, finishing at a height of about one thousand feet. Here the steamer comes to anchor for a few hours, to enable tourists to land and examine the tunnel. If the sea happens to be rough, however, this is not possible. A steep and rather trying climb over the spongy moss and rubble stones, where there is no definite path, brings one at last to the mouth of the opening, which is so regular in form that it would almost seem to have been constructed for some useful purpose by human hands, rather than by any freak of Nature. The floor of the tunnel is quite uneven and rough, being strewn with rocks that have fallen from the roof, owing to atmospheric disintegrating influences operating for many ages. It very naturally recalled the Grotto of Posilippo at Naples, surmounted by Virgil's tomb, though the Italian tunnel is artificial, while Torghatten is unmistakably natural. This tunnel is sixty feet high at the mouth, and between five and six hundred feet long, maintaining throughout about the same size. Through the large opening one gets a very curious, half-telescopic view of the sea and the many islands lying in range. Such a place would be quite incomplete as a unique resort, and particularly in Scandinavia, without its special legend attached; but the one we heard upon the spot was far too extravagant and foolish to repeat in these pages. This mountain island is said to contain caves which extend some distance beneath the surrounding waters, but which are nevertheless perfectly dry. A story is told of one of these being the bridal chamber of a famous Viking in the olden time, and which is said to be only accessible by diving beneath the surface of the sea. Soon after leaving the perforated insular mountain, the "Seven Sisters" come into view. These are elevations about three thousand feet high, located upon the island of Alsten, which forms the west side of Vefsenfjord. They are of remarkable similarity in form, with deep valleys and dark gorges separating them. From the group there rolled back across the waters a whole broadside of echoes in response to the single boom of our forecastle gun fired for the purpose. These "Sisters" have stood here, in their craggy and solitary grandeur, unexplored and untrodden for perhaps twice ten thousand years. The peaks are far too perpendicular for human access. The course in this region is along the shore of what is called Nordland, extending longitudinally about forty miles, the interior of which has not yet been explored.

We had already passed latitude 66° north, when the captain of the steamer casually remarked to a group of passengers that we must be on the look-out, for we should soon cross the line of the Arctic Circle. Young England was instantly on the alert, with his sticking eye-glass and fidgety manner, wanting to know what the "line" looked like. Intelligent glances were exchanged between a couple of gentlemen passengers, one of whom stepped into the captain's office and brought out a ship's spy-glass. After carefully sweeping the horizon with the instrument directed to the northwest, the gentleman thought that he discovered indications of the "line" already. In this supposition he was confirmed by his companion, after he also had taken a careful survey through the glass. Young England stood by, nervously jerking his eye-glass out of place and putting it back again, and anxious to get a peep; so he was kindly accommodated. He shouted almost immediately that he could see the "line," and indulged in rather boisterous demonstrations of satisfaction at the sight. Presently the gentleman who had borrowed the glass received it again; but before returning it to the captain's office he removed a small silk thread which had been extended across the object-glass. Young England in his simplicity never suspected the trick played upon his ignorance. The amateur photographer ("photographic fiend," as he was named by

the passengers) was also on board with his portable
machine, aiming it at everybody and everything. He
too was an English cockney of the shallowest kind;
but as regarded any pictorial results from the innocent
machine which he set up all over the ship, — now on
the bridge, now at the taffrail, and again on the forecastle, — there were none. Not a "negative" was produced during our eight days' voyage whereby one might
judge whether the whole affair was a "blind" or otherwise. This youth was one degree less verdant than he
with the sticking eye-glass, but yet he had an opinion to
offer upon every topic of conversation, and was, as he
believed, quite posted in all national and political matters at home and abroad. If he lives for a few years
he will doubtless have less faith in his own wisdom,
and will exhibit less conceit to others.

There is but one day in the year when the phenomenon of the midnight sun can be seen at the imaginary
line which we designate as the Arctic Circle, a point
twenty-three degrees and twenty-eight minutes from
the North Pole; but by sailing some three hundred
miles farther northward to the North Cape, the projecting point of the extreme north of Norway, it may
be observed under favorable circumstances, — that is,
when not obscured by clouds, — for over two months
dating from the middle of May. Soon after passing
the Arctic Circle, fourteen hundred and eight geo-
graphical miles from the North Pole, a singularly
formed island is observed, called by the natives Hest-
mandö, or Horseman's Island, — a rocky and moun-

tainous formation of two thousand feet in height, more or less. On approaching the island from the west, by a liberal aid from the imagination one can discern the colossal figure of a horseman wrapped in his cloak and mounted on a charger. It forms a well-known landmark to all navigating the coast. The summit, it is believed, has never been reached by human feet.

The fishing village or town of Bodöe, on the mainland, is one of the regular stopping places for the steamers that ply on the coast. It contains some fifteen hundred inhabitants, all toilers of the sea, and is the chief town of Nordland. Some few of the houses are large and comfortable, being of modern construction, forming a strong contrast to the low turf-roofed log-cabins which are to be seen in such close proximity to them. There is an ancient stone church here which the traveller should find time to visit, — a quaint building, with a few antique paintings upon the walls and an atmosphere of past ages permeating its dim interior. Only the sacred rust of this old temple makes it worthy of attention. In and about the humble settlement lovely wild-flowers were observed in profusion, — an agreeable surprise, for we had hardly expected to find these "smiles of God's goodness" so far north, within the Arctic Circle. Among them were the butterfly-orchis and Alpine lady's-mantle, besides a goodly crop of primroses, all the more attractive because of the seemingly unpropitious region where they were blooming. Here our earnest but simple old friend the botanist revelled in his specialty, indeed lost himself as it seemed, for when we sailed he was nowhere to be seen, and was surely left behind. " Did he take his baggage with him ? " we asked of an officer of the ship. " No, he had none," was the reply. And so we had parted from the absorbed gentle old scientist, without a word of farewell. Louis Philippe lived for a brief period at Bodöe when travelling as a refugee under the name of Müller, and visitors are shown the room which he occupied. Under favorable circumstances the midnight sun is visible here for a period of about four weeks each season, and many persons tarry at Bodöe to obtain the desired view without the trouble of travelling farther northward. By ascending the lofty hill called Lobsaas, one gets here also a grand though distant view of the remarkable Lofoden Islands.

After leaving Bodöe the course of the steamers lies directly across the Vestfjord to the islands just referred to, whose jagged outlines have been compared to the teeth which line a shark's mouth. They lie so close together, particularly on the side by which we approached them, that no opening was visible in their long undulating mountain-chain until the vessel came close upon them and entered a narrow winding passage among rocks and cliffs which formed an entrance channel to the archipelago. In crossing the open sea which lies between the main-land and the islands rough weather is often encountered, but once within the shelter of the group, the waters become calm and mirror-like in smoothness. The passage through the myriad isles and from one to another, now rounding sharp points and now making a complete angle in the course, renders it necessary to "slow down" the steamer, so that she glides silently over the immense depths of dark waters as if propelled by some strange mysterious power below her hull. The Lofodens, owing to the clearness of the atmosphere as seen from Bodöe, appear to be about fifteen or twenty miles away on the edge of the horizon, but the real distance is nearly or quite fifty. The play of light and shade is here so different from that of lower latitudes that the atmosphere seems at times to be almost telescopic, and the most experienced traveller finds himself often deceived in judging of distances.

A little to the westward of the steamer's course in coming hither from the main-land lies the famous vortex known as the Maelström, the theme of many a romance and wild conjecture which lives in the memory of every schoolboy. At certain stages of the wind and tide a fierce eddy is formed here, which is perhaps somewhat dangerous for very small boats to cross, but the presumed risk to vessels of the size of common coasting-craft under proper management is an error. At some stages of the tide it is difficult even to detect the exact spot which at other times is so disturbed. Thus we find that another fact of our credulous youth turns out to be a fable, with a very thin substratum of fact for its foundation. The tragedies recorded in connection with the Venetian Bridge of Sighs are proven to be mostly gross anachronisms; the episode of Tell and the apple was a Swiss fabrication; and now we know that neither ships nor whales were ever drawn into the Norwegian Maelström to instant destruction. There are several other similar rapids in and about these pinnacled islands, identical in their cause, though the one referred to is the most restless and formidable.

On close examination the Lofodens were found to consist of a maze of irregular mountain-peaks and precipices, often between two and three thousand feet in height, the passage between them being very tortuous, winding amid straits interspersed with hundreds of small rocky islets which were the home of large flocks of sea-birds. "It seemed," as was expressively remarked by a lady passenger, "like sailing through Switzerland." Dwarf-trees, small patches of green grass and moss grew near the water's edge, and carpeted here and there a few acres of level soil; but the high ridges were bleak and bare rock, covered in spots with never-melting snow and ice. Most of the coast of Norway is composed of metamorphic rock; but these islands are of granite, and for marvellous peaks and oddly-pointed shapes, deep, far-reaching gulches and cañons, are unequalled elsewhere. It seemed to us marvellous that a steamer could be safely navigated through such narrow passages and among such myriads of sunken rocks. These elevations from beneath the sea varied from mere turtle-backs, as the sailors called them, just visible above the water, to mountains with sky-kissing peaks. For a vessel to run upon one of the low hummocks would be simply destruction, the water alongside being rarely less than two or three hundred fathoms in depth. Fortunately the sea is mostly quite smooth within the shelter of the archipelago, otherwise steam-vessels would rarely enter it. The compass is brought but little into use. The pilots distinguish rocks and promontories by their peculiar physiognomy, and they steer from point to point with remarkable accuracy, arriving and departing from given stations with the variation of but a few minutes from the time laid down upon their schedules. Each steamer running upon the coast carries two pilots, independent of the other officers of the ship, one of whom is always at the wheel when the vessel is under way. They are chosen for their responsible character and their knowledge of the route, and they very justly command high wages. We stopped briefly at Henningsvær, the centre of the Lofoden cod-fishery establishments. It is a small town situated at the base of the Vaagekelle Mountain, an elevation between three and four thousand feet high. The place smells rank to heaven of dried fish and cod-liver oil, the combined stench of which articles, with that of decaying refuse lying everywhere, was truly overpowering. The hardy fishermen work nearly all winter at their rough occupation, braving the tempestuous Northern ocean in frail undecked boats, which to an inexperienced eye seem utterly unfit for such exposed service. The harvest-time to the cod-fishers here is from January to the middle of April. Casualties are of course frequent, but we were told that they are not remarkably so. Winter fishing on the banks of Newfoundland is believed to be the annual cause of more fatalities than are experienced among the Lofoden fishermen. Sometimes this region is visited by terrible hurricanes, as was the case in 1848, on which occasion five hundred fishermen were swept into eternity in one hour. Their boats are built of Norway spruce or pine, and are very light, scarcely more seaworthy than a Swampscott dory. Each has a single, portable mast which carries one square sail. The crew of a boat generally consists of six men. These live when on shore in little log-huts, each containing a score or more of bunks ranged along the sides one above another. The men come hither, as has been intimated, from all parts of the North, and return home at the close of the fishing season.

It should be made clear to the reader's mind that these matchless islands off the northwest coast of Norway consist of two divisions, — the Lofoden and Vesteraalen isles. The Vestfjord separates the former from the main-land and the Ofotenfjord; and a prolongation of the Vestfjord separates the latter from Norway proper. These two groups are separated from each other by the Raftsund. All the islands on the west of this boundary belong to the Lofoden, and those on the east and north to the Vesteraalen group. The total length of all these islands is about a hundred and thirty miles, and the area is computed at fifteen hundred and sixty square miles. These estimates, we were informed, had lately been very nearly corroborated by actual government survey. The population of the islands will not vary much from twenty thousand. The entire occupation of the people is fishing, curing the fish, and shipping them southward. Some of the shrewdest persons engaged in this business accumulate moderate fortunes in a few years, when they naturally seek some more genial home upon the main-land. The large islands contain rivers and lakes of considerable size, but the growth of trees in this high latitude is sparse, and when found they are universally dwarfed. There is, however, as the product of the brief summer season, an abundance of fresh green vegetation, which is fostered by the humidity of the atmosphere. Still the prevailing aspect is that of towering, jagged rocks. Though the winters are long, they are comparatively mild, so much so that the salt water does not freeze in or about the group at any time of the year. As to the scenery, the Lofodens must be admitted to surpass in true sublimity and grandeur anything of their nature to be found in southern Europe. There is ample evidence showing that in long past ages these islands were much more extensive than at present, and that they were once covered with abundant vegetation. But violent convulsions in the mean time must have rent them asunder, submerging some entirely, and elevating others into their present irregular shapes.

In pursuing her course towards the North Cape, the steamer for a distance of twenty miles and more glides through a strait remarkable for its picturesqueness and unique beauty, which is called the Raftsund. Here the shore is studded by the tiny red cabins of the fishermen, surrounded by green low-growing 'foliage, the earth-covered roofs of the huts often spread with purple heather-bloom, mingled about the eaves with moss of intensely verdant hue. The high slopes of the hills are covered with Alpine moss, and the upper cliffs with snow, whose yielding tears, persuaded by the warm sun, feed opalescent cascades; while below and all about the ship are the deep dark waters of the Polar Sea. Neither the majestic Alps, the glowing Pyrenees, nor the commanding Apennines ever impressed us like these wild, wrinkled, rock-bound mountains in their virgin mantles of frost. The sensation when gazing in wonder upon the far-away Himalayas, the loftiest range on the earth, was perhaps more overpowering; but the nearness to these abrupt cliffs, volcanic islands, mountains, and glaciers in boreal regions made it seem more like Wonderland. The traveller looks heavenward from the deck of the steamer to see the apex of the steep walls, stern, massive, and immovable, which line the fjords, lost in the blue sky, or wreathed in gauzy mantles of mist-clouds, as he may have looked upward from the deep, green valley of the Yosemite at the lofty crowns of Mount Starr King, El Capitan, or Sentinel Dome. On again approaching the main-land the varying panorama is similarly impressive, though differing in kind. It will be remembered that the coast of Norway extends three hundred miles north of the Arctic Circle, projecting itself boldly into the Polar Sea, and that two hundred miles and more of this distance is north of the Lofoden Island group. Now and then reaches of country are passed affording striking and beautiful landscape effects, where valleys open towards the sea, affording views sometimes capped by glaciers high up towards the overhanging sky, where they form immense level fields of dazzling ice embracing hundreds of square miles. The enjoyment of a trip along the coast is largely dependent upon the condition of the weather, which is frequently very disagreeable. In this respect the author was greatly favored. The absence of fog and mist was remarkable, while the water most of the time was as smooth as a pleasure pond. With a heavy, rolling sea and stormy weather, the trip northward from Bodöe, and especially among the Lofodens, would be anything but enjoyable. Sometimes fancy led us to gaze lazily over the bulwarks into the mirroring sea for long distances, where mountains, gorges, foaming torrents, and sheer precipices were even more sharply depicted than when gazing directly at them. A feeling of loneliness is sure to creep over the solitary traveller at such times, a longing for some congenial companion with whom to share all this glowing experience. "Joy was born a twin." Fulness of appreciation and delight can be reached only by being shared.

Amid such scenes as we have described rises the enormous Svartisen glacier, its ice and snow defying the power of the sun. This glacier is many miles in length and nearly as wide as it is long, covering a plateau four thousand feet above the level of the sea. The dimensions given the author upon the spot were so mammoth that he hesitates to record them; but it is by far the most extensive one he has ever seen. Sulitelma, the highest mountain in Lapland, six thousand feet above the sea, crowned by a shroud of eternal snow, comes into view, though it is nearly fifty miles inland. The snow-level about this latitude of 69° north is five hundred feet above that of the sea, below which, wherever the earth can find a foothold on the rocks, all is delightfully green, — a tender delicate green, such as marks the early spring foliage of New England, or the leaves of the young locust. The heat of the brief summer sun is intense, and insect life thrives marvellously in common with the more welcome vegetation. Birch and willow trees seem best adapted to withstand the rigor of these regions, and they thrive in the warm season with a vitality and beauty of effect which is heightened by the ever-present contrast. Every hour of the voyage seemed burdened with novelty, and ceaseless vigilance possessed every faculty. A transparent haze at mid-day or midnight lay like a golden veil over land and sea; objects even at a short distance presented a shadowy and an unreal aspect. The rough and barren islands which we passed in our midnight course often exhibited one side glorified with gorgeous roseate hues, while casting sombre and mysterious shadows behind them, which produced a strangely weird effect, half of delight, half of awe, while the long superb trail of sunlight crept towards us from the horizon.

The attractions of Norway to the artist are many, and in a great measure they are unique, especially in the immediate vicinity of the west coast. No two of the many abrupt elevations resemble each other, all are erratic; some like Alpine cathedrals seemingly rear their fretted spires far heavenward, where they echo the hoarse anthems played by the winters' storms. One would think that Nature in a wayward mood had tried her hand sportively at architecture, sculpture, and castle-building, — constructing now a high monumental column or a mounted warrior, and now a Gothic fane amid regions strange, lonely, and savage. There are grand mountains and glaciers in Switzerland, but they do not rise directly out of the ocean as they do here in Scandinavia; and as to the scenery afforded by the innumerable fjords winding inland, amid forests, cliffs, and impetuous waterfalls, nowhere else can these be seen save on this remarkable coast. Like rivers, and yet so unlike them in width, depth, and placidity, with their broad mouths guarded by clustering islands, one can find nothing in Nature more grand, solemn, and impressive than a Norwegian fjord. Now and again the shores are lined for brief distances by the greenest of green pastures, dotted with little red houses and groups of domestic animals, forming bits of verdant foreground backed by dark gorges. Down precipitous cliffs leap cascades, which are fed by ice-fields hidden in the lofty mountains so close at hand. These are not merely pretty spouts like many a little Swiss device, but grand, plunging, restless torrents, conveying heavy volumes of foaming water. An artist's eye would revel in the twilight glory of carmine, orange, and indigo which floods the atmosphere and the sea amid such scenery as we have faintly depicted.

CHAPTER VIII.

Birds of the Arctic Regions. — Effect of Continuous Daylight. — Town of Tromsöe. — The Aurora Borealis. — Love of Flowers. — The Growth of Trees. — Butterflies. — Home Flowers. — Trees. — Shooting Whales with Cannon. — Pre-Historic Relics. — About Laplanders. — Eider Ducks. — A Norsk Wedding Present. — Gypsies of the North. — Pagan Rites. — The Use of the Reindeer. — Domestic Life of the Lapps. — Marriage Ceremony. — A Gypsy Queen. — Lapp Babies. — Graceful Acknowledgment.

WE have said nothing about the feathered tribes of Norway, though all along this coast, which is so eaten and corroded by the action of the sea, the birds are nearly as numerous as the fishes. They are far more abundant than the author has ever seen them in any other part of the world. Many islands, beginning at the Lofodens and reaching to the extreme end of the peninsula, are solely occupied by them as breeding places. Their numbers are beyond calculation; one might as well try to get at the aggregate number of flies in a given space in midsummer. They consist of petrels, swans, geese, pelicans, grebes, auks, gulls, and divers; these last are more particularly of the duck family, of which there are over thirty distinct species in and about this immediate region. Curlews, wandering albatrosses, ptarmigans, cormorants, and ospreys were also observed, besides some birds of beautiful plumage whose names were unknown to us. Throughout all Scandinavia the many lakes, so numerous as to be unknown by name, also abound with water-fowl of nearly every description habitual to the North. These inland regions afford an abundance of the white grouse, which may be called the national bird of Norway, where it so much abounds. The author has nowhere seen such fine specimens of this bird except in the mountains of Colorado, where it is however very rarely captured. In Scandinavia it changes the color of its plumage very curiously, from a summer to a winter hue. In the first named season these birds have a reddish brown tinge, quite clear and distinctive; but in winter their plumage becomes of snowy whiteness,—a fact from which naturalists are prone to draw some fine-spun deductions.

As we advanced farther and farther northward our experiences became more and more peculiar. It seemed that humanity, like Nature about us, was possessed of a certain insomnia in these regions during the constant reign of daylight. People were wide awake and busy at their various occupations during all hours, while the drowsy god seemed to have departed on a long journey to the southward. The apparent incongruity of starting upon a fresh enterprise "in the dead vast and middle of the night" was only realized on consulting one's watch.

To meet the temporary exigency caused by continuous daylight, as to whether one meant day or night time in giving the figure on the dial, the passengers adopted an ingenious mode of counting the hours. Thus after twelve o'clock midday the count went on thirteen, fourteen, and fifteen o'clock, until midnight, which was twenty-four o'clock. This is a mode of designation adopted in both China and Italy.

Tromsöe is situated in latitude 69° 38' north, upon a small but pleasant island, though it is rather low compared with the surrounding islands and the nearest main-land, but clothed when we saw it, in July, to the very highest point with exquisite verdure. It is a gay and thrifty little place built upon a slope, studded here and there with attractive villas amid the trees; but the business portion of the town is quite compact, and lies closely about the shore. It is the largest and most important settlement in northern Norway, being the capital of Norwegian Lapland, and having about six thousand inhabitants. It rises to the dignity of a cathedral, and is the seat of a bishopric. In the Market Place is a substantial Town Hall, and a neat though small Roman Catholic church. There is also here an excellent Museum, principally of Arctic curiosities and objects relating to the history of the Lapps and Finlanders, with a fair zoölogical department, also possessing a fine collection of Alpine minerals. There are several schools, one of which is designed to prepare teachers for their special occupation, somewhat after the style of our Normal Schools. It must be admitted, however, that the lower order of the people here are both ignorant and superstitious; still, the conclusion was that Tromsöe is one of the most interesting spots selected as a popular centre within the Arctic Circle. Both to the north and south of the town snow-clad mountains shut off distant views. During the winter months there are only four hours of daylight here out of each twenty-four, — that is, from about ten o'clock A. M. until two o'clock P. M.; but the long winter nights are made comparatively light by the glowing and constant splendor of the Aurora Borealis. The pride of Tromsöe is its cathedral, which contains some really fine wood-carving; but the structure is small and has no architectural merit. Though regular services are held here on the Sabbath, that is about the only apparent observation of the day by the people. Games and out-door sports are played in the very churchyard, and balls and parties are given in the evening of the Lord's Day; evidently they do not belong to that class of people who think Sunday is a sponge with which to wipe out the sins of the week. The streets are ornamented by the mountain-ash, birch-trees, and the wild cherry, ranged uniformly on either side of the broad thoroughfares. In one place it was noticed that a miniature park had been begun by the planting of numerous young trees. The birches in this neighborhood are of a grandly developed species, the handsomest indeed which we remember to have seen anywhere. Just outside the town there was observed a field golden with buttercups, making it difficult to realize that we were in Arctic regions. A pink-blooming heather also carpeted other small fields; and here for a moment we were agreeably surprised at beholding a tiny cloud of butterflies, so abundant in the warm sunshine and presenting such transparency of color, as to suggest the idea that some rainbow had been shattered and was floating in myriad particles on the buoyant air. The short-lived summer perhaps makes flowers all the more prized and the more carefully tended. In the rudest quarters a few pet plants were seen, whose arrangement and nurture showed womanly care and tenderness. Every window in the humble dwellings had its living screen of drooping many-colored fuchsias, geraniums, forget-me-nots, and monthly roses. The ivy is especially prized here, and is picturesquely trained to hang gracefully about the architraves of the windows. The fragrant sweet-pea, with its combined snow-white and peach-blossom hues, was often mingled prettily with the dark green of the ivy, the climbing propensities of each making them fitting companions. In one or two windows was seen the brilliant flowering bignonia (Trumpet-vine), and an abundance of soft green, rose-scented geraniums. Surely there must be an innate sense of refinement among the people of these frost-imbued regions, whatever their seeming, when they are actuated by such delicate appreciations. "They are useless rubbish," said a complaining husband to his hard-working wife, referring to her little store of flowers. "Useless!" replied the true woman, "how dare you be wiser than God?"

Vegetation within the Arctic Circle is possessed of an individual vitality which seems to be independent of atmospheric influence. Plants seem to have thawed a little space about them before the snow quite disappeared, and to have peeped forth from their frost-surrounded bed in the full vigor of life, while the grass springs up so suddenly that its growth must have been well started under cover of the snow. One of the most interesting subjects of study to the traveller on the journey northward is to mark his progress by the products of the forest. The trees will prove, if intelligently observed, as definite in regard to fixing his position as an astronomical observation could do. From the region of the date and the palm we come to that of the fig and the olive, thence to the orange, the almond, and the myrtle. Succeeding these we find the walnut, the poplar, and the lime; and again there comes the region of the elm, the oak, and the sycamore. These will be succeeded by the larch, the fir, the pine, the birch, and their companions. After this point we look for no change of species, but a diminution in size of these last enumerated. The variety of trees is of course the result of altitude as well as of latitude, since there are mountain regions in southern Europe, as well as in America, where one may pass in a few hours from the region of the olive to that of the stunted pine or fir.

The staple commodities of Tromsöe are Lapps, reindeer, and midnight sun. The universal occupation is that of fishing for cod, sharks, and whales, to which may be added the curing or drying of the first and the " trying out " of the latter, supplemented by the treatment of cods' livers. From this place vessels are fitted out for Polar expeditions, which creates a certain amount of local business in the ship chandlery line. French, German, English, Russian, and Danish flags were observed floating from the shipping in the harbor, which presented a scene of considerable activity for so small a port. Some of these vessels were fitting for the capture of seals and walruses among the ice-fields of the Polar Sea, and also on the coast of Spitzbergen and Nova Zembla. A small propeller was seen lying in the stream fitted with a forecastle gun, from whence to fire a lance at whales, — a species of big fishing which is profitably pursued here. A huge carcass of this leviathan was stranded on the opposite side of the harbor from where we were moored, and it is hardly necessary to add that its decaying condition rendered the atmosphere extremely offensive. As we lay at anchor little row-boats, with high bows and sterns, flitted about the bay like sea-birds on the wing, and rode as lightly on the surface of the water. These were often "manned" by a couple of sturdy, bronzed women, who rowed with great precision and stout arms, their eyes and faces glowing with animation. These boats, of the same model as that thousand-year old Viking ship at Christiania, seemed to set very low in the water amidship, but yet were remarkable for their buoyancy, sharp bows and sterns, and the ease with which they were propelled. The tall wooden fish-packing houses which line the wharves suggest the prevailing industry of the place. A long, low white building upon the hill-side also showed that the manufacture of rope and cordage is a prominent industry of the locality.

The Lapps in their quaint and picturesque costumes surrounded the newly arrived steamer in their boats, offering furs, carved horn implements, moccasons, walrus-teeth, and the like for sale. These wares are of the rudest type, and of no possible use to civilized people; but they are curious, and serve as mementos of the traveller's visit to these northern latitudes. In the town there are several stores where goods, manufactured by the better class of Lapps, can be had of a finer quality than is offered by these itinerants, who are very ready to pass off inferior articles upon strangers. Their drinking-cups, platters, and dishes generally are made of the wood of the birch. Spoons and forks are formed of the horns and bones of the reindeer. In the fancy line they make some curious bracelets from the roots of the birch-tree. These Lapps are very shrewd in trade, and are not without plenty of low cunning hidden behind their brown, withered, and expressionless faces.

On the main-land near by, as we were told, there are some singular relics of antiquity, such as a series of large stones uniformly arranged in circles, and high cairns of stone containing in their centres one or more square chambers. At one place in this district there is a remarkable mound of reindeer's horns and human bones, mingled with those of unknown species of animals. It is believed that here, centuries ago, the

Lapps sacrificed both animals and human beings to their Pagan deities. There are also some deep earth and rock caves found in the same vicinity, which contain many human bones with others of huge animals, which have excited great interest among scientists. In the neighborhood of Tromsöe, and especially still farther north, large numbers of eider-duck are found, so abundant that no reliable estimate can be made of their number. The eggs are largely used by the natives for food, the nests being also regularly robbed of the down, while the birds with patient resignation continue for a considerable period to lay eggs and to renew the soft lining of their nests. The birds themselves are protected by law, no one being permitted to injure them. The male bird is white and black, the female is brown. In size they are larger than our domestic ducks. Landing almost anywhere in this sparsely inhabited region along the coast, but more particularly upon the islands, one finds the eider-ducks upon their low accessible nests built of marine plants among the rocks, and during incubation the birds are quite as tame as barn-yard fowls. The down of these birds forms a considerable source of income to many persons who make a business of gathering it. It has always a fixed value, and is worth, we were told, in Tromsöe, ten dollars per pound when ready for market. The waste in preparing it for use is large, requiring four pounds of the crude article as it comes from the nest to make one pound of the cleansed, merchantable down. Each nest during the breeding season produces about a quarter of a pound of the uncleansed article. When thoroughly prepared, it is so firm and yet so elastic that the quantity which can be pressed between the two hands will suffice to properly stuff a bed-quilt. It is customary for a Norsk lover to present his betrothed with one of these quilts previous to espousal, the contents of which he is presumed to have gathered with his own hands. A peculiarity of eider-down, as we were informed, is that if picked by hand from the breast of the dead bird it has no elasticity whatever. The natural color is a pale-brown. Many of the localities resorted to by the birds for breeding purposes are claimed by certain parties, who erect a cross or some other special mark thereon to signify that such preserves are not to be poached upon. The birds, like the people, get their living mostly by fishing, and are attracted hither as much by the abundance of their natural food as by the isolation of their breeding haunts.

The Lapps are to be seen by scores in the streets of Tromsöe. They are small in stature, being generally under five feet, with high cheek-bones, snub-noses, oblique Mongolian eyes, big mouths, large ill-formed heads, faces preternaturally aged, hair like meadow hay, and very scanty beards. Such is a photograph of the ancient race that once ruled the whole of Scandinavia. By taking a short trip inland one comes upon their summer encampment, formed of a few crude huts, outside of which they generally live except in the winter months. A Lapp sleeps wherever fatigue or drunkenness overcomes him, preferring the ground, but often lying on the snow. He rises in the morning refreshed from an exposure by which nearly any civilized human being would expect to incur lasting if not fatal injury. They are the gypsies of the North, and occupy a very low place in the social scale, certainly no higher than that of the Penobscot Indians of Maine. Their faculties are of a restricted order, and missionary efforts among them have never yet yielded any satisfactory results. Unlike our western Indians they are of a peaceful nature, neither treacherous nor revengeful, but yet having many of the grosser failings of civilized life. They are greedy, avaricious, very dirty, and passionately fond of alcoholic drinks, but we were told that serious crimes were very rare among them. No people could be more superstitious, as they believe that the caves of the half-inaccessible mountains about them are peopled by giants and evil spirits. They still retain some of their half-pagan rites, such as the use of magical drums and tom-toms for conjuring purposes, and to frighten away or to propitiate supposed devils, malicious diseases, and so on. The most advanced of the race are those who inhabit northern Norway. The Swedish Lapps are considered as coming next, while those under Russian dominion are thought to be the lowest.

An old navigator named Scrahthrift, while making a voyage of discovery northward, more than three centuries ago, wrote about the Lapps as follows: " They are a wild people, which neither know God nor yet good order; and these people live in tents made of deerskins, and they have no certain habitations, but continue in herds by companies of one hundred or two hundred. They are a people of small stature and are clothed in deerskins, and drink nothing but water, and eat no bread, but flesh all raw." They may have drunk nothing but water three hundred years ago, but they drink alcohol enough in this nineteenth century to make up for all former abstemiousness. Scrahthrift wrote in 1556, and gave the first account to the English-speaking world of this peculiar race whom modern ethnologists class with the Samoyedes of Siberia and the Esquimaux, the three forming what is called the Hyperborean Race. The word *Samoyedes* signifies "swamp-dwellers," and *Esquimau* means "eater of raw flesh."

The Lapps are natural nomads, their wealth consisting solely in their herds of reindeer, to procure sustenance for which necessitates frequent changes of locality. A Laplander is rich, provided he owns enough of these animals to support himself and family. A herd that can afford thirty full-grown deer for slaughter annually, and say ten more to be sold or bartered, makes a family of a dozen persons comfortably well off. But to sustain such a draft upon his resources, a Lapp must own at least two hundred and fifty head. There is also a waste account to be considered. Not a few are destroyed annually by wolves and bears, notwithstanding the usual precautions against such casualties, while in very severe winters numbers are sure to die of starvation. They live almost entirely on the so-called reindeer moss; but this failing them, they eat the young twigs of the trees. When the snow covers the ground to a depth of not more than three or four feet, these intelligent creatures dig holes in order to reach the moss, and guided by some strong instinct they rarely fail to do so in just the right place. The Lapps themselves would be entirely at a loss for any indication where to seek the animal's food when it is covered by the deep snow.

What the camel is to the Arab of the desert, the reindeer is to the Laplander. Though found here in a wild state, they are not common, and are very shy sometimes occupying partially inaccessible islands near the main-land, swimming back and forth as necessity may demand. The domestic deer is smaller than those that remain in a state of nature, and is said to live only half as long. When properly broken to harness, they carry lashed to their backs a hundred and thirty pounds, or drag upon the snow, when harnessed to a sledge, two hundred and fifty pounds, travelling ten miles an hour, for several consecutive hours, without apparent fatigue. Some of the thread prepared by the Lapp women from the sinews of the reindeer was shown to us, being as fine as the best sewing-silk, and much stronger than any silk thread made by modern methods.

These diminutive people are not so poorly off as one would at first sight think them to be. The climate in which they live, though terrible to us, is not

USES OF THE REINDEER.

so to them. They have their games, sports, and festive hours. If their hardships were very trying they would not be so proverbially long-lived. Though an ill-formed race, they are yet rugged, hardy, and self-reliant. Their limbs are crooked and out of proportion to their bodies; one looks in vain for a well-shaped or perfect figure among them, and indeed it may be safely doubted whether a straight-limbed Lapp exists. They are one and all bow-legged. The country over which these people roam is included within northern Norway, Sweden, Russia, and Finland, say extending over seven thousand square miles; but the whole race will hardly number thirty thousand in the aggregate. Lapland in general terms may be said to be the region lying between the Polar Ocean and the Arctic Circle, the eastern and western boundaries being the Atlantic Ocean and the White Sea, two thirds of which territory belong to Russia, and one third is about equally divided between Norway and Sweden.

We repeat that the reindeer is to the Lapp what the camel is to the Arab. This small creature is the Lapp's cow, horse, food, clothing, tent, everything. Food is not stored for the animals, as they are never under cover even in the severest weather, and they must procure their own food or starve. The females give but a small quantity of milk, not more than the amount yielded by a well-fed goat, but it is remarkably rich and nourishing. Oddly enough, as it seemed to us, they are milked but twice a week; and when this process is performed, each animal must be lassoed and firmly held by one person while another milks. Many of the doe on the occasion of our visit were accompanied by their fawns, of which they often have two at a birth. These little creatures are able to follow their dam twenty-four hours after birth. We were told that the bucks are inclined to kill the fawns when they are first born, but are fiercely attacked by the dams and driven away. A Swiss chamois is not more expert in climbing mountains than are these Norway deer; and were it not for the efficient help of their dogs, which animals are as sagacious as the Scotch sheep-dogs, the Lapps would often find it nearly impossible to corral their herds for milking and other purposes. In their nature deer are really untamable, being never brought into such complete subjection as to be quite safe for domestic use. Even when broken to harness, that is when attached to the snow-sledge or carrying burdens lashed to their backs, they will sometimes without any premonition break out into rank rebellion and violently attack their masters. We were told by an intelligent resident of Tromsöe that the Lapps never abuse these animals, even when they are attacked by them. They only throw some garment upon the ground upon which the buck vents his rage; after which the owner can appear and resume his former control of the animal, as though nothing had happened out of the common course of events.

The Lapps live in low, open tents during the summer season, moving from place to place as food is found for their herds, but keeping near the sea-coast for purposes of trade, as well as to avoid those terrible pests the gad-fly and the mosquito, insects too obnoxious for even the endurance of a Laplander. In the winter they retire far inland, where they build temporary huts of the branches of the trees, plastering them inside and out with clay, but leaving a hole in the top to act as a chimney and convey away the smoke, the fire being always built upon a broad flat stone in the centre of the hut. In these rude, and according to our estimate comfortless, cabins they hibernate rather than live the life of civilized beings for eight months of the year. Hunting and fishing occupy a portion of their time; and to kill a bear is considered a most honorable achievement, something to boast of for life, rendering the successful hunter quite a hero among his associates. Though the forest, river, and sea furnish this people with more or less food throughout the year, still the Lapp depends upon his herd for fixed supplies of sustenance. The milk made into cheese is his most important article of food, and is stored for winter use. Few are so poor as not to own forty or fifty reindeer. The Norwegians and Swedes who live in their neighborhood have as great a prejudice against the Lapps as our western citizens have against the North American Indians. This as regards the Lapps is perhaps more especially on account of their filthiness and half-barbarous habits. It must be admitted that a visit to their huts near Tromsöe leads one to form an extremely unfavorable opinion of the race. When a couple of young Lapps desire to become married a priest is sometimes employed, but by common acceptation among them the bride's father is equally qualified to perform the ceremony, which is both original and simple. It consists in placing the hands of the two contracting parties in each other, and the striking of fire with a flint and steel, when the marriage is declared to be irrevocable. Promiscuous as their lives seem to be in nearly all respects, we were told that when a Lapp woman was once married the attendant relationship was held sacred. Though it was our fate to just miss witnessing a marriage ceremony here, the bride and groom were pointed out to us, appearing like two children, so diminutive were they. The dress of the two sexes is so similar that it is not easy for a stranger to distinguish at a glance men from women, except that the latter are not so tall as the former. Polygamy is common among them. Men marry at the age of eighteen, women at fifteen; but as a race they are not prolific, and their numbers, as we were informed, are steadily decreasing. The average Laplander is less than five feet in height, and the women rarely exceed four feet. The latter are particularly fond of coffee, sugar, and rye flour, which the men care nothing for so long as they can get corn brandy, — a local distillation quite colorless but very potent. The Norwegians have a saying of reproach concerning one who is inclined to drink too much: "Don't make a Lapp of yourself." Both men and women are inveterate smokers, and next to money you can give them nothing more acceptable than tobacco.

Nature is sometimes anomalous. Among the group of Lapp men and women whom we met in the streets of Tromsöe, there stood one, a tall stately girl twenty-two years of age, more or less, who presented in her really fine person a singular contrast to her rude companions. Unmistakable as to her race, she was yet a head and shoulders taller than the rest, but possessing the high cheek-bones, square face, and Mongolian cast of eyes which characterizes them. There was an air of dignified modesty and almost of beauty about this young woman, spite of her leather leggins, queer moccasons, and rough reindeer clothes. Her fingers were busily occupied, as she stood there gracefully leaning against a rough stone-wall in the soft sunshine, twisting the sinews of the deer into fine thread, while she carelessly glanced up now and again at the curious eyes of the author who was intently regarding her. One could not but imagine what remarkable possibilities lay hidden in this individual; what a change education, culture, and refined associations might create in her; what a social world there was extant of which she had never dreamed! It was observed that her companions of both sexes seemed to defer to her, and we fancied that she must be a sort of queen bee in the Lapps' hive.

There is one thing observable and worthy of mention as regards the domestic habits of these rude Laplanders, and that is their apparent consideration for their women. The hard work is invariably assumed by the men. The women carry the babies, but the men carry all heavy burdens, and perform the rougher labor contingent upon their simple domestic lives. The women milk, but the men must drive the herds from the distant pasturage, lasso the doe, and hold the animals by the horns during the process. It is not possible to tame or domesticate them so as to submit to this operation with patience like a cow. Up to a certain age the Lapp babies are packed constantly in dry moss, in place of other clothing during their infancy, this being renewed as occasion demands, — thus very materially economizing laundry labor. The little creatures are very quiet in their portable cradles, consisting of a basket-frame covered with reindeer hide, into which they are closely strapped. The cases are sometimes swung hammock fashion between two posts, and sometimes hung upon a peg outside the cabins in the sunshine. It is marvellous to what a degree of seeming neglect semi-barbarous babies will patiently submit, and how quietly their babyhood is passed. Probably a Japanese, Chinese, or Lapp baby *can* cry upon occasion; but though many hours have been passed by the author among these people, he never heard a breath of complaint from the wee things.

Some of the Lapps are quite expert with the bow and arrow, which was their ancient weapon of defence as well as for hunting, it being the primitive weapon of savages wherever encountered. Few of this people possess firearms. The long sharp knife and the steel-tipped arrow still form their principal arms. With these under ordinary circumstances, when he chances upon the animal, a Lapp does not hesitate to attack the black bear, provided she has not young ones with her, in which case she is too savage a foe to attack single-handed. In starting out upon a bear-hunt, several Lapps combine, and spears are taken with the party as well as firearms if they are fortunate enough to possess them.

As we were standing among the Lapps in Tromsöe, with some passengers from the steamer, a bevy of children just returning from school joined the group. A blue-eyed, flaxen-haired girl of ten or eleven years in advance of the rest attracted the attention of a gentleman of the party, who presented her with a bright silver coin. The child took his hand in both her own, pressed it with exquisite natural grace to her lips, courtesied and passed on. This is the universal act of gratitude among the youth of Norway. The child had been taken by surprise, but she accepted the little gift with quiet and dignified self-possession. There is no importunity or beggary to be encountered in Scandinavia.

CHAPTER IX.

Experiences Sailing Northward. — Arctic Whaling. — The Feathered Tribe. — Caught in a Trap. — Domestic Animals. — The Marvellous Gulf Stream. — Town of Hammerfest. — Commerce. — Arctic Mosquitoes. — The Public Crier. — Norwegian Marriages. — Peculiar Bird Habits. — A Hint to Naturalists. — Bird Island. — A Lonely Habitation. — High Latitude. — Final Landing at the North Cape. — A Hard Climb. — View of the Wonderful Midnight Sun.

AFTER leaving Tromsöe our course was north by east, crossing broad wild fjords and skirting the main-land, passing innumerable islands down whose precipitous sides narrow waterfalls leaped hundreds of feet towards the sea. Along the shore at intervals little clusters of fishermen's huts were seen with a small sprinkling of herbage and patches of bright verdure. Here and there were partially successful attempts at vegetable culture, but the brief season which is here possible for such purposes is almost prohibitory. Whales, sometimes singly, sometimes in schools, rose to the surface of the sea, and casting up tiny fountains of spray would suddenly disappear to come up again, perhaps miles away. These leviathans of the deep are always a subject of great interest to persons at sea, and were certainly in remarkable numbers here in the Arctic Ocean. As we have said, small steamers are in use along the coast for catching whales; and these are painted green, to enable them to approach the animal unperceived. They are armed with small swivel-guns, from which is fired a compound projectile, consisting of a barbed harpoon to which a short chain is affixed, and to that a strong line. This special form of harpoon has barbs, which expand as soon as they have entered the body of the animal and he pulls upon the line, stopping at a certain angle, and rendering the withdrawal of the weapon impossible. Besides this an explosive shell is attached, which bursts within the body of the monster as soon as the flukes expand, producing almost instant death. A cable is then affixed to the head, and the whale is towed into harbor to be cut up and the blubber tried out upon the shore in huge kettles. This business is carried on at Vadsö and Hammerfest as well as at Tromsöe. The change was constant, and the novelty never ceasing. Large black geese, too heavy it would seem for lofty flight, rose awkwardly from the surface of the waves, and now and again skimmed across the fjords, just clearing the surface of the dark blue waters. Oyster-catchers, as they are familiarly called, decked with scarlet legs and bills, were abundant. Now and then that daring highwayman. among sea-birds, — the skua, or robber-gull, — was seen on the watch for a victim. He is quite dark in plumage, almost black, and gets a predatory living by attacking and causing other birds to drop what they have caught up from the sea, seizing which as it falls, he sails swiftly away to consume his stolen prize.

The movements of this feathered creature through the air when darting towards its object are almost too rapid to follow with the human eye. Not infrequently six or eight gulls of the common species club together and make a combined onslaught upon this daring freebooter, and then he must look out for himself; for when the gull is thoroughly aroused and makes up his mind to fight, he distinctly means business, and will struggle to the last gasp, like the Spanish game-cock. There is proverbially strength in numbers, and the skua, after such an organized encounter, is almost always found floating lifeless upon the surface of the sea.

We were told of an interesting and touching experience relating to the golden eagle which occurred near Hammerfest, in the vicinity of which we are now speaking. It seems that a young Norwegian had set a trap far up in the hills, at a point where he knew that these birds occasionally made their appearance. He was prevented from visiting the trap for some two weeks after he had set and placed it; but finally when he did so, he found that one of these noble creatures had been caught by the foot, probably in a few hours after the trap had been left there. His efforts to release himself had been in vain, and he lay there dead from exhaustion, not of starvation. This was plain enough, since close beside the dead eagle and quite within his reach was the half-consumed body of a white grouse, which must have been brought to him by his mate, who realizing her companion's position thus did all that was in her power to sustain and help him. Occasionally domestic animals in small numbers are seen at the fishing hamlets, though this is very rarely the case above Hammerfest. Goats, cows, and sheep find but a poor supply of vegetable sustenance, mostly composed of reindeer moss; but, strange to say, these animals learn to eat dried fish, and to relish it when mixed with moss and straw. The cows are small in frame and quite short in the legs, but they are hardy and prolific, and mostly white. All domestic animals seem to be dwarfed here by climatic influences.

Long before we reached Hammerfest the passengers' watches seemed to be bewitched, for it must be remembered that here it is broad daylight through all the twenty-four hours which constitute day and night elsewhere. No wonder that sleep became little more than a subterfuge, since everybody's eyes were preternaturally wide open.

The Gulf Stream emerging from the tropics thousands of miles away constantly laves these shores, and consequently ice is here unknown. At first blush it seems a little queer that icebergs here in latitude 70° north are never seen, though we all know them to be plenty enough in the season on the coast of America at 41°. The entire coast of Norway is warmer by at least twenty degrees than most other localities in the same latitude, owing to the presence and influence of the Gulf Stream,— that heated, mysterious river in the midst of the ocean. It also brings to these boreal regions quantities of floating material, such as the trunks of palm-trees and other substances suitable for fuel, to which useful purpose they are put at the Lofoden fishing hamlets and also on the shores of the main-land. By the same active agency West Indian seeds and woods are found floating on the west coast of Scotland and Ireland.

Hammerfest, the capital of the province of Finmark, is situated in latitude 70° 40' north, upon the island of Kvalöe, or "Whale Island." It is overshadowed by Tyvfjeld,—that is, "Thief Mountain," thus fancifully named because it robs the place of the little sunshine it might enjoy were this huge elevation not at all times intervening. It is the most northerly town in all Europe, and is located about sixty-five miles southwest of the North Cape. It is a compactly-built town of about three thousand inhabitants, who appear to be exceptionally industrious and intelligent. Even here, in this far-off region of frost, there are good schools and able teachers. There is also a weekly newspaper issued, and some authorities claim a population of nearly six thousand, which seemed to be an excessive estimate.

The harbor presents a busy scene, with its queer Norwegian boats formed after the excellent but antique shape of the galleys of old. On a little promontory near the entrance of the harbor is erected a stone pillar, indicating the spot where the measurement of the degrees of latitude between the mouth of the Danube and Hammerfest was perfected. It is called the Meridianstötte. The trading-vessels are many, and they fly the flags of several commercial nations; but most numerous of all is the flag of Russia, whose trading-ships swarm on the coast during the summer season. Many of these vessels were from far-off Archangel and the ports of the White Sea, from whence they bring cargoes of grain to exchange for dried fish. Truly has it been said that commerce defies every wind, outrides every tempest, and invades every zone. Hammerfest, consisting mostly of one long, broad street, is neat and clean; but the odor of fish-oil is very sickening to one not accustomed to it. We were twice compelled to beat a retreat from certain localities, being unable to endure the stench. Many of the people were seen to be shod in heavy leather boots or shoes, similar in form to the fishing-boats, being curiously pointed and turned up at the toes. Certain tokens in and about the town forcibly reminded one of New Bedford in Massachusetts. On the north promontory of the island is situated a picturesque lighthouse, from which a fine view may be enjoyed of the rocky shore, the myriads of islands, and the mountainous main-land. The mosquitoes, that inexplicable pest even in this high latitude, scarcely wait for the snow to disappear before they begin their vicious onslaught upon humanity. The farther one goes inland the greater this annoyance becomes, and some protection to face, neck, and hands is absolutely necessary. The public crier pursues his ancient vocation at Hammerfest, not however with a noisy bell, but with a more melodious trumpet. After blowing a few clear, shrill notes thereon calculated to awaken attention, he proclaims that there will be a missionary meeting held at a certain hour and place, or that a steamer will sail on the following day at a given time, the favorite hour being at twelve midnight. The crier here understands his vocation, and by introducing a certain melodious expression to his words, chanting them in fact, he commands the pleased attention of the multitude.

A wedding-feast in Norway is always looked upon as a grand domestic event, and is ever made the most of by all parties concerned; but at Hammerfest and the north part of the country generally, it becomes a most important and demonstrative affair. No expense is spared by the bride's parents to render the event memorable in all respects. The revels are sometimes kept up for a period of three weeks, until at last every one becomes quite exhausted with the excitement and with dancing, when the celebration by common consent is brought to a close. During the height of the revels, street parades constitute a part of the singular performances, when bride, bridegroom, family and friends, preceded by a band of musicians, march gayly from point to point; or a line of boats is formed, with the principals in the first, the musicians in the second, and so on, all decked with natural and artificial flowers and bright-colored streamers. As we started out of Hammerfest harbor we chanced upon one of these aquatic bridal parties, accompanied by instrumental music and a chorus of many pleasant voices, the diaphanous dresses of bride and bridesmaids looking like mist-wreaths settled about the boats. It was easy to distinguish the bride from her attendants, by the tall, sparkling gilt crown which she wore.

In sailing along the coast after leaving the point just described, it is observed that vegetation grows more and more scarce. The land is seen to be useless for agricultural purposes; habitations first become rare, then almost entirely cease, bleakness reigning supreme, while one seems to be creeping higher and higher on the earth. In ascending lofty mountains, say in the Himalayan range, we realize that there are heights still above us; but in approaching the North Cape a feeling comes over us that we are gradually getting to the very apex of the globe. Everything seems to be beneath our feet; the broad, deep, unbounded ocean alone makes the horizon. Day and night cease to be relative terms, while the strange effect and the magic brightness of a Polar night utterly beggar description. As we rounded one of the many abrupt rocky islets in our course, which came up dark, steep, and inaccessible from an unknown depth, there flew up from the smooth waters into which the steamer ploughed her way a couple of small ducks, each with a young bird snugly ensconced upon its back, between the broad-spread, narrow wings. This was to the writer a novelty, though an officer of the ship said it was not unusual to see certain species of Arctic ducks thus transporting their ducklings. One reads of woodcock at times seizing their young in their talons, and bearing them away from impending danger; but a web-footed bird could not effectually adopt this mode in any exigency. It seems however that Nature has taught the ducks another fashion of transporting their helpless progeny. The birds we had disturbed did not fly aloft with their tiny burdens, but skimmed over the surface of the fjord into some one of the sheltering nooks along the irregular shore. We were further told a curious fact, if fact it be, that the young ducks of the female species, almost as soon as they are able to fly, begin to practise the habit of carrying something upon their backs. That is to say, they are not infrequently found skimming along the surface of the water with a small wad of sea-weed, such as is used by aquatic birds in nest-building, carefully supported between their wings. Just so little girls are prone to pet a doll, the maternal instinct exhibiting itself in early childhood. The male and female birds are easily distinguished from each other by the difference in their plumage. The former do not show this inclination for carrying baby burdens, neither do young boys display a predilection for dolls! We commend these facts to the notice of naturalists.

About forty miles northward from Hammerfest is situated what is called Bird Island, a hoary mass of rock, famous as a breeding place of various sea-birds, and where the nests of many thousands are to be seen. This huge cliff rises abruptly to the height of over a thousand feet from the surrounding ocean.

Its seaward face being nearly perpendicular is yet so creviced as to afford lodgement for the birds, and it is literally covered by their nests from base to top. The Norwegians call the island Sværholtklubben. It is customary for excursion steamers to "make" this island in their course to the North Cape, and to stand off and on for an hour to give passengers an opportunity to observe the birds and their interesting habits. The ship's cannon is fired also, when the echoes of its single report become myriad, reverberating through the caves and broad chasms of the rock, starting forth the feathered tribes, until the air is as full of them as of flakes in an Arctic snow-storm. The echoes mingle with the harsh, wailing screams, and roar of wings become almost deafening as the birds wheel in clouds above the ship, or sail swiftly away and return again like a flash to join their young, whose tiny white heads may be seen peeping anxiously above the sides of the nests. One or two dwelling-houses, surrounded by a few small sheds, are to be seen in a little valley near the water's edge on the lee side of Bird Island, where a dozen persons more or less make their dreary home. These residents send off fresh milk by a boat to the passing steamer, though how the cows can find sustenance here is an unsolved riddle. They also make a business of robbing the birds'-nests of the eggs, by means of ladders, but do not injure the birds themselves. Of course there are but comparatively few of the nests which they can manage to reach at all.

The North Cape is in reality an island projecting itself far into the Polar Sea, and which is separated from the main-land by a narrow strait. The highest point which has ever been reached by the daring Arctic explorer was eighty-three degrees twenty-four minutes, north latitude; this Cape is in latitude seventy-one degrees ten minutes. The island is named Magerœ, which signifies a barren place; and it is certainly well named, for a wilder, bleaker, or more desolate spot cannot be found on the face of the earth. Only a few hares, ermine, and sea-birds manage to subsist upon its sterile soil. The western and northern sides are absolutely inaccessible from their rough and precipitous character. The Arctic Sea thundered hoarsely against its base as we approached the wind-swept, weather-worn cliff of the North Cape in a small landing-boat. It was near the midnight hour, yet the warm light of the sun's clear, direct rays enveloped us. A few sea-birds uttered dismal and discordant cries as they flew lazily in circles overhead. The landing was soon accomplished amid the half impassable rocks, and then began, the struggle to reach the top of the Cape, which rises in its only accessible part at an angle of nearly forty-five degrees. For half an hour we plodded wearily through the débris of rubble-stones, wet soil, and rolling rocks, until finally the top was reached, after which a walk of about a third of a mile upon gently rising ground brings one to the point of observation, — that is, to the verge of the cliff. We were now fully one thousand feet above the level of the sea, standing literally upon the threshold of the unknown.

No difference was observed between the broad light of this Polar night and the noon of a sunny summer's day in the low latitudes. The sky was all aglow and the rays of the sun warm and penetrating, though a certain chill in the atmosphere at this exposed elevation rendered thick clothing quite indispensable. This was the objective point to reach which we had voyaged thousands of miles from another hemisphere. We looked about us in silent wonder and awe. To the northward was that unknown region to solve the mysteries of which so many gallant lives had been sacrificed. Far to the eastward was Asia; in the distant west lay America, and southward were Europe and Africa. Such an experience may occur once in a lifetime, but rarely can it be repeated. The surface of the cliff, which is quite level where we stood (near the base of the small granite column erected to commemorate the visit of Oscar II. in 1873), was covered by soft reindeer moss, which yielded to the tread like a rich carpet of velvet. There was no other vegetation near, not even a spear of grass; though as we climbed the steep path hither occasional bits of pea-green moss were seen, with a minute pink blossom peeping out here and there from the rubble-stones. Presently the boom of a distant gun floated faintly upwards. It was the cautionary signal from the ship, which was now seen floating far below us, a mere speck upon that Polar sea.

The hands of the watch indicated that it was near the hour of twelve, midnight. The great luminary had sunk slowly amid a glory of light to within three degrees of the horizon, where it seemed to hover for a single moment like some monster bird about to alight upon a mountain peak, and then changing its mind, slowly began its upward movement. This was exactly at midnight, always a solemn hour; but amid the glare of sunlight and the glowing immensity of sea and sky, how strange and weird it seemed!

Notwithstanding they were so closely mingled, the difference between the gorgeous coloring of the setting and the fresh hues of the rising sun was clearly though delicately defined. Indeed, the sun had not really set at all. It had been constantly visible, though it seemed to shine for a few moments with slightly diminished power. Still, the human eye could not rest upon it for one instant. It was the mingling of the golden haze of evening with the radiant, roseate flush of the blushing morn. At the point where sky and ocean met there was left a boreal azure resembling the steel-white of the diamond; this was succeeded by pearly gray, until the horizon became wavy with lines of blue, like the delicate figures wrought upon a Toledo blade. In the Yellow Sea the author has seen a more vivid sunset, combining the volcanic effects of lurid light; but it lacked the sublime, mysterious, mingled glory of evening and morning twilight which characterized this wondrous view of the Arctic midnight sun.

CHAPTER X.

Journey Across Country. — Capital of Sweden. — Old and New. — Swedish History. — Local Attractions. — King Oscar II. — The Royal Palace. — The Westminster Abbey of Stockholm. — A Splendid Deer Park. — Public Amusements. — The Sabbath. — An Official Dude. — An Awkward Statue. — Swedish Nightingales. — Linnæus and Swedenborg. — Dalecarlia Girls. — A Remarkable Group in Bronze. — Rosedale Royal Cottage. — Ancient Oaks. — Upsala and its Surroundings. — Ancient Mounds at Old Upsala. — Swedenborg's Study.

THE reader will remember that we spoke in our early pages of the inland trip across Norway and Sweden, — that is, from Gottenburg to Stockholm. After visiting the North Cape, one returns by nearly the same route along the coast to Trondhjem, thence to Christiania. Our next objective point being the capital of Sweden, we took passage by rail, crossing the country by way of Charlottenborg, which is the frontier town of Sweden. Here there is a custom-house examination of baggage; for although Norway and Sweden are under one crown, yet they have a separate tariff, so that custom-house rules are regularly enforced between them. As regards others than commercial travellers however this is a mere form, and is not made a source of needless annoyance, as is too often the case in other countries. In crossing the peninsula by rail one does not enjoy the picturesque scenery which characterizes the Gotha Canal route. The railroad journey takes one through a region of lake and forest by no means devoid of interest, and which is rich in mines of iron and other ores. Some important viaducts, iron bridges, and tunnels are passed, and as we approach Lake Maelaren on the east coast a more highly cultivated country is traversed, some of the oldest towns in Sweden being also passed, each of which is strongly individualized. There is a considerable difference observable between the architecture of the Norwegians and that of the Swedes, the former affecting the style of the Swiss châlet, while the latter build much more substantially. Their dwellings as a rule are better finished, and always neatly painted, in town or country.

Stockholm is a noble capital, in many respects exceptionally so. It is situated on the Baltic at the outlet of Lake Maelaren, and is built on several islands, all of which are connected by substantial bridges, — the finest of which is the Norrbro, which has several grand arches of stone, the whole measuring four hundred feet in length by at least sixty in width, though we have no statistics at hand by which to verify these figures. The city has a population of over a hundred and eighty thousand, covering an area of five square miles, and taken as a whole it certainly forms one of the most cleanly and interesting capitals in Europe. It is a city of canals, public gardens, broad squares, and gay cafés. It has two excellent harbors, one on the Baltic and one on Lake Maelaren. Wars, conflagrations, and the steady progress of civilization have entirely changed the city from what it was in the days of Gustavus Vasa,— that is, about the year 1496. It was he who founded the dynasty which has survived for three hundred years. The streets in the older sections of the town are often crooked and narrow, like those of Marseilles, or of Toledo in Spain, where in looking heavenward one does not behold enough of the blue sky between the' roofs for the measure of a waistcoat pattern, but in the more modern-built parts there are fine straight avenues and spacious squares, with large and imposing public and private edifices. Here as in most of the other Scandinavian cities, in consequence of various sweeping fires, the old timber-built houses have gradually disappeared, being replaced by those of brick or stone, and there is now enforced a municipal law which prohibits the erection of wooden structures within the precincts of the city proper.

Stockholm is the centre of the social and literary activity of Scandinavia, hardly second in these respects to Copenhagen. It has its full share of scientific, artistic, and benevolent institutions, such as befit a great European capital. The stranger should as soon as convenient after arriving ascend an elevation of the town called the Mosebacke, whereon has been erected a lofty iron framework and look-out, which is surmounted by means of a steam elevator. From this structure an admirable view of the city is obtained and its topography fixed clearly upon the mind. At a single glance as it were, one overlooks the charming marine view of the Baltic with its busy traffic, while in the opposite direction the hundreds of islands that dot Lake Maelaren form a wide-spread picture of varied beauty. The bird's-eye view obtained of the environs of the capital is unique, since in the immediate vicinity of the city lies the primeval forest, undisturbed and unimproved. This seems the more singular when we realize how ancient a place Stockholm is, having been fortified and made his capital by Birger Jarl, between seven and eight hundred years ago. Though Sweden unlike Norway has no heroic age, so to speak, connecting her earliest exploits with the fate of other countries, still no secondary European power has enacted so brilliant a part in modern history as have those famous Swedish monarchs Gustavus Vasa, Gustavus Adolphus, and Charles XII. The latter fought all Europe, — Danes, Russians, Poles, Germans, — and gave away a kingdom before he was twenty years of age. It was he who at his coronation snatched the crown from the hand of the archbishop and set it proudly on his head with his own hands.

Some of the local attractions of the city are the National Museum, built of granite and marble in the Venetian Renaissance style, the Academy of Sciences, the Art Museum, the Town Hall, and the Royal Palace; but we will not weary the reader with detailed accounts of them. The Royal Palace, like that at Christiania, is an exceedingly plain building, with a granite basement and stuccoed bricks above, forming an immense quadrangular edifice. Though it is very simple externally, it is yet finely proportioned, and stands upon the highest point of the central island. Its present master, King Oscar II., is an accomplished artist, poet, musician, and an admirable linguist, nobly fulfilling the requirements of his responsible position. He has been justly called the ideal sovereign of the age, and the more the world knows of him the more fully this estimate will be confirmed. His court, while it is one of the most unpretentious, is yet one of the most refined in Europe. It is not surprising therefore that the King enjoys a popularity among his subjects characterized by universal confidence, respect, and love. The State departments of the palace are very elegant, and are freely shown to strangers at all suitable times. In the grand State Hall is the throne of silver originally occupied by Queen Christina, while the Hall of Mirrors appears as though it might have come out of Aladdin's Palace. Amid all the varied attractions of art and historic associations, the splendid Banqueting Hall, the galleries of painting and statuary, the Concert Room, audience chambers, saloons hung with Gobelin tapestry, and gilded boudoirs, one simple chamber impressed us most. It was the bed-room of Charles XIV. (Marshal Bernadotte), which has remained unchanged and unused since the time of his death, his old campaign cloak of Swedish blue still lying upon the bed. The clock upon the mantle-piece significantly points to the hour and the minute of the monarch's death. The life and remarkable career of the dead King flashed across the memory as we stood for a moment beside these suggestive souvenirs. It was recalled how he began life as a common soldier in the French army, rising with rapidity by reason of his military genius to be a Marshal of France, and finally to sit upon the Swedish throne. Bernadotte, Prince of Ponte Corvo, is the only one of Napoleon's generals whose descendants still occupy a throne.

The Royal Library is said to be a very choice collection of books in all modern languages, occupying a hall which extends over nearly the entire length of one wing of the palace, and contains a hundred thousand bound volumes. One of the most conspicuous objects seen from its windows is the Riddarsholm Church, a lofty, Gothic structure of red brick, and the Westminster Abbey of the metropolis. Its tall openwork spire of iron tracery reaches towards the sky as though it would pierce the blue vault, forming a conspicuous object for the eye of the traveller who approaches the city by water. This old church, with its banner-hung arches, possesses considerable historic interest. There is significance in the fact that its chime of bells is only heard on the occasion of royal funerals. The broad aisle is filled with grand colossal statuary by Sergel, Bystrom, and other native sculptors. In one of the chapels is the tomb of Gustavus Adolphus, and in another repose the ashes of the youthful hero Charles XII. A long line of Swedish

monarchs also rest beneath the Riddarsholm Church.
The central floor is covered with gravestones bearing
the titles of historic characters and of heroic names,
in the study of which and recalling of their mingled
histories hours glide swiftly away. There is a chapel
of relics attached to the church which contains many
valuable historic souvenirs. In the large square bearing the name of Birger Jarl's Torg, near by the church
just described, stands a bronze statue of this former
ruler and founder of the city, who was a great reform-
er in his day, living until 1266. It was modelled by
Fogelberg, and represents the famous original in the
armor which was common in the twelfth century, the
general effect being artistic and impressive; but it is
by no means faultless. The pedestal is formed by a
heavy dwarfed pillar, which places the statue too far
above the line of sight for good effect. The church of
Adolphus Frederick is built in the form of a cross, and
is rendered quite conspicuous by its large tower, which
is crowned by a copper dome. This church is just a
century old. A monument was observed within its
walls erected to the memory of Descartes, the famous
French philosopher, who died at Stockholm in 1650,
but whose remains were finally removed to Paris.
The most conspicuous dome and tower in the city is
that of the Ladugardslands Church, surmounting an
octagon structure two centuries old. St. Catherine's
Church is the highest in the metropolis, and is built
in the Grecian cross shape, with a lofty dome and five
spires. Its erection dates back two hundred years.

The population of Stockholm seems to consist of a cheerful, prosperous, and contented people, though few remarkable signs of luxury or opulence meet the eye of a stranger. The shops on the principal streets are elegantly arrayed, and in the spacious windows choice merchandise, books, pictures, and jewelry are tastefully displayed. There are not better supplied or more attractive shops on the Rue de la Paix or the Italian Boulevard of Paris. A ceaseless activity reigns along the thoroughfares, among the little steam gondolas upon the many water-ways, and the myriad of passenger steamers which ply upon the lake. Many pleasure seekers throng the small parks in the city, while others seek the more extensive and distant Djurgard, or "Deer Park," in the environs. These are the finest grounds of the sort and by far the most extensive devoted to such a purpose which the author has chanced to see. This remarkable pleasure resort, originally laid out as a deer park by Gustavus III., occupies an entire island by itself, and is some miles in circumference, beautified with inviting drives, grassy glades, rocky knolls, Swiss cottages, Italian verandas, and containing innumerable thrifty trees, among which are some of the noblest oaks to be found outside of England. Refreshment booths, cafés, music halls, marionette theatres, gymnastic apparatus, and various other means of public amusement are liberally distributed over the wide-spread area. It is the great summer resort of the populace for picnicing, pleasure outings, and Sunday holidays. The environs far and

PUBLIC AMUSEMENTS IN STOCKHOLM. 177

near, including the Deer Park, are easily and cheaply reached by small steam launches, or by tramway, at any hour of the day or evening.

No population known to the author is so thoroughly devoted to public amusement as are the citizens of the Swedish capital during the warm season; the brief summer is indeed made the most of by all classes in the enjoyment of out-door life. Beginning at an early hour of the day and continuing until past midnight, gayety reigns supreme from the middle of June until the end of August. To a stranger it seems to be one ceaseless holiday, leading one to ask what period the people devote to their business occupations. It is surprising to observe how many theatres, circuses, concerts, fairs, casinos, field sports and garden entertainments are liberally supported by a population of less than two hundred thousand. At night the tide of life flows fast and furious until the small hours, the town and its environs being ablaze with gas and electric lights. The little omnibus steamers which flit about like fire-flies are, like the tramways, taxed to their utmost capacity, while the air is full of music from military bands. It is the summer gayety of the Champs Elysées thrice multiplied by a community which does not number one tenth of the aggregated population of the great French capital. Not one but every day in the week forms a link in the continuous chain of revelling hours, until on the Sabbath the gayety culminates in a grand fête day of pleasure-outings for men, women, and children. Scores of steamers gayly dressed in flags and crowded with passengers start in the early morning of this day for excursions on Lake Maclaren, or to visit some pleasure resort on the Baltic, while the Deer Park and public gardens of the city resound all day and night with mirth and music.

The Royal Opera House is a plain substantial structure on the Gustaf-Adolf-Torg, built by Gustavus III. in 1775, and will seat fifteen hundred persons. A music-loving Swede told us of the début of Jenny Lind years ago in this dramatic temple, and also described that of Christine Nilsson, which occurred more recently. The excellent acoustic properties of the Stockholm Opera House are admitted by famous vocalists to be nearly unequalled. It was here, at a gay masquerade ball on the morning of March 15, 1792, that Gustavus III. was fatally wounded by a shot from an assassin, one of the conspirators among the nobility. Our place of sojourn while in Stockholm was at the Hotel Rydberg, which overlooks the Gustaf-Adolf-Torg. Directly opposite our windows, across the bridge where the waters of the Baltic and Lake Maclaren join, was the Royal Palace, situated upon a commanding site. On the right of the square and forming one whole side of it was the Crown Prince's palace; on the left was the Opera House, with an equal frontage; while in the centre stood the equestrian bronze statue of Gustavus Adolphus. On the low ground beside the bridge leading to the royal palace close to the water was one of those picturesque pleasure-gardens for which the town is famous, where under the trees hung with fancy lamps an animated crowd assembled nightly to enjoy the music of the military band and to partake of all sorts of refreshments, but mainly consisting of Swedish punch, Scandinavian beer, or coffee. The distance of this pleasure-garden from the hotel was just sufficient to harmonize the music with one's mood, and to lull the drowsy senses to sleep when the hour for retiring arrived.

Following the motley crowd one evening, indifferent as to where it might lead, the author found himself on board one of the little omnibus steamers, which in about fifteen minutes landed its passengers at the Deer Park, near the entrance to which a permanent circus establishment seemed to be the attraction; so purchasing a ticket in our turn, we entered with a crowd which soon filled the auditorium. Over two thousand spectators found accommodation within the walls. The performance was excellent and of the usual variety, including a ballet. Occupying a seat by our side was a man of about seventy years of age, whose white hair, mutton-chop whiskers, and snowy moustache were cut and dressed after the daintiest fashion. He was a little below the average size, and was in excellent preservation for one of his years. It was observed that his hands and feet were as small as those of a young school-girl. He was in full evening dress, with a button-hole bouquet in his coat lapel, held in place by a diamond clasp. On three of the fingers of each hand were diamond rings reaching to the middle joints. Diamonds mingled with rubies and pearls glistened upon his wrists, upon which he wore ladies' bracelets. His tawdry watch-chain was heavy with brilliants. In his necktie was a large diamond, and a star-shaped clustre of small ones furnished him with a breastpin. In short, this antique dude sparkled all over like a jeweller's shop-window. Each of the ballet-girls had a sign of recognition for the gay Lothario, who exchanged signals with several of the women performers. We felt sure that he must be some well-known character about town, and upon returning to the hotel described him and asked who he was. "Oh!" said the proprietor, "that was the Portuguese Minister!"

Some of the public streets of the city are quite steep, so as to be impassable for vehicles,—like those of Valetta in the island of Malta, and those in the English part of Hong Kong. The northern suburb is the most fashionable part of Stockholm, containing the newest streets and the finest private residences. Among the statues which ornament the public squares and gardens, that of Charles XII. in King's Park is perhaps the most remarkable,—he whom Motley called "the crowned gladiator." It stands upon a pedestal of Swedish granite, surrounded by four heavy mortars placed at the corners,—spoils which were taken by the youthful hero in battle. Touching the individual figure, which is of bronze and colossal, it struck us as full of incongruities, and not at all creditable to the well-known designer Molin.

THE DALECARLIAN GIRLS. 181

The Swedish and Norwegian languages are very similar, and, as we were assured by persons of both nationalities, they are becoming gradually amalgamated. The former is perhaps the softer tongue and its people the more musical, as those two delightful vocalists and envoys from thence, Jenny Lind and Christine Nilsson, would lead us to infer. Both countries are undoubtedly poor in worldly riches, but yet they expend larger sums of money for educational purposes in proportion to the number of their population than any other country except America. The result here is manifest in a marked degree of general intelligence diffused among all classes. One is naturally reminded in this Swedish capital of Linnæus and Swedenborg, both of whom were born here. The latter graduated at the famous University of Upsala, the former in the greater school of out-door Nature. Swedenborg was as eminent a scientist as religionist, and to him was first intrusted the engineering of the Gotha Canal; but his visionary peculiarities growing upon him it was found necessary to substitute a more practical individual, so that the great work was eventually completed by Sweden's most famous engineer and mechanician, Kristofer Polhem.

The stranger often meets in the streets of Stockholm a conspicuous class of peasant women dressed very neatly but somewhat gaudily in stripes and high colors, wearing a peculiar head-gear. They are from Dalecarlia, with sun-burned cheeks, splendid teeth, bright serious eyes, soft light hair worn in braids hanging down their backs, and universally possessing sturdy, well-shaped forms. These women are from a favored province of Sweden, and for a long time enjoyed a monopoly of the many ferry-boats of the city, it having been accorded to them by royal consent in consideration of the patriotism exhibited by them, and of aid which the women of that ancient province gave to the cause of the throne at a critical moment in Swedish history. Dalecarlian girls on arriving at a suitable age have for many generations been in the habit of coming to the capital and remaining long enough to earn by their industry sufficient means to return home, become married, and set up their households for life. The small omnibus-steamers have superseded the row-boat ferries, but still the women of this province come to the city all the same, pursuing various occupations of a laborious character, but always retaining their native costumes. Swedish provinces have each to a certain extent a special style of dress to which they tenaciously adhere, as the several Highland clans of Scotland do to their plaids and colors. These girls are often engaged by wealthy families as nurses for their children; some few are to be seen at service in the cafés and public gardens, others are engaged as porters, who transport light packages while pushing before them a small two-wheeled handcart. They certainly form a very picturesque feature with their peculiar costume of striped aprons, party-colored waists, and tall caps, recalling the Italian models one sees on the Spanish Stairs of the Piazza di Spagna in Rome. As a rule, in point of morals they are represented to be beyond reproach ; but some of them inevitably drift into temptation, and become lost to their country and home ties. But even under these sad circumstances, the Dalecarlian girls adhere tenaciously to their peasant costume to the last. The pride which prevents them from returning to their village homes after the blandishments have faded which led them astray, often prompts them to seek a watery grave in the Lake Maelaren.

The National Museum is a fine modern structure three stories in height, the façade ornamented with appropriate statues and medallions, among which was one of Linnæus. On entering the edifice three colossal marble figures attract the eye, representing the chief deities of Scandinavian mythology, Odin, Thor, and Freyr; but as regards the curiosities collected here, they are in no way remarkable, being much like those of other collections. One exception should be made, however, in favor of the cabinet of ancient coins, which is very complete and attractive; it is claimed for it that there is no other in Europe of equal interest or importance. The collection of ancient Arabian coins is unique, and would delight the heart of the simplest numismatist. There is a large gallery of paintings in the upper story of the Museum, with a few examples of the old masters and many of the modern schools. In the open square before the National Museum is to be seen the original of the bronze group described in our chapter upon Gottenburg. This remarkable production, called the "Girdle-Duellists," is the masterpiece of the Swedish artist Molin, and is undoubtedly the finest piece of sculpture to be seen in the country. The pedestal is ornamented with four reliefs representing the origin and issue of the combat, with Runic inscriptions signifying "Jealousy," "Drinking," "Beginning of the Combat," and the "Widow's Lament." It seemed surprising to us that an artist capable of such admirable work as this justly famous group represents, could also have been the author of that hideous conception, the bronze statue of Charles XII., so conspicuously placed in the King's Park of Stockholm.

One of the most popular of the many cafés and pleasure-gardens either in the city proper or its environs, is that known as Hasselbacken, which is situated quite near to the Deer Park. This garden is crowded day and evening during the warm season with hundreds of visitors intent upon enjoying the various entertainments characterizing this resort, among which excellent instrumental and vocal music forms a specialty, while refreshments of every sort are served by an army of white-aproned and active waiters. A broad Turkish pavilion forms the principal concert-room at Hasselbacken, picturesquely fitted up for the purpose. In these grounds, under an ancient oak which reared its tall head proudly above all its neighbors, there was observed a fine statue of Bellman the composer, who, as we learned, was accustomed a century ago to sit in this spot and sing his compositions to his assembled friends, accompanying himself on his favorite instrument the cithern. The sculptor Nyström has reproduced the poet in bronze; and the composition is both beautiful as an ideal-historical monument and excellent in an artistic point of view. Fountains and flower-beds abound on all sides in these inviting grounds, the sylvan aspect being carefully and ingeniously preserved.

While driving in the Deer Park we accidentally came upon the royal cottage of Rosedale, which was built by Charles XIV. about sixty years ago, and was the favorite summer residence of the Queen-dowager Josephine. It is a most delightful rural retreat, surrounded by hothouses, graperies, flower-plots, broad gravelled walks, and trees in great variety. Some of the ancient oaks about Rosedale are of special beauty and of noble development, challenging the admiration of every stranger. In the rear of the royal cottage is a remarkable porphyry urn in three parts, foot, stem, and crown, — being nearly forty feet in circumference, and weighing, we were told, over fifty thousand pounds. Charles XIV. took great pride in perfecting the Deer Park as a place of public resort and pleasure, for which object he expended large sums from his private purse. From Rosedale one can return to the city by boat or by a drive over the pleasant, well-macadamized roads which intersect the country lying between the Baltic and Lake Maelaren.

Upsala is the oldest town in the country as well as the historical and educational centre of the kingdom, situated just fifty miles from Stockholm, and may be reached either by boat or by rail. Going in one way and returning by the other adds a pleasing variety to the trip, which by starting early in the morning can be satisfactorily consummated in a single day. This is the Cambridge of Sweden,—the name Upsala signifying the "Lofty Halls." It was the royal capital of the country for more than a thousand years, and was the locality of the great temple of Thor, now replaced by a Christian cathedral which was over two centuries in building. "The religion of one age is the literary entertainment of the next," says Emerson. The more modern structure is in the Gothic style, built of brick, and the site being on elevated ground renders it very effective. Originally it had three spires four hundred feet high; but these were destroyed by lightning in 1702, and were afterwards replaced by the present two incongruous towers of circumscribed elevation, and which do not at all accord with the original architectural design of the structure. This spot in the Pagan ages was a famous resort for sacrifices. History, or at least legend tells us that in those days the original temple was surrounded by a sacred grove wherein the sacrifices were made to propitiate the deities worshipped there,—human blood being considered the most acceptable. So powerful was the heathenish infatuation, that parents even immolated their children. An account is still extant of seventy-two bodies of human beings being seen here at one time, suspended and dead upon the trees. Odin was once a sacred deity here; now the name represents among the peasantry that of the Devil. The present temple in its architectural aspect is nearly a duplicate of Notre Dame in Paris, and is the largest cathedral in the north of Europe. The same architect, Étienne de Bonnevil, designed them both, and came to Upsala, accompanied by a small army of mechanics from France, to begin the work which was destined, from various causes, to linger along through two centuries. The interior is impressive from its severe simplicity. The flying buttresses inside the structure give a peculiarly striking effect. Between each of them is a small chapel. The vaulting is supported by twenty-four soaring pillars. The dead, cold walls are finished in glaring whitewash without any relief. Under the altar is an elaborate and much-venerated shrine of silver containing the ashes of Saint Eric, the patron saint of Sweden.

Upsala has often been the scene of fierce and bloody conflicts. Saint Eric was slain here in 1161. It has its university and its historical associations; but it has neither trade nor commerce of any sort beyond that of a small inland town,—its streets never being disturbed by business activity or the "fever of living," though there is a population here of at least fifteen or sixteen thousand persons. The University, founded in 1477 and richly endowed by Gustavus Adolphus, is the just pride of the country,—having to-day some fifteen hundred students and forty-eight competent professors. No one can enter the profession of law, medicine, or divinity in Sweden who has not graduated either at this University or at that of Lund. Its library contains nearly or quite two hundred thousand bound volumes and over seven thousand important manuscripts. Among the latter is a copy of the four Gospels, with movable silver letters placed on parchment at the chapter heads, the whole being in the old Gothic language. This book, named "Codex Argenteus," contains nearly two hundred folios, and was made by Bishop Ulphilas one thousand years before Gutenberg was born. It was in this University that Linnæus, the great naturalist, was professor of botany and zoölogy for nearly forty years. His statue still very properly ornaments the lecture-room, and his journal is shown to visitors in the large hall of the library.

The former dwelling house of Linnæus may be seen by tourists at Upsala, where he lived among his well-beloved flora, planted and tended by his own hands. His remains lie interred within the cathedral under a mural tablet of red porphyry, bearing upon the surface a portrait of the grand old naturalist by Sergel, in bas-relief. Many of the tombs and tablets in the aisles bore dates of more than five hundred years ago, but none interested us so much as that of Linnæus the great disciple of Nature. This humble shoemaker by force of his genius alone rose to be a prince in the kingdom of Science. Botany and Zoölogy have never known a more eminent exponent than the lowly-born Karl von Linné, whom the Swedes very appropriately denominate the King of Flowers. A certain knowledge of plants and of natural history forms a part of the primary education of every Swede. At Upsala one has abundant evidence to show how liberally the Government of the country fosters education among all classes, and also that special attention is given to the education of women.

About three or four miles from the University is the village of Old Upsala, where there are three huge tumuli said to contain the remains of Pagan deities. One is here forcibly reminded of the North American mound-builders. In Illinois the author has seen examples double the size of these at Upsala, while in the State of Ohio there are thousands of these tumuli to be seen. Adjoining the three mounds at Upsala is a quaint little church, more than two thousand years old, built of rough field-stones. It contains a monument to Anders Celsius the Swedish astronomer and some ancient ecclesiastical vessels, also some old pictures upon canvas nearly consumed by mould. The huge key with which the door was opened to admit the author bore a date of six centuries ago. We noticed some Pagan idols in wood preserved in an oaken chest inside the old church, which dated about the eleventh century. What a venerable, crude, and miraculously-preserved old pile it is! Who can say that inanimate objects are not susceptible to minute impressions which they retain? Has not the phonograph proven that it receives mechanically, through the waves of sound, spoken words, which it records and repeats? What then may possibly be retained in the memory of this old, old church, which has kept watch and ward on the footsteps of time, these two thousand years! Few temples are now in existence which are known to antedate the Christian era, but undoubtedly these gray old walls form one of them. The three mounds referred to — the tombs of heroes in their lifetime, gods in their death — are said to be those of Thor, Odin, and Freyr. They were found easy of ascent, and were covered with a soft, fresh verdure, from whence we gathered a bouquet of native thyme and various colored wild-flowers which were brought back with us to Stockholm. Near these mounds is also a hill of forty or fifty feet in height called Tingshog, from which all the kings down to Gustavus Vasa used to address their subjects. In this same neighborhood also are the famous Mora Stones, where in the Middle Ages the election ceremony and the crowning of the Swedish kings took place with great solemnity. Tangible evidence as well as the pages of history show Upsala to have been the great stronghold of Paganism, and here the apostles of Christianity encountered the most determined opposition. There are many other mounds in the vicinity of the three specified, all undoubted burial-places erected ages ago. The highest one, measuring sixty-four perpendicular feet, was cut through in 1874 to enable the Ethnological Congress then assembled here to examine the inside. There were found within it a skeleton and some fragments of arms and jewelry, which are now preserved in the Museum at Stockholm. We were told that another of these mounds was opened in a similar manner nearly fifty years ago, with a like result as to its contents.

Before leaving the Swedish capital a spot of more than passing interest was visited; namely, the garden and summer-house in which Emanuel Swedenborg, philosopher and theosophist, wrote his remarkable works. It seems strange that here in his native city this man as a religionist had no followers. It is believed to-day by many in Stockholm that he wrote under a condition of partial derangement of mind. The house which he owned and in which he lived has crumbled away and disappeared, but his summer-house study — a small close building fifteen feet in height and about eighteen feet square — is still extant. In most countries such a relic would be carefully preserved, and made to answer the purpose of an exhibition to the visiting strangers; but here no special note is taken of it, and not without some difficulty could it be found. One intelligent resident even denied the existence of this object of inquiry, but a little persistent effort at last discovered the interesting old study at No. 43 Hornsgatan, a few streets in the rear of the Royal Palace, from which it is about one half of a mile distant.

Every one is amenable to the influence of the weather. Had the same dull dripping atmosphere greeted us at Stockholm which was encountered at Bergen, perhaps the impression left upon the memory would have been less propitious, but the exact contrary was the case. The days passed here were warm, bright, and sunny; everything wore a holiday aspect; life was at its gayest among the citizens as seen in the public gardens, streets, and squares, even the big white sea-gulls that swooped gracefully over the many water-ways, though rather queer habitués of a populous city, seemed to be uttering cries of bird merriment. In short our entire experience of the Swedish capital is tinctured with pleasurable memories.

CHAPTER XI.

The Northern Mediterranean. — Depth of the Sea. — Where Amber comes From. — A Thousand Isles. — City of Åbo. — Departed Glory. — Capital of Finland. — Local Scenes. — Russian Government. — Finland's Dependency. — Billingsgate. — A Woman Sailor in an Exigency. — Fortress of Sweaborg. — Fortifications of Cronstadt. — Russia's Great Naval Station. — The Emperor's Steam Yacht. — A Sail Up the Neva. — St. Petersburg in the Distance. — First Russian Dinner.

EMBARKING at Stockholm for St. Petersburg one crosses the Baltic,—that Mediterranean of the North, but which is in reality a remote branch of the Atlantic Ocean, with which it is connected by two gulfs, the Cattegat and the Skager-Rack. It reaches from the south of the Danish archipelago up to the latitude of Stockholm, where it extends a right and left arm, each of great size, the former being the Gulf of Finland, and the latter the Gulf of Bothnia, the whole forming the most remarkable basin of navigable inland water in the world. The Finnish Gulf is two hundred miles long by an average width of sixty miles, and that of Bothnia is four hundred miles long averaging a hundred in width. The peninsula of Denmark, known under the name of Jutland, stands like a barrier between the Baltic and the North Sea, midway between the two extremes of the general western configuration of the continent of Europe. We have called the Baltic the Mediterranean of the North, but it has no such depth as that classic inland sea, which finds its bed in a cleft of marvellous depression between Europe and Africa. One thousand fathoms of sounding-line off Gibraltar will not reach the bottom, and two thousand fathoms fail to find it a few miles east of Malta. The maximum depth of the Baltic on the contrary is found to be only a hundred and fifty fathoms, while its average depth is considerably less than a hundred fathoms. It cannot be said that these waters deserve the expressive epithet which has been applied to the sea that laves the coast of Italy and the Grecian Isles; namely, "The cradle of the human race," but yet the ages ancient and modern have not been without their full share of startling episodes in these more northern regions.

It is a curious though familiar fact that the waters of the Baltic, or rather the bottom of the basin in which it lies, is rich in amber, which the agitated waters cast upon the shores in large quantities annually, — a process which has been going on here for three or four centuries at least. We all know that amber is an indurated fossil resin produced by an extinct species of pine; so that it is evident that where these waters ebb and flow there were once flourishing forests of amber pines. These were doubtless submerged by the gradual encroachment of the sea, or suddenly engulfed by some grand volcanic action of Nature. Pieces of the bark and the cones of the pine-tree are often found adhering to the amber, and insects of a kind unknown to our day are also found embedded in its yellow depths. The largest piece of amber extant is in the Berlin Museum, and is about the size of a child's head. This is dark and lacks transparency, a quality which is particularly sought for by those who trade in the article. It is known that the peninsula of Scandinavia is gradually becoming elevated above the surrounding waters at the north, and depressed in an equal ratio in the extreme south,— a fact which is held to be of great interest among geologists. The total change in the level has been carefully observed and recorded by scientific commissions, and the aggregate certified to is a trifle over three feet occurring in a period of a hundred and eighteen years.

We took passage on a neat little steamer of about four hundred tons which plies regularly between the capitals of Sweden and Russia, stopping on the way at Åbo and Helsingfors, a distance in all of about six hundred miles. By this route, after crossing the open sea, one passes through an almost endless labyrinth of picturesque islands in the Gulf of Finland, including the archipelago known as the Aland Isles, besides many isolated ones quite near to the coast of Finland. This forms a most delightful sail, the waters being nearly always smooth, except during a few hours of necessary exposure in the open Gulf. The islands are generally covered with a variety of trees and attractive verdure, many of them being also improved for the purpose of small farms, embracing appropriate clusters of buildings, about which were grouped domestic cattle and bevies of merry children, making memorable pictures as we wound in and out among them pursuing the course of the channel. The great contrast between these low-lying verdant islands and those lofty, frowning, jagged, and snow-capped ones which we had so lately encountered in the far North was striking indeed. By and by we enter the fjord which leads up to Åbo from the Gulf, which is also dotted here and there by the most beautiful, garden-like islands imaginable, and upon which are built many pretty châlets, forming the summer homes of the citizens of Finmark's former capital. It would be difficult to name a trip of a mingled sea-and-land character so thoroughly delightful; it constantly and vividly recalled the thousand islands of the St. Lawrence in North America, and the Inland Sea of Japan. The town of Åbo has a population of about twenty-five thousand, who are mostly of Swedish descent. It is thrifty, cleanly, and wears an aspect of quiet prosperity. The place is venerable in years, and has a record reaching back for over seven centuries. Here the Russian flag—red, blue, and white—first begins to greet one from all appropriate points, and more especially from the shipping; but we almost unconsciously pass from one nationality to another where the dividing lines are of so mingled a character. The most prominent building to catch the stranger's eye on entering the harbor is the long barrack-like prison upon a hillside. In front of us loomed up the famous old castle of Åbo, awkward and irregular in shape, and snow white. Here in the olden time Gustavus Vasa, Eric XIV., and John III. held royal court. The streets are few but very broad, which causes the town to cover an area quite out of proportion to the number of its inhabitants. The buildings are all modern, as the fire-fiend destroyed nearly the entire place so late as 1827, when nine hundred buildings and over were consumed within the space of a few hours.

The Russian Chapel is a conspicuous and characteristic building, and so is the Astronomical Observatory, situated on the highest eminence in the town. This structure has lately been converted into a scientific school. Crowds of pupils were filing out of its doors just as we made fast to the shore in full view. The cathedral is an object of some interest, and contains many curious relics. Åbo however is a very quiet little town, whose glory has departed since it ceased in 1819 to be the political capital of Finland. It formerly boasted a University, but that institution and its large library were swept away by the fire already mentioned.

Helsingfors is situated still farther up the Gulf, facing the ancient town of Revel on the Esthonian coast, and is reached from Åbo in about twelve hours' sail, also through a labyrinth of islands so numerous as to be quite confusing, but whose picturesqueness and beauty will not easily be forgotten. This is the present capital of Finland, and it contains from fifty to fifty-five thousand inhabitants, but has several times been partially destroyed by plague, famine, and fire. It was founded by Gustavus Vasa of Sweden, in the sixteenth century. The University is represented to be of a high standard of excellence, and contains a library of about two hundred thousand volumes. A gentleman who was himself a graduate of the institution and a fellow passenger on the steamer, entertained us with an interesting account of the educational system enforced here. The present number of students exceeds seven hundred, and there are forty professors attached to the institution, which is the oldest university in Russia, having been founded as far back as 1640. It is interesting to recall the fact that printing was not introduced into Finland until a year later.

The most striking feature of Helsingfors as one approaches it from the sea is the large Greek Church with its fifteen domes and minarets, each capped by a glittering cross and crescent with pendant chains in gilt, and as it is built upon high ground the whole is very effective. The Lutheran Church is also picturesque and notable, with its five domes sparkling with gilded stars upon a dark green ground, a style of finish quite new to us, but which became familiar after visiting the interior of Russia. The approach to the entrance of this church is formed by many granite steps, which extend across the base of the façade and are over two hundred feet in width. The streets of the town are handsomely and evenly paved, of good width, and bordered with excellent raised side-walks, — a convenience too generally wanting in old European cities and towns. Through the centre of some of the main streets a broad walk is constructed, lined on either side by trees of the linden family, and very ornamental. The buildings are imposing architecturally, being mostly in long uniform blocks, quite Parisian in effect. Several large buildings were observed in course of construction, and there were many tokens of prosperity manifest on all hands. The Imperial Palace is a plain but substantial building, with heavy Corinthian pillars in front. Its situation seemed to us a little incongruous, being located in a commercial centre quite near the wharves.

We need hardly remind the reader that Finland is a dependency of Russia; yet it is nearly as independent as is Norway of Sweden. Finland is ruled by a governor-general assisted by the Imperial Senate, over which a representative of the Emperor of Russia presides. There is also resident at St. Petersburg a Secretary of State, so to designate the official, for Finland. Still, the country pays no tribute to Russia. It imposes its own taxes, and forms its own codes of law; so that Norway, as regards constitutional liberty, is scarcely freer or more democratic. When Finland was joined to Russia, Alexander I. assured the people that the integrity of their constitution and religion should be protected; and this promise has thus far been honestly kept by the dominant power.

The port of Helsingfors is defended by the large and famous fortress of Sweaborg, which repelled the

English and French fleets during the Crimean war. It was constructed by the Swedish General Ehrenswärd, who was a poet as well as an excellent military engineer. The fort is considered to be one of the strongest in the world, and is situated upon seven islands, each being connected with the main fortress by tunnels under the waters of the harbor constructed at enormous expense, mostly through ledges of solid granite. The natural rock of these islands has, in fact, been utilized somewhat after the elaborate style of Gibraltar. An extensive and most substantial granite quay extends along the water in front of the town, where a large fleet of fishing-boats managed mostly by women is moored daily, with the freshly caught cargoes displayed for sale, spread out in great variety both upon the immediate shore and on the decks of their homely but serviceable little vessels. The energy of the fishwomen in their efforts to trade with all comers, accompanied by loud expressions and vociferous exclamations, led us to think that there might be a Finnish Billingsgate as well as an English. While we stood watching the busy scene on and near the wharves, a fishing-boat of about twenty tons, with two masts supporting fore and aft sails and a fore-staysail, was just getting under way outward bound. The boat contained a couple of lads and a middle-aged woman, who held the sheet of the mainsail as she sat beside the tiller. The little craft had just fairly laid her course close-hauled towards the mouth of the bay, and was hardly a quarter of a mile from the dock when one of the sudden squalls so common in this region, accompanied by heavy rain, came down upon the craft like a flash, driving her lee gunwales for a moment quite under water. The main sheet was instantly let go, so also with the fore and stay sails, and the boat promptly brought to the wind, while the woman at the helm issued one or two orders to her boy-crew which were instantly obeyed. Ten minutes later, under a close-reefed foresail, the boat had taken the wind upon the opposite tack and was scudding into the shelter of the dock, where she was properly made fast and her sails quietly furled to await the advent of more favorable weather. No experienced seaman could have managed the boat better under the circumstances than did this woman.

After leaving Helsingfors we next come upon Cronstadt, formed by a series of low islands about five miles long by one broad, which are important only as fortifications and as being the acknowledged key of St. Petersburg, forming also the chief naval station of the great empire. The two fortifications of Sweaborg and Cronstadt insure to Russia the possession of the Gulf of Finland. The cluster of islands which form the great Russian naval station are raised above the level of the sea barely sufficient to prevent their being overflowed, while the foundations of many of the minor works are considerably below the surrounding waters, which are rather shallow, being less than two fathoms in depth. The fortifications are of brick faced with granite, and consist mainly of a rounded structure with four stories of embrasures, from the top of which rises a tall signal-mast supporting the Muscovite flag. The arsenals and docks here are very extensive, and unsurpassed of their kind in completeness. The best machinists in the world find employment here, the latest inventions a sure market. In all facilities for marine armament Russia is fully abreast of if it does not surpass most of the nations of Europe. The quays of Cronstadt are built of granite and form a grand monument of engineering skill, facing the mouth of the Neva, less than twenty miles from the Russian capital. Six or eight miles to the south lies Istria, and about the same distance to the north is the coast of Carelia. The population of the adjoining town will aggregate nearly fifty thousand persons, more than half of whom belong either directly or indirectly to the army or navy. The Russian fleet, consisting of iron-clads, rams, torpedo-boats, and sea-going steamers of heavy armament, lies at anchor in a spacious harbor behind the forts. The united defences here are so strong that the place is reasonably considered to be impregnable. An enemy could approach only by a narrow winding passage, which is commanded by such a cross-fire from the heaviest guns as would sink any naval armament now afloat. As we have intimated, every fresh improvement in ordnance is promptly adopted by Russia, whose army and navy are kept at all times if not absolutely upon what is called a war-footing, still in a good condition for the commencement of offensive or defensive warfare.

As we came into the river from the Gulf we passed the Emperor's private steam-yacht, which is a splendid side-wheel steamer of about two thousand tons burden. She was riding quietly at anchor, a perfect picture of nautical beauty. Yet a single order from her quarter-deck would instantly dispel this tranquillity, covering her decks with sturdy seamen armed to the teeth, opening her ports for huge death-dealing cannon, and peopling her shrouds with scores of sharp-shooters. The captain of our own vessel told us that she was the fastest sea-going steamer ever built. Behind the royal yacht, some little distance upon the land, the Palace and surroundings of Peterhoff were lit up by the sun's rays playing upon the collection of gilded and fantastic domes. It was a fête day. A baby of royal birth was to be christened, and the Emperor, Empress, and royal household were to assist on the auspicious occasion; hence all the out-door world was dressed in national flags, and the passenger steamers were crowded with people bent upon making a holiday. The sail up that queen of northern rivers presented a charming panorama. Passenger steamers flitting about with well-peopled decks; noisy tug-boats puffing and whistling while towing heavily-laden barges; naval cutters propelled by dozens of white-clad oarsmen, and steered by officers in dazzling uniforms; small sailing yachts glancing hither and thither, — all gave life and animation to the maritime scene. Here and there on the river's course long reaches of sandy shoals would appear covered with myriads of white sea-gulls, scores of which would occasionally rise, hover over our steamer and settle in her wake. As we approached nearer and nearer, hundreds of gilded domes and towers of the city flashing in the warm light came swiftly into view. Some of the spires were of such great height in proportion to their diameter as to present a needle-like appearance. Among these reaching so bravely heavenward were the slender spire of the Cathedral of Peter and Paul within the fortress, nearly four hundred feet in height, and the lofty pinnacle of the Admiralty.

Notwithstanding its giddy towers and looming palaces rising above the level of the capital, the want of a little diversity in the grade of the low-lying city is keenly felt. Like Berlin or Havana, it is built upon a perfect level, the most trying of positions. A few custom-house formalities were encountered, but nothing of which a person could reasonably complain; and half an hour after the steamer had moored to the wharf, we drove to the Hôtel d'Angleterre, on Isaac's Square. Then followed the first stroll in a long-dreamed-of city. What a thrilling delight! Everything so entirely new and strange; all out-of-doors a novelty, from the Greek cross on the top of the lofty cupolas to the very pavement under one's feet; and all permeated by a seductive Oriental atmosphere, as stimulating to the imagination as hashish.

We will not describe in detail the bill of fare at the first regular meal partaken of in Russia, but must confess to a degree of surprise at the dish which preceded the dinner; namely, iced soup. It was certainly a novelty to the author, and by no means palatable to one not initiated. As near as it was possible to analyze the production, it consisted of Russian beer, cucumbers, onions, and slices of uncooked fish floating on the surface amid small pieces of ice. With this exception, the menu was not very dissimilar to the sparse service of northern European hotels. But let us dismiss this mention of food as promptly as we did that odious, frosty soup, and prepare to give the reader the impressions realized from the grandest city of Northern Europe.

CHAPTER XII.

St. Petersburg. — Churches. — The Alexander Column. — Principal Street. — Cathedral of Peter and Paul. — Nevsky Monastery. — Russian Priesthood. — The Canals. — Public Library. — Cruelty of an Empress. — Religious Devotion of the People. — A Dangerous Locality. — Population. — The Neva and Lake Ladoga. — The Nicholas Bridge. — Winter Season. — Begging Nuns. — Nihilism. — Scandal Touching the Emperor. — The Fashionable Drive. — St. Isaac's Church. — Russian Bells. — Famous Equestrian Statue. — The Admiralty. — Architecture.

ST. PETERSBURG is a city of sumptuous distances. There are no blind alleys, no narrow lanes, no ragfair in the imperial capital. The streets are broad, the open squares vast in size, the avenues interminable, the river wide and rapid, and the lines of architecture seemingly endless, while the whole is as level as a chess-board. One instinctively desires to reach a spot whence to overlook this broad area peopled by more than eight hundred thousand souls. This object is easily accomplished by ascending the tower of the Admiralty, from whose base the main avenues diverge. The comprehensive view from this elevation is unique, studded with azure domes decked with stars of silver and gilded minarets. A grand city of palaces and spacious boulevards lies spread out before the spectator. The quays of the Neva above and below the bridges will be seen to present as animated a scene as the busy thoroughfares. A portion of this Admiralty building is devoted to school-rooms for the education of naval cadets. The rest is occupied by the civil department of the service and by a complete naval museum, to which the officers of all vessels on their return from distant service are expected to contribute. There are over two hundred churches and chapels in the city, most of which are crowned with four or five fantastic cupolas each, and whose interiors are opulent in gold, silver, and precious stones, together with a large array of priestly vestments elaborately decked with gold and ornamented with gems. It is a city of churches and palaces. Peter the Great and Catherine II., who has been called the female Peter, made this brilliant capital what it is. Everything that meets the eye is colossal. The superb Alexander Column, erected about fifty years ago, is a solid shaft of mottled red granite, and the loftiest monolith in the world. On its pedestal is inscribed this simple line: "To Alexander I. Grateful Russia." It is surmounted by an angelic figure, — the whole structure being one hundred and fifty-four feet high, and the column itself fourteen feet in diameter at the base; but so large is the square in which it stands that the shaft loses much of its colossal effect. This grand column was brought from the quarries of Pytterlax, in Finland, one hundred and forty miles from the spot where it now stands. It forms a magnificent triumph of human power, which has hewn it from the mountain mass and transported it intact over so great a distance. Arrived complete upon the ground where it was designed to be erected, to poise it safely in the air was no small engineering triumph. The pedestal and capitol of bronze is made of cannon taken from the Turks in various conflicts. It was swung into its present upright position one August day in 1832, in just fifty-four minutes, under direction of the French architect, M. de Montferrand. Just opposite the Alexander Column, on the same wide area, are situated the Winter Palace, — the Hermitage on one side; and on the other, in half-moon shape, are the State buildings containing the bureaus of the several ministers, whose quarters are indeed, each one, a palace in itself. This is but one of the many spacious squares of the city which are ornamented with bronze statues of more or less merit, embracing monuments of Peter, Catherine, Nicholas, Alexander I., and many others.

The Nevsky Prospect is the most fashionable thoroughfare and the street devoted to the best shops. It is from two to three hundred feet in width, and extends for a distance of three miles in nearly a straight line to the Alexander Nevsky Monastery, forming all together a magnificent boulevard. On this street may be seen the churches of several dissenting sects, such as Roman Catholics, Protestants, Armenians, and a Mahometan mosque. Hereon also are the Imperial Library, the Alexander Theatre, and the Foreign Office. The metropolitan cathedral of St. Petersburg is also situated upon this main artery of the city, and is called Our Lady of Kazan, — finished with an elegant semi-circular colonnade, curving around a large square much like that of St. Peter's at Rome. This edifice is superb in all its appointments, no expense having been spared in its construction. The aggregate cost was three millions of dollars. One item of costliness was observed in the massive rails of the altar, which are formed of solid silver. The church contains between fifty and sixty granite columns brought from Finland, each one of which is a monolith of forty feet in height, with base and capitol of solid bronze. Why the architect should have designed so small a dome as that which forms the apex of this costly temple with its extended façade, was a question which often occurred to us. Within, upon the altar, is an aureole of silver bearing the name of God, inscribed in precious stones of extraordinary value. The sacred images before which lamps are always burning are literally covered with diamonds, rubies, emeralds, and sapphires. One of the diamonds in the crown of Our Lady of Kazan is of fabulous value, and dazzling to look upon. Within these walls was observed the tomb of Kutuzof, the so-called "Savior of Russia" on the occasion of the French invasion of 1812. Outside, in front of the cathedral, are two admirable statues in bronze standing before the bending corridor of each wing, representing historical characters in Russian story, but whose names are quite unpronounceable in our tongue. The cosmopolitan character of the population of St. Petersburg is indicated by the fact that preaching occurs weekly in twelve different languages in the several churches and chapels of the city.

In the Cathedral of Peter and Paul rest the ashes of the founder of the city; and grouped about his tomb are those of his successors to the Russian throne, with the exception of Peter II., whose remains are interred at Moscow. These sarcophagi are quite simple, composed of white marble tablets raised three feet above the level of the floor, with barely a slight relief of gilded ornamentation. At the time of our visit they were covered with an abundance of fresh flowers and wreaths of immortelles. Peter and Paul is a fortress as well as a church; that is to say, it stands within a fortress defended by a hundred guns and garrisoned by between two and three thousand men. It is more venerable and interesting in its associations than the grander Cathedral of St. Isaac's, while its mast-like, slender spire, being fifty or sixty feet higher than any other pinnacle in the city, is more conspicuous as a landmark. The immediate surroundings constitute the nucleus about which the founder of the city first began to rear his capital, being an island formed by the junction of the Neva and one of its natural branches, but connected with the main-land by bridges. We were told that the present Emperor sometimes visits incognito the tombs of his predecessors here, where kneeling in silence and alone, he seems to pray long and fervently, — and that he had done so only a few days previous to the time of our visit. That

Alexander III. is actuated by devout religious convictions, of which he makes no parade, is a fact well known to those habitually near his person, and that he seeks for higher guidance than can be expected from mortal counsellors is abundantly proven. It was in the prison portion of this fortress that the Czarowitz Alexis, the only son of Peter the Great that lived to manhood, died under the knout while being punished for insubordination and open opposition to his father's reforms. What fearful tragedies are written in lines of blood upon every page of Russian history! Peter's granddaughter, the Princess Tarakanof, was also drowned in the Fortress of Peter and Paul by an overflow of the Neva while confined in one of the dreary subterranean dungeons. About the pillars and upon the walls inside the cathedral hang the captured battle-flags of many nations,— Turkish, Persian, Swedish, French, and Prussian, besides the surrendered keys of several European capitals, including Paris, Dresden, Hamburg, Leipsic, and others. The National Mint of Russia is within this fortress-prison and cathedral combined.

A brief visit to the Monastery of St. Alexander Nevsky was productive of more than ordinary interest, and it chanced to be at an hour when the singing was especially impressive and beautiful, being conducted, as is always the case in the Greek Church, by a male choir. As already intimated, this institution is situated at the extremity of the Nevsky Prospect, about three miles from the heart of the city, occupying a large space enclosed by walls within which are fine gardens, thrifty groves, churches, ecclesiastical academies, dwelling-houses for the priests, and the like. The main church is that of the Trinity, which is appropriately adorned with some fine paintings, among which one by Rubens was conspicuous. Hither the Emperor comes at least once during the year to attend the service of Mass in public. This monastery was founded by Peter the Great in honor of Alexander surnamed Nevsky, who vanquished the Swedes and Livonians, but who in turn succumbed to the Tartar Khans. This brave soldier, however, was canonized by the Russian Church. His tomb, we were told, weighs nearly four thousand pounds, and is of solid silver. Close beside his last resting-place hang the surrendered keys of Adrianople. The treasury of this monastery contains pearls and precious stones of a value which we hesitate to name in figures, though both our eyes and ears bore witness to the aggregate as exhibited to us. The value of the pearls is said to be only exceeded as a collection by that in the Troitea Monastery, near the city of Moscow. We were here shown the bed upon which Peter the Great died, across which lay his threadbare dressing-gown and night-cap. In the crypt, among the tombs, is one which bears a singular inscription, as follows: "Here lies Souvarof, celebrated for his victories, epigrams, and practical jokes." This brave and eccentric soldier made the Russian name famous on many a severely contested battlefield. He was also quite as noted for his biting epigrams as for his victorious warfare. He lies buried here in the Alexander Nevsky Monastery, as this peculiar inscription indicates; and the curious stranger is quite as eager in seeking his tomb as that of the canonized soldier whose name the institution bears. This monastery is the coveted place of burial to the soldier, statesman, and poet. In the cemetery attached there is seen a white marble column raised to the cherished memory of Lomonosof, called the father of Russian poetry, who was born a serf, but whose native genius won him national renown. He was made Councillor of State in 1764.

The monks who inhabit this and all other Russian monasteries are of the one Order of St. Basil. They wear a black pelisse extending to the feet and broad-brimmed dark hats, permitting their hair and beards to grow quite long. They pretend never to eat meat, their ordinary food consisting of fish, milk, eggs, and butter; but on fast days they are allowed to eat only fruit or vegetables. They take vows of chastity, to which they are doubtless as recreant as the Roman Catholic priests of Italy and elsewhere. The Government gives to each member of the Order an annuity of forty roubles per annum, which forms their only fixed income; and consequently they must depend largely on the liberality of their congregations and the fees for attendance upon funerals, marriages, and christenings. The priesthood is divided into two classes, — the parish priests, called the white clergy; and the monks, who are called the black clergy; but the latter are comparatively circumscribed in number. We have seen that dissenters are as common in Russia as in other countries; religious intolerance apparently does not exist.

In returning from the monastery, the whole length of the Nevsky Prospect was passed on foot. It was a warm summer afternoon of just such temperature as to invite the citizens who remained in town for a stroll abroad, and there was a world of people crowding the sidewalks of this metropolitan road-way. The brilliant Russian signs in broad gilt letters — so very like the Greek alphabet — which line the street, must often be renewed to present so fresh an appearance. It is a thoroughfare of alternating shops, palaces, and churches, the most frequented and the most animated in the great city of the Neva. Four canals cross but do not intercept this boulevard, named successively the Moika, the Catherine, the Ligawa, and the Fontanka. These water-ways, lined throughout by substantial granite quays, are gay with the life imparted to them by pleasure and freight boats constantly furrowing their surface. In our early morning walks, pausing for a moment on the street bridges, large barges were seen containing forests of cut-wood loaded fifteen feet high above their wide decks, delivering all along the banks of the canals the winter's important supply of fuel. Others, with their hulls quite hidden from sight, appeared like immense floating hay-stacks moving mysteriously to their destination with horse-fodder for the city stables. Barges containing fruit, berries, and vegetable produce were numerous, and these were often followed by flower-boats propelled with oars by women and filled with gay colors, bound to the market square. The canals seemed as busy as the streets they intersected. From one o'clock to five in the afternoon the Nevsky Prospect, with the tide of humanity pouring either way through its broad space, was like the Rue Rivoli or the Rue Vivienne Paris on a fête day.

The Imperial Library of St. Petersburg is justly entitled to more than a mere mention, for it is one of the richest collections of books in all Europe, both in quality and quantity. The number of bound volumes aggregates a little over one million, while it is especially rich in the rarest and most interesting manuscripts. In a room specially devoted to the purpose there is a collection of incunabula, or books printed previous to the year 1500, which is considered unique. The noble building exclusively appropriated to this purpose has several times been enlarged to meet the demand for room to store and classify the accumulating treasures. So late as 1862 there was added a magnificent reading-room, quite as spacious and well appointed as that of the British Museum at London. One division of the manuscript department relates particularly to the history of France, consisting of the letters of various kings of that country, and those of their ambassadors at foreign courts, with many secret State documents and a great variety of historical State papers. These interesting documents were dragged from the archives of Paris by the crazed mob during the French Revolution, and sold to the first bidder. They were bought by Peter Dubrowski, and thus found their way into this royal collection. Some of the Latin manuscripts of the fifth century, nearly fourteen hundred years old are still perfectly preserved, and are of great interest to antiquarians. The stranger visiting St. Petersburg will be sure to return again and again to this treasure-house, whose intrinsic riches surpass all the gems of the Winter Palace and those of the Hermitage, marvellous as their aggregate value is when measured by a criterion of gold.

The Alexander Theatre and the Imperial Public Library both look down upon a broad square which contains an admirable statue of Catherine II. in bronze. This fine composition seemed to us to be the boldest and truest example of recorded history, breathing the very spirit of the profligate and cruel original, whose ambitious plans were even paramount to her enslaving passions. History is compelled to admit her exalted capacity, while it causes us to blush for her infamy. This square opens on the right side of the Nevsky Prospect, and is the spot where the Countess Lapuschkin received her terrible punishment for having spoken lightly of the amours of the Empress Elizabeth. The Countess is represented to have been as lovely in person as in mind, the very idol of the court, and surrounded by admirers to the last moment. She struggled bravely with her fate, mounting the scaffold in an elegant undress which heightened the effect of her delicate charms; and when one of the executioners pulled off a shawl which covered her bosom, her modesty was so shocked that she turned pale and burst into tears. Her clothes were soon stripped to her waist, and before the startled eyes of an immense concourse of people she was whipped until not one inch of the skin was left upon her back, from the neck downward. The poor lady of course became insensible before this was entirely accomplished. But her inhuman punishment did not end here. Her tongue was cut out, and she was banished to Siberia!

The people of no city in Europe exhibit so much apparent religious devotion as do the inhabitants of this Muscovite capital; and yet we do not for a moment suppose that they are more deeply influenced in their inner lives by sacred convictions than are other races. The humblest artisan, the drosky driver, the man of business, the women and children, all bow low and make the sign of the cross when passing the churches, chapels, or any of the many religious shrines upon the streets. No matter how often these are encountered, or in how much of a hurry the passers may be, each one receives its due recognition of devout humility. In the churches the people, men and women, not only kneel, but they bow their bodies until the forehead touches the marble floor, repeating this again and again during each service. It was observed that children, seemingly far too young to understand the purport of these signs of humility, were nevertheless sure to go through with them precisely like their elders. As regards the multiplicity of shrines, they are frequently set up in the private houses of the common people, consisting of a picture of some saint gaudily framed and set in gilt, before which a lamp is kept constantly burning. Some of the shops also exhibit one of these shrines, before which the customer on entering always takes off his hat, bows low, and makes the sign of the cross. A custom almost precisely similar was observed by the author as often occurring at Hong Kong, Canton, and other parts of China, where images in private houses abound, and before which there was kept constantly burning highly-flavored pastilles as incense, permeating the very streets with a constant odor of musk, mingled with fragrant spices.

St. Petersburg is the fifth city in point of population in Europe, but its very existence seemed to us to be constantly threatened on account of its low situation between two enormous bodies of water. A westerly gale and high tide in the Gulf of Finland occurring at the time of the annual breaking up of the ice in the Neva, would surely submerge this beautiful capital and cause an enormous loss of human life. The Neva, which comes sweeping with such resistless force swiftly through the city, is fed by that vast body of water Lake Ladoga, covering an area of over six thousand square miles at a level of about sixty feet above the sea. In 1880 the waters rose between ten and eleven feet above the ordinary level, driving people from their basements and cellars, as well as from the villas and humbler dwellings of the lower islands below the city. However, St. Petersburg has existed for one hundred and eighty years, and it may last as much longer, though it is not a city of Nature's building, so to speak. It is not a healthy city; indeed the death rate is higher than that of any other European capital. The deaths largely exceed the births, as in Madrid; and it is only by immigration that the population of either the Spanish or the Russian capital is kept up. Young men from the rural districts come to St. Petersburg to better their fortunes, and all the various nationalities of the empire contribute annually to swell its fixed population. In the hotels and restaurants many Tartar youth are found, being easily distinguished by their dark eyes and hair, as well as by their diminutive stature, contrasting with the blond complexion and stout build of the native Slav. Preference is given to these Tartars in situations such as we have named because of their temperate habits, which they manage to adhere to even when surrounded by a people so generally given to intoxication. Among the mercantile class there is a large share of Germans, whose numbers are being yearly increased; and we must also add to these local shopkeepers, especially of fancy goods, a liberal sprinkling of French nationality, against whom popular prejudice has subsided.

What the Gotha Canal is to Sweden, the Neva and its joining water-ways are to Russia. Through Lake

Ladoga and its extensive ramifications of connecting waters it opens communication with an almost unlimited region of inland territory, while its mouth receives the commerce of the world. The Lake system of Russia presents a very similar feature to that of the northern United States, though on a miniature scale. They are mostly found close to one another, intersected by rivers and canals, and bear the names of Ladoga, Onega, Peipous, Saima, Bieloc, Ilmen, and Pskov, — the first named being by far the largest, and containing many islands. The two important lakes of Konevetz and Valaam have two famous mountains, whose stream-falls and cascades are swallowed up in their capacious basins. The sea-fish and the beds of shell found in Lake Ladoga show that it must once have been a gulf of the Baltic. Vessels of heavy burden have heretofore been obliged to transfer their cargoes at Cronstadt, as there was not sufficient depth of water in the Neva to float them to the capital; but a well constructed channel has just been completed, and vessels drawing twenty-two feet of water can now ascend the river to St. Petersburg. Since the perfection of this ship-canal another marine enterprise of importance has been resolved upon; namely, a large open dock is being prepared by deepening the shallow water near the city, covering an area of twenty acres more or less, in order that the merchant shipping heretofore anchoring within the docks of Cronstadt may find safe quarters for mooring, loading, and unloading contiguous to the city. The spacious docks thenceforth at the mouth of the Neva will be devoted with all their marine and mechanical facilities to the accommodation of the rapidly growing Russian navy.

The Neva is no ordinary river, though its whole length is but about thirty-six miles. It supplies the city with drinking water of the purest description, and is thus in this respect alone invaluable, as there are no springs to be reached in the low marshy district upon which the metropolis stands, resting upon a forest of piles. The river forms a number of canals which intersect the town in various directions, draining away all impurities, as well as making of the city a series of closely-connected islands. In short, the Neva is to this Russian Venice in importance what the Nile is to the Egyptians, though effective in a different manner. The entire course of the river from its entrance to its exit from the city is a trifle over twelve miles, lined the whole distance by substantial stone embankments, finished with granite pavements, parapets, and broad stone steps leading at convenient intervals from the street to the water's edge, where little steam-gondolas are always in readiness to convey one to any desired section of the town. Many officials and rich private families have their own boats, propelled by from two to eight oarsmen. On Sundays especially a small fleet of boats is to be seen upon the river, which is almost a mile in width opposite the Winter Palace, where the shores are united by a long bridge of boats, the depth in mid channel being over fifty feet. The main branch of the Neva divides the city into two great sections, which are connected by four bridges. The principal of these is the Nicholas Bridge, a superb piece of marine architecture which was fifteen years in the process of building, having been begun by the Emperor in 1843 and finished in 1858. It crosses the river on eight colossal iron arches resting on mammoth piers of granite. By patient engineering skill the difficulties of a shifting bottom, great depth, and a swift current were finally overcome, giving lasting fame to the successful architect, Stanislas Herbedze. The Nicholas is the only permanent bridge, the others being floating structures supported by pontoons, or boats, which are placed at suitable distances to accommodate the demands of business. Notwithstanding the populous character of the city, the avenues and squares have a rather deserted aspect in many sections, but this is mainly owing to their extraordinary size. A marching regiment on the Nevsky Prospect seems to be scarcely more in number than does a single company in most European thoroughfares. We may mention, by the way, that the garrison of St. Petersburg never embraces less than about sixty thousand troops of all arms, quite sufficient to produce an ever-present military aspect, as they are kept upon what is called a war-footing. In the event of a sudden declaration of war this garrison is designed as a nucleus for an efficient army.

The winter season, which sets in about the first of November, changes the aspect of everything in the Russian capital, and lasts until the end of April, when the ice generally breaks up. In the mean time the Neva freezes to a depth of six feet. But keen as is the winter cold the Russians do not suffer much from it, being universally clad in skins and furs. Even the peasant class necessarily wear warm sheep-skins, or they would be liable often to freeze to death on the briefest exposure. In the public squares and open places before the theatres large fires in iron enclosures are lighted and tended by the police at night, for the benefit of the drosky drivers and others necessarily exposed in the open air. The windows of the dwelling-houses are all arranged with double sashes, and each entrance to the house is constructed with a double passage. So also on the railroad cars, which are then by means of large stoves rendered comparatively comfortable. Ventilation is but little regarded in winter. The frosty air is so keen that it is excluded at all cost. The nicely spun theories as to the fatal poison derived from twice-breathed air are unheeded here, nor do the people seem to be any the worse for disregarding them. The animal food brought to market from the country is of course frozen hard as stone, and will keep sweet for months in this condition, having finally to be cut up for use by means of a saw or axe; no knife could sever it. But in spite of its chilling physical properties, the winter is the season of gayety and merriment in this peculiar capital. With the first snow, wheels are cheerfully discarded, and swift-gliding sleighs take the place of the uncomfortable droskies; the merry bells jingle night and day a ceaseless tune; the world is robed in bridal white, and life is at its gayest. Balls, theatres, concerts, court fêtes, are conducted upon a scale of magnificence unknown in Paris, London, or Vienna. Pleasure and reckless amusement seem to be the only end and aim of life among the wealthier classes, — the nobility as they are called, — who hesitate at nothing to effect the object of present enjoyment. Morality is an unknown quantity in the general calculation. When that Eastern monarch offered a princely reward to the discoverer of a new pleasure, he forgot to stipulate that it should be blameless.

If there are poverty and wretchedness existing here it is not obvious to the stranger. More or less of a secret character there must be in every large community; but what we would say is that there is no street begging, and no half-starved women or children obstruct the way and challenge sympathy, as in London or Naples. There is to be sure a constant and systematic begging just inside the doors of the churches, where one passes through a line of nuns dressed in black cloaks and peaked hoods lined with white. These individuals are sent out from the religious establishments to which they belong to solicit alms for a series of years, until a certain sum of money is realized by each, which is paid over to the sisterhood, — and which, when the fixed sum is obtained, insures them a provision for life. This to the writer's mind forms the very meanest system of beggary with which he has yet been brought in contact. These women, mostly quite youthful, are apparently in perfect health and quite able to support themselves by honest labor, like the rest of their sisterhood. As we have intimated, there is no St. Giles, Five Points, or North Street in St. Petersburg. The wages paid for labor are very low, amounting, as we were told, to from forty to fifty cents per day in the city, and a less sum in the country. The necessities of life are not dear in the capital, but the price of luxuries is excessive. The common people are content with very simple food and a share of steaming hot tea. The drosky drivers are hired by companies who own the horses and vehicles, and receive about eight dollars per month on which to support themselves. They pick up a trifle now and then from generous passengers in the way of *pourboire*, and as a class they are the least intelligent to be found in the metropolis. There is a local saying applied to one who is deemed to be a miserable, worthless fellow. They say of him, "He is only fit to drive a drosky." The Paris, New York, London, and Vienna cab-drivers are cunning and audacious, but the Russian drosky-driver is very low in the scale of humanity, so far as brains are concerned, and does not know enough to be a rogue.

Discontent among the mass of the people does not exist to any material extent; those who represent the case to be otherwise are seriously mistaken. It is the few scheming, partially educated, idle, disappointed, and useless members of society who ferment revolution and turmoil in Russia, — people who have everything to gain by public agitation and panic; men actuated by the same spirit as those who were so lately condemned to death for wholesale murder in our own country. Nine tenths and more of the people of Russia are loyal to "father the Tzar," — loyal to his family and dynasty. Nihilism is almost entirely stimulated from without. England is more seriously torn by internal dissensions to-day than is Russia, and the German people have a great deal more cause for dissatisfaction with their government than have the Russian. To hold up the Russian government as being immaculate would be gross folly; but for foreigners to represent it to be so abhorrent as has long been the fashion to do, is equally incorrect and unjust. Nihilism means *nothingness;* and never was the purpose of a mad revolutionary combination more appropriately named. This murderous crew has been well defined by an English writer, who says, "The Nihilists are simply striving to force upon an unwilling people the fantastic freedom of anarchy." The very name which these restless spirits have assumed is an argument against them. Some have grown sensitive as to having the title of Nihilists applied to them, and prefer that of Communists or Socialists, which are in fact synonymous names that are already rendered odious in Europe and America. When Elliott, the Corn-law rhymer was asked, "What is a Communist?" he answered: "One who has yearnings for equal division of unequal earnings. Idler or burglar, he is willing to fork out his penny and pocket your shilling." Socialism is the very embodiment of selfishness; its aim is that of legalized plunder. Communists, Socialists, Nihilists, are one and all disciples of destruction. Just after the terrible explosion in the Winter Palace, two of the conspirators met in St. Isaac's Square. " Is all blown up ? " asked one of the other. " No, " was the reply, " the Globe remains." " Then let us blow up the globe !" added the other. When these vile conspirators are discovered, as in the case of those lately detected in an attempt to burn the city of Vienna, they are found to be composed of escaped convicts, forgers, and murderers, who naturally array themselves against law and order. It was not when Russia was little better than a military despotism under the Emperor Nicholas, that Nihilism showed its cloven foot. Alexander II. was assassinated in the streets of St. Petersburg after the millions of grateful serfs had been given their liberty, the press granted greater freedom of discussion, the stringent laws mitigated, and when the country was upon its slow but sure progress towards constitutional government. National freedom is not what these anarchists desire; they seek wholesale destruction. The devotion to the Tzar evinced by the common people is not slavish, or the result of fear ; it is more of childlike veneration. Whatever the Emperor commands must be done ; no one may question it. The same respect exists for the property of the Tzar. No collector of government taxes fears for his charge in travelling through the least settled districts. The money he carries belongs to the Tzar and is sacred; no peasant would touch it. The Tzar is the father of his people, commanding parental obedience and respect. The author believes this sentiment to be largely reciprocal, and that the monarch has sincerely the best good of the people at heart.

A fresh scandal has lately been started in the columns of the European press, notably in the English and German papers,— that the Tzar is addicted to gross intemperance, and may at any time in a moment of excess plunge headlong into a foreign war. Of course no casual visitor to Russia can offer competent evidence to the contrary; but it was our privilege to see Alexander III. on several occasions, and at different periods of the day, being each time strongly impressed with a very different estimate of his habits. The Emperor presents no aspect of excess of any sort, but on the contrary appears like one conscious of his great responsibility and actuated by a calm conscientious resolve to fulfil its requirements. "What King so strong can tie the gall up in the slanderous tongue?" asks Shakspeare.

Our remarks as to the honesty of the peasantry in all matters relating to the Tzar must not be taken as indicating the honesty of the Russian masses generally, as regards strangers and one another, especially those of the large cities and the habitués of the great fairs. There are no more adroit thieves in Christendom than those of St. Petersburg and Moscow. Some of the anecdotes relating to these gentry seem almost incredible for boldness, adroitness, and success. There is a familiar proverb here which says, "The common Russian may be stupid, but he would only make one mouthful of the Devil himself!"

Intemperance is the great bane of the lower classes, and the aggregate quantity of spirit consumed by the people is almost beyond belief, though St. Petersburg is not to be compared with Moscow in this very objectionable respect. The chief means of intoxication is the drinking of Vodka, brandy made from grain. The drunken Russian however is not as a rule quarrelsome, he only becomes more lovingly demonstrative and foolish. A ludicrous though sad evidence of this peculiarity was observed in front of the Hôtel d'Angleterre. A well-dressed and intelligent appearing citizen paused opposite the principal entrance, took off his hat, and quietly but tenderly apostrophized it, smoothing the crown affectionately, which he petted and kissed. It was then replaced properly upon his head, and the wearer passed on to the next corner, where his chapeau was again made the recipient of his fond caresses and gentle assurances, ending as before with a devoted kiss. This process was repeated several times as he passed along the big square of St. Isaac's totally indifferent to all observers. Singular to say, this behavior was the only manifest evidence of the individual's inebriety; but the truth is, our Muscovite was very drunk.

Nearly every nationality of Europe and many of Asia are represented on the business streets of St.

Petersburg, — Persians, English, Arabs, Greeks, Circassians, and so on, each more or less strongly individualized. The close observer is not long in discovering that the northern being the sunny side of the streets radiating from the Admiralty, on that side are to be found the finest shops. The summer days are long; twilight is not a period between light and darkness, but between light and light. The street lamps are nearly useless at this season of the year. Friday is the sacred day of the Moslem, the turbaned Turk, and the black-bearded Persian; Saturday the Jews appear in holiday attire (though they are not in favor here), Sunday being appropriated by the professed Christian. Nowhere else is there such an array of white palatial residences, such an airy metropolitan aspect, such grand and costly statues of bronze, such broad and endless boulevards. The English Quay is a favorite promenade and drive; it is surrounded by the grand residences of wealthy Russians, who live on a scale of splendor and expense equal to petty sovereigns. A marked feature in the windows, balconies, and entrances of these dwellings was the long, wavy, green leaves of tropical plants, which must require a world of care to insure their healthful existence in this climate. Handsome four-in-hand vehicles dash through the fashionable streets, and though one sees both sexes in public, there seems to be a half-Oriental exclusiveness surrounding womanhood in the realm of the Tzar. Glare and glitter are manifest on all sides, but the domestic virtues are little cultivated in any class of society, marriage being scarcely more than a matter of form, hardly ever one of sentiment. As in France and at Continental courts generally, intrigue and sensuality prevail in those very places to which the common people look for their example. Gaming is a prevailing vice among the women, if we may credit what we were told and judge from what little we saw. As to gentlemen, they have practised that vice almost from boyhood; it is the universal habit of Russian youth. But to all such general remarks there are noble exceptions, and if these are rare they are all the more appreciable.

We were speaking of the English Quay, which recalls the beauty and spirited action of the Russian horses. No stranger will fail to notice them. The author has seen animals more beautiful in form among the Moors; but taken as a whole the horses of St. Petersburg, whether we select them from those kept for private use, or from the cavalry of the army, or the artillery attached to the garrison, are the finest equine specimens to be seen anywhere. The dash of Tartar blood in their veins gives them all the vigor, spirit, and endurance that can be desired. The five islands of the city separated by the arms of the Nevka and Neva, are named the "Garden Islands," which form the pleasure-drive of the town. They have quite a country aspect, and are a series of parks in fact, where the fine roads wind through shady woods, cross green meadows, and skirt transparent lakes. Here every variety of villa and châlet is seen embowered in attractive verdure, where one is sure in the after part of the day to meet the best equipages of the citizens, occupied by merry family parties.

The city of the Neva is the most spacious capital ever built by the hand of man, and one cannot but feel that many of its grand squares presided over by some famous monument are yet dismally empty. The millions of the Paris populace could find space sufficient here without enlarging the present area. As we look upon it to-day, it probably bears little resemblance to the city left by the great Peter its founder, except in its grand plan; and yet it extends so little way into the past as to have comparatively no root in history. The magnificent granite quays, the gorgeous palaces, the costly churches and monuments do not date previous to the reign of Catherine II. The choice of the locality and the building of the capital upon it, is naturally a wonder to those who have not thought carefully about it, since it seems to have been contrary to all reason, and to have been steadily pursued in the face of difficulties which would have discouraged and defeated most similar enterprises. Ten thousand lives were sacrificed among the laborers annually while the work was going on, owing to its unhealthy nature; but still the autocratic designer held to his purpose, until finally a respectable but not unobjectionable foundation may be said to have been achieved upon this Finland marsh. Yet there are those who reason that all was foreseen by the energetic founder; that he had a grand and definite object in view of which he never lost sight; and moreover that the object which he aimed at has been fully attained. The city is necessarily isolated, the environs being nearly unavailable for habitations, indeed incapable of being much improved for any desirable purpose. Like Madrid, it derives its importance from the fact that it is the capital, — not from its location, though it has a maritime relation which the Spanish metropolis cannot boast. The great interest of the city to the author was its brief but almost magical history, and the genius of him who founded it, of whom Motley said that he was the only monarch who ever descended from a throne to fit himself properly to ascend it. In population and its number of houses St. Petersburg is exceeded by several European cities; but its area is immense.

St. Isaac's Cathedral was begun in 1819 and completed in 1858, being undoubtedly the finest structure of its class in Northern Europe. So far as its architecture is concerned, its audacious simplicity amounts to originality. It stands upon the great square known as Isaac's Place, where a Christian church formerly stood as early as the time of Peter. Its name is derived from a saint of the Greek liturgy, — St. Isaac the Delmatian, — and is altogether distinct from the patriarch of that name in the Old Testament. As the Milan Cathedral represents a whole quarry of marble, this church may be said to be a mountain of granite and bronze. Nor is it surprising that it occupied forty years in the process of building; its completion was only a question of necessary time, never one of pecuniary means. Whatever is undertaken in this country is carried to its end, regardless of the cost. The golden cross on the dome is three hundred and thirty-six feet from the ground, the form of the structure being that of a Greek cross with four equal sides, surmounted by a central dome, which is covered with copper overlaid with gold. Two hundred pounds of the precious metal, we were told, were required to complete the operation. The dome is supported by a tiara of polished granite pillars. Each of the four grand entrances, which have superb peristyles, is reached by a broad flight of granite steps. The four porches are supported by magnificent granite columns sixty feet in height, with Corinthian capitals in bronze, these monoliths each measuring seven feet in diameter. The entire architectural effect, as already intimated, is one of grandeur and simplicity combined; but the impressive aspect of the interior, when the lamps and tapers are all lighted, is something so solemn as to be quite beyond description, — illumination being a marked feature in the Greek, as in the Roman Catholic Church. No interment, baptism, or betrothal takes place in Russia without these tiny flames indicative of the presence of the Holy Spirit; and thus it is that the humblest cabin of the peasant or city laborer supports one ever-burning lamp before some hallowed and saintly picture. Instrumental music is not permitted in the Greek Church, but the human voice forms generally the most effective portion of the service; and of course the choir of St. Isaac's is remarkable for its excellence. Some idea of the cost of this cathedral may be found in the fact that to establish a suitable foundation alone cost over a million roubles; and yet at this writing a hundred skilled workmen are endeavoring to secure the heavy walls so as to stop the gradual sinking which is taking place at three of the corners! It is feared that these walls before many years will have to come down all together, and a fresh and more secure foundation created by the driving of another forest of piles. It is to be hoped that St. Isaac's may be indefinitely preserved in all its purity of design and splendor of material; and with its foundation established this may reasonably be expected. Architecture has been called the printing press of all time, from the period of the Druids to our own day. Future generations will perhaps read in this noble edifice a volume of history relating to the state of society, the degree of culture existing, and the iron despotism which entered into its construction.

Russia has always been famous for its church bells. That of St. Isaac's, the principal one of the city, weighs over fifty-three thousand pounds and gives forth sounds the most sonorous we have ever chanced to hear. These great Russian bells are not rung by swinging; a rope is attached to the clapper, or tongue, and the operator rings the bell by this means. Our hotel was on Isaac's Place, and our sleeping apartment nearly under the shadow of the lofty dome of the church. It seemed as though the bell was never permitted to rest,— it was tolling and ringing so incessantly, being especially addicted to breaking forth at the unseemly hours of four, five, and six o'clock A. M. Of course sleep to one not accustomed to it was out of the question, while fifty-three thousand pounds of bell-metal were being so hammered upon. It was not content to give voice sufficient for a signal to the specially devout, but its outbursts assumed chronic form, and having got started it kept it up for the half-hour together, causing the atmosphere to vibrate and the window sashes to tremble with thrills of discomfort. Sometimes it would partially subside in its angry clamor, and one hoped it was about to become quiet, when it would suddenly burst forth again with renewed vigor, and with, as we fancied, a touch of maliciousness added. Then, — then we did not ask that blessings might be showered upon that bell, but — well, we got up, dressed, and took a soothing walk along the banks of the swiftly flowing river!

On the right of Isaac's Place as one looks towards the Neva is the spacious Admiralty, reaching a quarter of a mile to the square of the Winter Palace. On the left is the grand and effective structure of the Senate House. Immediately in front of the cathedral, between it and the river, surrounded by a beautiful garden, stands the famous equestrian statue of Peter the Great in bronze. The horse is seventeen feet high, and the rider is eleven. Horse and rider rest upon a single block of granite weighing fifteen hundred tons, which was brought here from Finland at great cost and infinite labor. The effect of this group struck us as being rather incongruous and far from artistic; but it is only fair to add that many able judges pronounce it to be among the grandest examples of modern sculpture. Falconet, the French artist, executed the work at the command of Catherine II. On the opposite side of the cathedral is the more modern equestrian statue and group reared in memory of the Emperor Nicholas, one of the most elaborate, costly, and artistic compositions in bronze extant. At each corner of the profusely-embossed pedestal stands a figure of life size, moulded after busts of the Empress and her three daughters. We had not chanced to know of this work of art before we came full upon it on the morning following our arrival in the city; but certainly it is the most remarkable and the most superb monument in St. Petersburg. Well was the man it commemorates called the Iron Emperor, both on account of his great strength of body and of will. His was a despotism which permitted no vent for public opinion, and which for thirty years kept an entire nation bound and controlled by his single will. It was the misfortunes which befell Russia through the Crimean war that finally broke his proud self-reliance. He died, it is said, of a broken heart on the 2d of March, 1855.

Before leaving the subject of St. Isaac's Cathedral, let us refer to its interior, which is very beautiful, and to us seemed in far better taste than the gaudy though costly embellishments of the Spanish and Italian churches. The Greek religion banishes all statues, while it admits of paintings in the churches, as also any amount of chasing, carving, and gilding. The various columns of malachite and lapis-lazuli, together with the abundant mosaic and bronze work, are characterized by exquisite finish. The many life-size portraits of the disciples and saints in the former material present an infinite artistic detail. The small circular temple which forms the inmost shrine was the costly gift of Prince Demidof, who is the owner of the malachite mines of Siberia. The steps are of porphyry, the floor of variegated marble, the dome of malachite, and the walls of lapis-lazuli, — the whole being magnificently gilded. The intrinsic value of this unequalled shrine is estimated at a million dollars. Many others of the superb decorations of the interior are the gifts of wealthy citizens of St. Petersburg. The numerous battle-trophies which enter into the decoration of the interior of this cathedral seemed to us a little incongruous, though quite common in this country, and indeed in other parts of Europe. The banners of England, France, Turkey, and Germany are mingled together, telling the story of Russia's struggles upon the battlefield and of her victories. The keys of captured fortresses are also seen hanging in clusters upon the walls, flanked here and there by a silver lamp burning dimly before some pictured saint. The cost of constructing and furnishing St. Isaac's was over fifteen million dollars.

All art decorations and objects of *virtu* which one finds in Russia seem to partake of other and various nationalities, a fact, which is perhaps easily accounted for. The Empire is located between the East and the West, and has derived her tastes and art productions from both, as the influence of Asia and Europe are mingled everywhere. Assyria, China, India, Greece, Byzantium, France, and England, all contribute both artists and materials to adorn the Russian palaces, churches, and public buildings. The more practical Americans first built her railroads and first established her now famous machine-shops. Of originality there is very little; all is borrowed, as it were. There is no such thing as Russian art pure and simple; and yet over the broad territory which forms the dominion of the Tzar, we know there have been in the past centuries large, self-dependent communities, who must have been more or less skilled in the various arts, but of whom we know only what may be gathered from half-obliterated ruins of temples and of tombs. The obscurity which envelops the early periods of Russian history is well known to be more impenetrable than that of nearly any other civilized region of the globe. If there can be said to be a Russian style of architecture, it is a conglomerate, in which the Byzantine predominates, brought hither from Constantinople with Christianity.

St. Petersburg is not without its triumphal arches. Two very noble and elaborate structures of this character connect the city with its most important territories, — the one on the road to Narva, the other on that leading to Moscow. The first named is specially noticeable, and was built to commemorate the victorious return of the Russian troops in 1815. The arch is supported by lofty metal columns, and surmounted by a triumphal car drawn by six bronze horses, which have never made a journey abroad like those in the piazza of St. Mark. In the car is a colossal figure of Victory crowned with a laurel wreath and holding emblems of war.

CHAPTER XIII.

The Winter Palace. — The Hermitage and its Riches. — An Empress and her Fancies. — A Royal Retreat. — Russian Culture. — Public Library. — The Summer Garden. — Temperature of the City. — Choosing of the Brides. — Peter's Cottage. — Champ de Mars. — Academy of Fine Arts. — School of Mines. — Precious Stones. — The Imperial Home at Peterhoff. — Curious and Interesting Buildings. — Catherine's Oak. — Alexander III. at Parade. — Description of the Royal Family. — Horse-Racing. — The Empress's Companions.

ONLY Rome and Constantinople contain so many imperial residences as does St. Petersburg, within whose borders we recall twelve. Some idea may be formed of the size of the Winter Palace, from the fact that when in regular occupancy it accommodates six thousand persons connected with the royal household. With the exception of the Vatican and that at Versailles, it is the largest habitable palace in the world, and is made up of suites of splendid apartments, corridors, reception saloons, banqueting rooms, galleries, and halls. Among them is the Throne Room of Peter the Great, the Empress's Reception-Room, the Grand Drawing-Room, Hall of St. George, the Ambassadors' Hall, the Empress's Boudoir, and so on. The gem of them all, however, is the Salle Blanche, so called because the decorations are all in white and gold, by which an almost aërial lightness and fascination of effect is produced. It is in this apartment that the court fêtes take place; and it may safely be said that no royal entertainments in Europe quite equal those given within the walls of the Winter Palace. One becomes almost dazed by the glare of gilt and bronze, the number of columns of polished marble and porphyry, the gorgeous hangings, the carpets, mosaics, mirrors, and candelabra. Many of the painted ceilings are wonderfully perfect in design and execution; while choice works of art are so abundant on all hands as to be confusing. The famous Banqueting Hall measures two hundred feet in length by one hundred in breadth. As we came forth from the grand entrance upon the square, it was natural to turn and scan the magnificent façade as a whole, and to remember that from the gates of this palace Catherine II. emerged on horseback, with a drawn sword in her hand, to put herself at the head of her army.

The Hermitage, of which the world has read and heard so much, is a spacious building adjoining the Winter Palace, with which it is connected by a covered gallery, and is of itself five hundred feet long. It is not, as its name might indicate, a solitude, but a grand and elaborate palace in itself, built by Catherine II. for a picture-gallery, a museum, and a resort of pleasure. It contains to-day one of the largest as well as the most precious collections of paintings in the world, not excepting those of Rome, Florence, or Paris. The catalogue shows twenty originals by Murillo, six by Velasquez, sixty by Rubens, thirty-

THE HERMITAGE AND ITS RICHES. 243

three by Vandyke, forty by Teniers, the same number by Rembrandt, six by Raphael, and many by other famous masters. The Spanish collection, so designated, was sold to the Russian Government by the late King of Holland. The more modern French and Dutch schools are also well represented in this collection, particularly the latter. Among the many pieces of antique sculpture in the halls devoted to statuary, is the remarkable Venus known as the Venus of the Hermitage, found at Castle Gandolfo, and which is favorably compared by professional critics to the Venus di Medici. The series of Greek and Etruscan vases, with many superb examples of malachite from Siberia (over one thousand in all), are quite unequalled elsewhere, and embrace the famous vase of Cumæ from the Campana collection, as well as the silver vase of Nicopol and the golden vase of Kertch. The treasury of gems exhibited to the visitor is believed to be the finest and most valuable collection in the world. It includes the well-known Orlof diamond, whose history is as interesting as that of the Kohinoor (Mountain of Light), now in the English Royal Treasury, and which it exceeds in weight by a little over eight carats. This brilliant stone was bought by Count Orlof for the Empress Catherine of Russia, and is considered to have an intrinsic value of about eight hundred thousand dollars. The intimate relation of Russia with Persia and India in the past has made her the recipient of vast treasures in gems; while of late years the mines of the Urals, within her own territory, have proved an exhaustless Fortunatus's purse. The interior of the Hermitage is decorated with Oriental luxuriance tempered by Western refinement. The gilding is brilliant, the frescos elaborate to the last degree, and the masses of amber, lapis-lazuli, gold, silver, and precious gems are a never-ending surprise. Here are also preserved the private libraries that once belonged to Zimmermann, Voltaire, and Didcrot, besides those of several other men of letters. There is a Royal Theatre under the same roof, where plays used to be performed by amateurs from the court circles for the gratification of the Empress Catherine, the text of which was not infrequently written by herself.

The Empress indulged her royal fancy to its full bent in the use she made of the Hermitage. On the roof was created a marvellous garden planted with choicest flowers, shrubs, and even trees of considerable size. This conservatory was heated in winter by subterranean fires, and sheltered by glass from the changeable weather at all times. At night these gardens were illumined by fancy-colored lamps; and report says that in the artificial groves and beneath the screen of tropical plants scenes not quite decorous in a royal household were often enacted. The will of the Empress was law; no one might question the propriety of her conduct. Famous men from far and near became her guests, musicians displayed their special talents, and various celebrities their wit. With all her recklessness, dissipation, and indelicacy,

Catherine II. was a woman of great intellectual power and of keen insight, possessing remarkable business capacity. Well has she been called the Semiramis of the North. One evidence of her practical character was evinced by her promotion of emigration from foreign countries. By liberal gratuities transmitted through her diplomatic agents in Western Europe, she induced artisans and farmers to remove to her domain, and placing these people in well-selected centres did much towards civilizing the semi-barbarous hordes over whom she ruled. The visitor to the Academy of Arts at St. Petersburg will not fail to regard with interest a fine original portrait of the Empress, representing a woman of commanding presence, with a large handsome figure, big gray eyes, and blooming complexion.

Among other royal residences the Marble Palace erected by Catherine for Prince Gregory Orlof stands but a short distance from the Hermitage eastward. The Castle of St. Michael situated near the Fontanka Canal was built by the Emperor Paul; and here he met his sanguinary death. This structure is magnificently decorated. Close at hand on the canal is the modern Michael Palace, before which Alexander II. fell shattered by a Nihilist bomb on the 13th day of March, 1881. Fortunately it also killed the miserable assassin who threw it. The Taurida Palace presented by Catherine to her favorite Potemkin is still a wonder of elegance, and is considered an object of much interest to strangers, to whom it is freely shown at

the expense of the usual gratuities, though it is now
occupied by an humble branch of the imperial family.
The ball-room is of enormous proportions: here the
musicians were originally suspended in the chande-
liers! When this gorgeous apartment was fully prepared for a public entertainment, it required twenty
thousand candles to light it properly. The Amirtchkoff
Palace situated on the Nevsky Prospect is a favorite
town residence of the Emperor Alexander III. To
the newly arrived visitor it would seem that one half
the town belongs to the Crown, and consists of public
offices, military schools, charitable institutions and
palaces. In the immediate environs of the city, within an extensive grove, is located what is called Catherine's House, being little more than a cottage in a
small forest. It is a low wooden building two stories
in height, and was shown to us as containing the
same furniture and belongings that surrounded the
Empress, who often retired here as a secluded spot
where to indulge in her erratic revels. The ceilings of
the apartments are so low that one can easily reach
them with the hands when standing upright. There
are exhibited some pictures upon secret panels set
in the walls, which are of a character corroborative
of the lewd nature attributed to Catherine II. The
situation of the cottage is really lovely, surrounded
by woods, lakes, and gardens. The rooms contain a
number of souvenirs of the Great Peter, manufactured
by his own hands, and who must certainly have been
one of the most industrious of mortals. One of these

original productions was especially interesting, being a large map some five or six feet square, drawn and colored upon coarse canvas, and representing his dominions in considerable detail. This map though somewhat crude in execution was yet an evidence of Peter's versatile skill and tireless industry, modern survey having in many respects corroborated what must have been originally only conjecture drawn from the scantiest sources of information.

In passing the Imperial Public Library already mentioned, one could not but feel that its vast resources of knowledge must not be considered as typifying the general intelligence of the mass of the Russian people. That must, we are sorry to say, be placed at a low estimate. The difference between Scandinavia and Russia in this respect is very marked and entirely in favor of the former. A large majority of the common people of St. Petersburg cannot read or write, while eight out of ten persons in Norway and Sweden can do both creditably. So can nearly the same ratio of the inhabitants of Canton and Pekin. It is not surprising that a people having no mental resort will seek animal indulgences more or less disgraceful.

Let us be careful, however, not to give a wrong impression relative to this matter of education. Until the time of Alexander II. the village priests controlled all schools in the country, though often they were utterly incompetent for teaching. But that liberal monarch changed this, and gave the schools into the hands of the most capable individuals, whether they were priests or otherwise. A manifest improvement has been the consequence. Thirty years ago there were but about three thousand primary schools in all Russia; to-day there are nearly twenty-four thousand. This increase has been gradual, but is highly significant. Reading, writing, arithmetic, and geography are the branches which are taught in these schools. Statistics show that in 1860 only two out of one hundred of the peasants drafted into the army could read and write. Ten years later, in 1870, the proportion had increased to eleven in a hundred, and in 1882 it had reached nineteen in a hundred. Government organizes these village schools, and holds a certain supervision over them, contributing a percentage of their cost, the balance being realized by a small tax upon the parents of the children attending them. Finland has an educational system quite distinct from the empire, supporting by local interest high schools in all the principal towns, and primary schools in every village.

In St. Petersburg the common signs over and beside the doors of the shops are pictorially illustrated, indicating the business within, these devices taking the place of lettered signs, which the common people could not read. Thus the butcher, the barber, the pastry-cook, and the shoemaker put out symbols of their trade of a character intelligible to the humblest understanding. At times these signs are very curious, forming ludicrous caricatures of the business which they are designed to indicate, so laughable indeed that one concludes they are designedly made ridiculous in order the more readily to attract attention. There is a large population of well-educated native and foreign-born people whose permanent home is here, among whom a German element is the most conspicuous. Nor is America unrepresented. There are good Russian translations of most of the standard English and American authors, poets, and novelists. We saw excellent editions of Shakspeare, Longfellow, and Tennyson; also of Byron, Macaulay, Scott, and Irving. This list might be extended so as to embrace many other names. The modern school of Russian romance writers is not formed upon the vicious French standard, but rather upon the best English; not upon that of Balzac and Dumas, but upon Thackeray and George Eliot. Toorgenef, Gogol, Pisanski, and Goncharov are Russian names whose excellence in literature have familiarized them to English readers. There is upon the bookshelves of nearly every cultured family in St. Petersburg and Moscow a translation of Homer into Russian, the scholarly work of an assistant in the Imperial library of St. Petersburg. Competent persons have pronounced this to be equal to the best rendering which we possess in the English language. The native Universities at Moscow, Kiev, St. Petersburg, Kharkov, Odessa, Kazan, and Warsaw are all kept fully up to modern requirements, and are all well attended.

The Mineralogical Academy of St. Petersburg is extremely interesting, where the various riches of the

Ural Mountains are especially displayed in all their natural beauty. Topazes, rubies, opals, garnets, pearls, and diamonds are to be seen here as large and as perfect as the world can produce. Many of these gems are now as delicately and scientifically cut in Siberia as at Amsterdam or New York. One golden nugget was observed here which weighed over eighty pounds. This remarkable specimen of the precious metal was dug out of the earth exactly in its present form and condition. It would seem that the mineral riches of Russia rival those of all the rest of the world; and we ceased to wonder, after visiting this exhibition of native mineral products, at the lavish use of gems and the precious metals in the palaces and churches.

The extensive and remarkably beautiful promenade on the banks of the Neva near the Trinity Bridge called the Summer Garden it would be hard to equal elsewhere. The ever recurring surprise is that so many acres of land in the very heart of a great capital can be spared for a delightful pleasure-ground. It is laid out with long avenues of fine trees, interspersed with lovely blooming flowers and musical fountains. A grand specimen of the fuchsia, developed into a tree ten or twelve feet in height, attracted our attention. It was laden with its ever gracefully drooping flowers in dainty purple, scarlet, and white. Marble statues are appropriately distributed representing the Seasons, the goddess Flora, Neptune, and others, recalling the Prado at Madrid, which is similarly ornamented. There is here also a fine statue in memory of Kriloff, the La Fontaine of Russia. This remarkable fabulist died as late as 1844. In the autumn these statues are all carefully enclosed in boxes, and those of the shrubs and trees which are not housed are also packed securely to protect them from the extreme severity of the climate. It must be remembered that although the thermometer rises here to 99° Fahrenheit in summer, it also descends sometimes to 40° below zero in winter, — a range not exceeded by the temperature of any other city in the world. It would seem as though nothing which is exposed can withstand this frosty climate. Even the granite monolith which forms the shaft of the Alexander Column has been seriously affected by it. The same may be said of the heavy stone-work which forms the embankment bordering the Neva and the canals; so that workmen must rebuild annually what the frost destroys.

In this famous and popular Summer Garden, on Monday the second day of Whitsuntide, a ceremony used to take place of which we have all heard and many doubted; it was called "The Choosing of the Brides." Young girls, mostly of the middling class, dressed for the occasion in their finest clothes and ornaments, came hither with their mothers and were marshalled in line upon the broad paths. In front paraded the young men accompanied by their fathers, walking back and forth and freely examining with earnest eyes the array of blushing maidens. If signs of mutual attraction were exhibited, the parents of such would engage in conversation, which was intended to introduce the young people to each other. This often led to an acquaintance between those who had heretofore been perfect strangers, and, being followed up, it finally led to betrothal and marriage. This annual custom was looked upon with favor by all the common people, and was continued until late years; but as a recognized formality it has become a thing of the past. We were told, however, that it is still indirectly pursued by maidens appearing in the garden on that special day dressed in their best, where they are sought by young men who are matrimonially inclined. No indelicacy is thought to attach itself to this admission of purpose on the maiden's part, who is as of yore not only incited but always chaperoned by her mother.

Near the Summer Garden is the little log building which was occupied by Peter the Great while he superintended personally the work he inaugurated here, and more especially the important part of laying the foundations of the great city, so far back as 1703, — to use the words attributed to him, while he was creating "a window by which the Russians might look into civilized Europe." It is a rude affair built of logs, the ceiling absolutely too low for a tall visitor to stand under comfortably. The inside is lined with leather, and the structure is preserved by a substantial brick house erected over and about it, within which a few of the simple utensils that belonged to the energetic autocrat are also to be seen. Among these articles was a well made and still serviceable small-boat constructed by his own hands, and in which he was accustomed to row himself about the Neva. It will be remembered that Peter served an apprenticeship to this trade in his youth. The apartment which was originally the workshop of the royal carpenter has been transformed into a chapel, where the common people crowd to witness the daily service of the Greek Church. Some of these were seen to kiss the venerated walls,— an act of devotion which it was difficult clearly to understand. True, the Russians, like the Japanese and early Scandinavians, make saints of their heroes; but we believe they forgot to canonize Peter the Great.

Close at hand is situated the spacious Champ de Mars, where the troops of the garrison of all arms are exercised,— a never-ending occupation here, one taking precedence of all others in a nation so thoroughly military. The Russians make the best of soldiers, — obedient, enduring, faithful, and brave. It is true that there are but few "thinking bayonets" in the ranks; yet for the duty they are trained to perform, perhaps such qualification is neither required nor particularly desirable. Stories are often told of the hardship and rigid severity of the Russian military service, but many of them are gross exaggerations. The knout, of which such cruel stories are told, has long been banished as a punishment in the army and navy. The Champ de Mars is a square and perfectly level field where twenty thousand troops — cavalry, artillery, and infantry — can be manœuvred at a time.

On the border of this parade-ground stands a fine bronze statue in memory of Marshal Souvarof, the ablest Russian general of his day, and who died so late as the year 1800. The figure, heroic in size, is represented wielding a sword in the right hand and bearing a shield in the left.

On the Vassili Ostrof stands the spacious Academy of Arts, the front on the Neva measuring over four hundred feet in length; and though it is adorned with many columns and pilasters, its architectural effect is not pleasing to the eye. Its size, however, makes it rather imposing as a whole. The central portico is surmounted by a graceful cupola, upon which a figure of Minerva is seated; beneath are seen statues of Flora and Hercules. Two large and quite remarkable granite sphinxes brought from Egypt stand in front of the Academy upon the stone embankment of the river; but the broad business thoroughfare between them and the building isolates these figures so that one would hardly think they were in any way connected with the institution. This Academy of Fine Arts is just one century old, having been erected in 1786 after a design by a French architect. The lower floor forms a series of halls devoted to sculpture, the examples of which are arranged chronologically in various rooms beginning with the early Greek and Roman schools and terminating with the productions of the nineteenth century. In apartments over these are the galleries devoted to paintings. One very interesting and instructive division is that which is

THE MINING SCHOOL. 255

devoted to drawings illustrating the progress of architecture. This gallery also affords an admirable opportunity for studying the growth of what is termed the Russian school of painting.

At the western extremity of the Vassili Ostrof is located the Institution of Mines, or the Mining School, which is a resort of special interest to strangers, being in fact a technological college conducted by the Government upon the most liberal principles, and designed to fit its students for becoming accomplished mining engineers. It contains the finest collection of models and mineralogical specimens we have ever seen collected together, not excepting those of the British Museum. This institution will accommodate about three hundred pupils, and is always improved to its fullest educational capacity. The specimens of native gold alone which are here exhibited have an intrinsic value of nearly a hundred thousand dollars, while the beryls, tourmalines, amethysts, topazes, and other minerals from Siberia are unequalled in any other collection. The interested visitor cannot fail to receive a correct impression of the great mineral wealth of this wide-spread empire, and which will be found to exceed all previously conceived ideas. A very beautiful rose-colored rubellite from the Urals was observed, also a green beryl valued at twenty-five thousand dollars. Specimens of the Alexandrite, named after Alexander I., are also to be seen here in beautiful form and clearness. A printed list of the gems and treasures generally which are gathered here would prove of great interest. In the garden of the institution there is a model of a mine, through the winding passages of which a guide bearing a lighted taper conducts the visitor, while he explains the Russian process of mining in Siberia and the Urals.

The Palace of Peterhoff is situated about sixteen miles from the city of St. Petersburg, on the shore of the Neva where the river assumes a width of eight or ten miles. It has always been famous for the magnificent fêtes given here since the days when it was built by the Great Peter. The main structure has no special merit in point of architecture, but the location and the surroundings are extremely beautiful. From the terrace, the great yellow Palace being built upon a natural elevation some sixty feet above the level of the sea, one gets a fine though a distant view of the coast of Finland, — a portion of the Tzar's dominion which alone exceeds in size Great Britain and Ireland, a widespread barren land of lakes and granite rocks, but peopled by over two millions of souls. The parks, gardens, fountains, hothouses, groves, flower-beds, and embowered paths of Peterhoff are kept in the most perfect order by a small army of household attendants. The whole forms a resort of regal loveliness and of endless sylvan variety. The artificial water-works, cascades, and fountains are arranged somewhat like those of St. Cloud, and nearly equal to those of Versailles. In front of the Palace is a fountain named Samson, which throws water to the height of eighty feet, and is also constructed to form various fountains.

It is called Samson from the colossal bronze figure forcing open the jaws of a lion, and from whence the water rushes copiously. The fountains are so arranged that on the occasion of holidays and grand fêtes artificial lights can be placed behind the liquid sheets, thus producing novel effects even more wonderful than the golden waters of Parizade. Here the famous Peter used to resort, and stroll about the gardens with his humble favorite, a Polish girl, forgetting the cares of State. This lowly companion besides great personal beauty possessed much force of character, and exercised great influence over her melancholic and morose master. Many instances are related of her interference in behalf of mercy long before her final elevation, which showed a kind and loving nature.

There are several other royal residences in these spacious grounds. One near the sea-shore is that of Montplaisir, a long, low, one-story brick structure with tiled floors and numbers of Dutch pottery stoves. It is an exceedingly plain residence but still very comfortable, containing many Dutch pictures which the Tzar brought from that country. Peter was very much attached to this comparatively humble dwelling, and he breathed his last in it. While standing in the little chamber where he slept and where he died, his last words were recalled: "I believe, and I trust." Here the Empress Elizabeth occasionally spent the brief summer days, amusing herself, as we were told, by cooking her own dinner. The low building is shaded by tall sky-reaching old pines, whose odor pleasantly permeated the air as we wandered about the grounds among the choice flowers and the carefully tended undergrowth, half expecting to come upon the Talking Bird and Singing Tree of the Arabian fable. One or two cypress avenues in the palace grounds are matchless in sylvan effect, producing those charming lines of perspective which trees alone can afford. Here the local guide pointed out an oak which Catherine II. discovered springing from an acorn, and which she protected and planted where it now stands. This little incident occurred on the day before she ascended the throne; but her reign was long enough for the royal lady to see the tiny sprout grow into a lofty and vigorous tree.

There is another small palace near by Montplaisir which was built after the English style for the wife of the Emperor Nicholas, being called Znamenska, and it is occupied at times by the present Empress. The pictures in this summer resort are all of cabinet size and numerous, but not of a very delicate or refined character; how high-bred ladies could abide to have them constantly in sight was a surprise to the author. The furniture is rococo, and almost too delicate for domestic use. Two other small palaces at Peterhoff are upon the islands Isola Bella and Isola Madre. These last are in the Italian style, and as we saw them that soft, sunny July afternoon they were embedded in gorgeous colors, "a snow of blossoms and a wild of flowers." These may be enjoyed by strangers who understand that a golden key opens all doors in Russia. The domestic arrangements in these minor palaces are unique; the bathing apparatus in Montplaisir is very curious, where the royal personages come even to-day to enjoy steam baths, cold baths, and baths of every conceivable nature, often submitting to a discipline which one would think might try the physical powers of an athlete.

One building which we visited within the royal grounds was a very homely square structure of wood, with a brick basement. The house was surrounded by a deep broad moat which could be flooded at will; the little foot-bridge being then raised, the spot was completely isolated. In this building there were but two large rooms, one above the other, the whole being from a design by Catherine II., and was called by her the Peterhoff Hermitage. Hither the fanciful Empress would retire to dine with her ministers of State or the foreign ambassadors. The table was so arranged that the servants had no occasion to enter the apartment where the meal was partaken of. In front of each person sitting at table there was a circular opening, through which at a signal the dishes could descend upon a small dumb-waiter to the carving and cooking room below, and fresh ones be raised in their places. Thus any number of courses could be furnished and no servants be seen at all; nor was there any danger that State secrets could be overheard or betrayed by the attendants. The whole machinery of this automatic table is still operative, and was put in motion for our amusement, — dishes appearing and disappearing as if by magic at the will of the exhibitor.

The author's visit to Peterhoff occurred on a warm, bright Sabbath day. Passage was taken at the English Quay on a steamer which plies regularly between the two places. The decks were thronged with well-dressed, well-behaved citizens, many of whom had wife and children with them, to share the pleasure of a river excursion. Our course was straight down the channel of the Neva; but long before the landing was made, the gilded spires of the royal chapel and some other surrounding golden minarets were discovered blazing under the intense rays of the sun. At present, this beautiful retreat forms the summer residence of the royal family. Lying half a mile off the shore, above and below the landing at Peterhoff, was a light-draft naval steamer, fully manned and armed, acting as a coast-guard. No strange vessel or craft of even the smallest dimensions would be permitted to pass within the line of these vessels. After driving through the widespread royal gardens, dotted with flower-beds, fountains, and mirror-like lakes shaded by a great variety of grand old trees, we finally came upon the Champ de Mars, — and at an opportune moment, just as the Emperor and Empress, with the Prince Imperial and his brother next of age, came upon the ground in an open barouche, to witness a review of the troops which are stationed here. The Emperor, dressed in full uniform, alighted at once, and with military promptness, began to issue his orders. As he moved

here and there, his tall commanding figure was quite
conspicuous among his attending suite. The Empress,
who it will be remembered is the daughter of the
King of Denmark and sister of the Princess of Wales,
retained her seat in the vehicle, looking very quiet and
composed; but the young princes, dressed in white
linen coats and caps of a semi-military character, kept
a little in the rear, though close to the Emperor, as he
walked back and forth directing the movements of
the troops. The Empress is tall and stately in figure,
her fair and really handsome features bearing no traces
of age or care. If she has secret pangs to endure, —
common to both the humble and the exalted, — her
features record, like the dial-plate in the piazza of St.
Mark, only the sunny hours. Her dark eyes lighted
up with animation, and a pleased smile hovered about
her lips, while the whole corps d'armée, as with one
voice, greeted the Emperor when he alighted, and gave
the military salute.

The level parade-field was between thirty and forty
acres in extent, and the manœuvres evinced the perfection of military drill. The Queen of Greece and
the Duchess of Edinburgh, with sóme attendant ladies
of the court, were also present in a carriage behind
that occupied by the Empress. The whole party, while
it was of so distinguished a character, was yet marked
by great simplicity of dress and quietness of manners.
Nochili, brother of the late Emperor and uncle to the
present Tzar, was in the royal suite, wearing the full
uniform of an Admiral of the Russian navy, of which

he is the present efficient head. The Prince Imperial is a quiet, dignified lad of seventeen, with features hardly yet sufficiently matured to express much character. He bids fair to be like his parents, tall and commanding in figure; a pleasant smile lighted up his face as he watched with evident interest every detail of the parade. His brother who accompanied him is about three years his junior, but was, we thought, the more dignified of the two. When the whole body of infantry passed the reviewing point at the double-quick, the admirable precision of the movement elicited from the multitude of civilians unlimited applause. In the several stages of the review which the Emperor directed personally, he passed freely close by the lines of the assembled citizens who were drawn hither from St. Petersburg and elsewhere; also in and among the lines of soldiery. He was calm, cool, and collected, the expression upon his features being that of firmness, dignity, and assured power. The stories bruited about concerning his hermit-like seclusion, caused by a realizing sense of personal danger, are mostly exaggerations of the grossest character. They are manufactured and set afloat by the cowardly revolutionists, who strive in many subtle ways to create a false sentiment against the Emperor. Here in St. Petersburg such stories are known to be lies, but it is hoped that among the hidden nests of anarchists in other parts of Europe, and even in America, they may have their effect. That Alexander III. is popular with the masses of Russia, both civil and military, there is no doubt. Of course the avowed enmity of secret revolutionists renders it necessary to take the usual precautions against outrage; consequently guards and detectives are at all times on duty in large numbers, not only at Peterhoff, but wherever the Emperor and royal family may happen to be on public occasions. These detectives are composed of picked men devoted to their duty, chosen for their known loyalty, courage, and discretion, not one of whom but would lay down his life if called upon so to do in order to protect that of the Emperor. The necessity for employing such defensive agents is to be deplored; but it is not confined to the court of Russia. Germany and Austria adopt similar precautions; and even Victoria, amid all the boasted loyalty of her subjects, is exercised by a timidity which leads to similar precautions whenever she appears in public.

After the review had taken place on the occasion which we have described, a slight change in the arrangements of the grounds transformed the level field into an admirable race-course. The Empress is over-fond of the amusement of horse-racing, and is herself an excellent horsewoman, said to have the best "seat" in the saddle of any royal lady in Europe, not even excepting that remarkable equestrienne the Empress of Austria. She remained with her lady-companions and the princes to witness the races, while the Emperor with his military suite retired to the Imperial Palace half a mile away. The ladies in the Empress's immediate company were very refined in appearance, possessing strong intellectual faces and much grace of manners; but as to personal beauty among the Russian ladies generally, one must look for it in vain, the few vivid exceptions only serving to emphasize the rule. While the men have fine regular features and are generally remarkable for their good looks, their mothers, sisters, and wives are apt to be positively homely; indeed, it has passed into an axiom that nowhere are the old women so ugly and the old men so handsome as in this country.

It will be remembered that Alexander III. succeeded to the throne on the assassination of his father, March 13, 1881; and that he is far more liberal and progressive than any of his predecessors is universally admitted. We were told by influential Russians that a constitutional form of government even may be established under his rule, if his life is spared for a series of years. Though a true soldier and an able one, he has not the ardent love for military affairs which absorbed Nicholas I. While he is sensitive to national honor as regards his relations with other countries, his home policy is eminently liberal and peaceful. He has ably seconded his father's efforts for the improvement of the judicial system, the mitigation of the censorship of the press, the abolishment of corporal punishment in the army and navy, and the improvement of primary educational facilities. In such a country as Russia, progress in these directions must be gradual; any over-zealousness to promote great reforms would defeat the object.

CHAPTER XIV.

Power of the Greek Church. — Freeing the Serfs. — Education Needed. — Mammoth Russia. — Religion and Superstition. — Memorial Structures. — Church Fasts. — Theatres and Public Amusements. — Night Revels. — A Russian Bazaar. — Children's Nurses in Costume. — The one Vehicle of Russia. — Dress of the People. — Fire Brigade. — Red Tape. — Personal Surveillance. — Passports. — Annoyances. — Spying Upon Strangers. — The Author's Experience. — Censorship of the Press.

It is not alone her military organization, colossal and complete as it is, which forms the sole strength of the great Russian Empire, embracing nearly two thirds of the earth's surface, and covering an area of eighty millions of square miles. There is a power behind the army which is nearly as potent as any other element in maintaining the absolute sovereignty of the Emperor, and that is the Church which recognizes him as its head; and where physical control might prove inadequate to enforce the wishes of the Tzar, religious influence, as directed by the priesthood, would undoubtedly accomplish as much with the masses of the population as would force of arms. The clergy of the Greek Church are the faithful servitors of absolutism, and from the nature of things must always be hearty supporters of the reigning monarch. It requires no remarkable insight for them to realize that their very existence as a priesthood depends upon the stability of the Empire. The Anarchists, who entertain but one distinctive idea, admit of no fealty to God or man, and cherish as little respect for the Church as for the State.

Alexander III. has probably at this writing one hundred millions of subjects, embracing the most remarkable diversity of nationalities and races of which it is possible to conceive. Since March 3, 1861, there have been no serfs in the Empire. Twenty millions of human beings who were slaves the day before, on that auspicious date were proclaimed freemen. All honor to the memory of him who made this bold and manly stride towards universal emancipation against the combined influence of the entire Russian nobility! Whatever of political restlessness there may be existing among the upper classes of the Tzar's subjects is traceable in its origin to this freeing of the peasantry of the country. Like slavery in our own Southern States serfdom died hard, and its supporters are not yet all "reconstructed." Like the American negroes, the serfs were sold from master to master and treated like chattels; humanity was not a relative term between noble and serf. Masters sent them to Siberia to work in the mines, or to serve in the army, or exchanged them for cattle or money, and often gambled them away by the dozen in a single night. They made or unmade families according to the heartless caprice of the moment, and unhesitatingly outraged every domestic tie. Before the abolishment of serfdom the Government and the nobles owned all the land in Russia; but to-day the former serfs own at least one third of the land whereon they live and which they cultivate, and for every acre (to their honor be it said) they have paid a fair market value, having accumulated the means by industry and rigid economy. An intelligent native merchant informed the author that self-respect seemed to have been at once implanted among the common people by the manifesto of March, 1861, and that a rapid social improvement has been clearly observable ever since. The better education of the rising generation is what is now most required to supplement the great act of emancipation; and though this is being attempted in the various districts to a limited extent as we have shown, still it is but a slow condition of progress. Not until the Government takes the matter seriously in hand, using its authority and lending its liberal pecuniary aid, will anything of importance be accomplished in this direction.

The Tzar's dominion embraces every phase of religion and of civilization. Portions of the Empire are as barbaric as Central Africa; others are semi-civilized, while a large share of the people inhabiting the cities assume the highest outward appearance of refinement and culture. This diversity of character spreads over a country extending from the Great Wall of China on one side to the borders of Germany on the other; from the Crimea in the South to the Polar Ocean in the far North. As to the national or State religion,—that of the Greek Church,— it seems to be based upon gross superstition, and is therefore all the more effective as a restraining principle from evil-doing among the great mass of poor ignorant creatures who respect scarcely anything else. Much genuine piety is observable among the Russians, a large proportion of the educated people being zealous church-goers, strictly observing all the outward forms of the religion they profess. In the churches there is no distinction of person; all are deemed equal before the Almighty Father. There are no seats in the temples of worship; all the congregation stand or kneel, and during the services often prostrate themselves upon the marble floor. The monks and nuns conduct a thriving business in the sale of sacred tapers, holy relics, images, wedding-rings, and also indulgences and prayers, as in the Roman Catholic Church. Indeed, the resemblance in the forms and ceremonies of the two are to one not initiated almost identical.

To commemorate such an event as leads other nations to erect triumphal arches, Russia builds churches. In St. Petersburg, the Church of St. Alexander commemorates the first victory won by the Russians over the Swedes; St. Isaac's, the birth of Peter the Great; Our Lady of Kazan, the triumph of Russian arms against the Persians and the Turks. In Moscow, St. Basil commemorates the conquest of Kazan; the Donskoi Convent, the victory over the Crim Tartars; and St. Saviour's, the expulsion of Napoleon. *Slava Bogu!* — " Glory to God," — is an expression ever upon the lips of the devout Russian, and he is only consistent to his Oriental instincts in the multiplication of fane and altar throughout his native-land. If fasting and prayer are indications of sincerity, he must be actuated by honest convictions, since he has twice the number of days in the year devoted to self-denial which are known to other religionists. Every Wednesday and Friday, be his situation or condition what it may, he must abstain from meat. More than one half the days in a Russian year are devoted to fasting and humiliation. During seven weeks before Easter no flesh or fish, no milk, no eggs, and no butter can be partaken of without outraging the familiar rules of the Church. For fifteen days in August a fast of great severity is held in honor of the Virgin's death. We do not pretend to give a list of the periods devoted to fast; these we have named are only examples. Every new house in which a man lives, every new shop which he opens for trade, must be formally blessed at the outset. So closely have religious passions passed into social life that the people are even more alive to its requirements than the priesthood, save in those instances where perquisites are anticipated.

The cost of everything in Russia, except the bare necessities, seemed to us to be exorbitant, — nice articles of dress or of simple wear being held at such prices as naturally leads foreigners to avoid all purchases which can conveniently be deferred. As to the native population who are able to expend money freely, they do not seem to care what price is charged them; their recklessness, indeed, in money matters has long been proverbial. So long as they have the means to pay with, they do so; when this is no longer the case, they seem to live with equal recklessness on credit. We were told that one third of the apparently affluent were bankrupt. Fancy articles which are offered for sale in the city stores are nearly all imported from Paris or Vienna; very few lines of manufactured goods are produced in the country. Opera and theatre tickets cost three times as much as in America; and all select public exhibitions are charged for in a similar ratio, except a few which are organized on a popular basis for the humbler classes, such as the tea and beer gardens. The theatres of St. Petersburg are after the usual European style of these structures, — all being large and convenient. As they are under the sole charge of the Government, they are conducted on a grand scale of excellence. Nothing but the choicest thing of its kind in dramatic representation is permitted, — only the best ballet and opera, aided by the most admirable scenery and mechanical effects. The establishment known as the Italian Opera accommodates three thousand spectators without crowding. In what is called the Michael Theatre the best French troupes only appear; and it may be safely said that the average performances excel those of Paris. A Government censor critically examines every piece before its performance. The prices paid by the directors for the services of the best European performers are almost fabulous; no private enterprise could afford to disburse such liberal compensations to artists. The necessity for paying such extravagant rates arises partly from the disinclination of prima-donnas and other dramatic artists to subject themselves to the arbitrary direction of a censorship which is sure to hold them strictly to the letter of their agreement, and which does not hesitate to inflict exemplary punishment for wilful departure from the same. Besides which, the rigor of the climate is such as to create a dread among women-artists to encounter its exigencies. It is only during the winter months that the theatres are open, as in the summer season the court and fashionable people generally are absent from the capital.

Here, as in Copenhagen and Stockholm, the people are assiduous in improving the short summer weeks by devoting themselves heart and soul to out-door amusements. Night is turned into day; the public gardens are crowded, — the entertainments consisting of light theatricals, music, acrobatic performances, dancing, and the like, which are kept up alternating with each other until long past midnight. The people in the mean time sit at little marble tables, and sip tea from tumblers, drink beer, coffee, and spirits, supplemented by various light condiments, until finally those who drink fermented liquors become more than jolly. These places of course draw together all classes of people, and more especially are the nightly resort of the demi-monde. In European cities, generally, such resorts are compelled to close at midnight; here they may last until daylight returns. The Sabbath is the most popular day of the seven at the public gardens, when day and evening performances take place. The Greek churches, like the Roman Catholic, are always open through the entire week, so that the devoutly-inclined can turn aside at any hour and bow before the altar, which to him typifies all that is holy. The Sabbath is therefore regarded here as it is in Rome, Paris, or Seville,— in the light of a holiday as well as a holy-day. After having attended morning Mass, a member of either church unhesitatingly seeks his favorite amusement. The horse-races of Paris, the bull-fights of Madrid, and the grand military-parades of St. Petersburg, all take place on Sunday. Few European communities find that repose and calmness in the day which seems best to accord with American sentiment. It cannot be supposed that a community which goes to bed so late,— seldom before two or three o'clock A. M.,— can be early risers, and they certainly are not. Only the bakers' and butchers' shops and the bar-rooms are open before ten o'clock A. M., while general business is not resumed before about midday. The plodding laborer only is seen wending his way to work as the church-bells chime out the six o'clock matins; and no matter how many churches, shrines, or chapels he may pass, at each one he lifts his hat, makes the sign of the cross upon his breast, and mutters a brief prayer.

Every Russian city has a Gostinnoi-Dvor, or Bazaar, meaning literally the "Stranger's Court,"— a sort of permanent fair, — a "bon-marché" on a large scale. That of St. Petersburg is situated on the Nevsky Prospect; or rather it fronts upon that thoroughfare, but extends through to Great Garden Street. The structure devoted to this purpose is two stories in height, the second floor being reserved for wholesale business, while the basement or ground-floor consists of a multitude of retail shops, where nearly every conceivable kind of goods is offered for sale. No fire is allowed in the bazaar even in winter, except the tiny silver lamps which burn before the pictures of saints. To suppose that these could be dangerous would be sacrilege. There is one excellent rule in the Gostinnoi-Dvor: while other city shops ask various prices, and sell for whatever they can get, this great bazaar has fixed prices, and is supposed to adhere to them. Regarding the quality of the goods sold here, truth compels us to say that the intelligent traveller will hardly feel inclined to invest much money in their purchase. Pictures of saints and packs of cards are the two articles which find the largest sale in such places. A propensity to gamble is as natural to this people as it is to the Chinese. The popular cry of the Spanish lower classes is "bread and bulls;" that of the Russians might be "saints and cards." Next to vodka, cards are the evil genius of the masses. Many are the dram-shops and potent the liquor where the idlers play with cards and liquid fire. We were speaking to a resident upon these matters, when he closed by saying: "Ah, yes, it is to be regretted; but what can you expect? It is so hard to be good, and so very easy to be bad!"

Coming out of the labyrinth of narrow alleys and long arcades of the bazaar upon the Nevsky Prospect side, we overtook a bevy of nursery girls with their juvenile charges bound for the shady paths and fragrant precincts of the Summer Garden. These maids are here quite a social feature, and in their showy distinctive dress recall those of the Tuileries at Paris, the Prado at Madrid, or the Ceylon nurses of English officers' children at Colombo. These St. Petersburg domestics much affect the old Russian costume, with added vividness of color, producing a theatrical and gala-day effect. It seems to be quite a mark of family distinction to have a nurse thus bedecked about the house, or abroad with its baby-representative, while there is evident rivalry between the matronly employers in regard to the richness of the dresses worn by the maids. These costumes consist often of a bonnet like a diadem of red or blue velvet, embroidered with gold, beneath which falls the hair in two long braids. The robe is of some wadded damask, the waist just below the arms, supplemented by a very short skirt. Plenty of gold cord decks these garments, which are usually braided in fantastic figures.

The one vehicle of Russia is the drosky, the most uncomfortable and unavailable vehicle ever constructed for the use of man, but of which there are, nevertheless, over fifteen thousand in the streets of the imperial city. It has very low wheels, a heavy awkward body, and is as noisy as a Concord coach. Some one describes it as being a cross between a cab and an instrument of torture. There is no rest for the occupant's back; and while the seat is more than large enough for one, it is not large enough for two persons. It is a sort of sledge on wheels. The noise made by these low-running ugly conveyances as they are hurried by the drivers over the uneven rubble-stones of the streets is deafening. Why the Russians adhere so tenaciously to this ill-conceived four-wheeled conveyance, we could not divine. It has no special adaptability to the roads or streets of the country that we could understand, while there are half-a-dozen European or American substitutes combining comfort, economy, and comeliness, which might be profitably adopted in its place. The legal charge for conveyance in droskies is as moderate as is their accommodation, but a foreigner is always charged three or four times the regular fare. The poor ill-paid fellows who drive them form a distinct class, dressing all alike, in a short bell-crowned hat, a padded blue-cloth surtout, or wrapper, reaching to their feet and folded across the breast. This garment is buttoned under the left arm with a row of six small, close-set silver buttons, while a belt indicates where the waist should be. These drivers are a miserably ignorant class, sleeping doubled up on the front of the droskies night and day, when not employed. The vehicle is at once their house and their bed, and if one requires a drosky he first awakens the driver, who is usually curled up asleep like a dog. It is the only home these poor fellows have, in nine cases out of ten. The horses are changed at night after a day's service, but the driver remains at his post day and night. Unlike the reckless drivers of Paris, Naples, and New York, the Russian rarely strikes his horse with the whip, but is apt to talk to him incessantly,— " Go ahead ! we are in a hurry, my infant;" or, "Take care of that stone !" " Turn to the left, my pigeon !" and so on.

All St. Petersburg wear top-boots outside the pantaloons. Even mechanics and common laborers adopt this style; but wherefore, except that it is the fashion, one cannot conceive. The common people universally wear red-cotton shirts hanging outside the pantaloons. It was surprising to see gentlemen wearing overcoats in mid-summer, when the temperature was such that Europeans would be perspiring freely though clad in the thinnest vestment. In winter the Russian covers himself up to the very eyes in fur, and perhaps the contrast between fur and woollen makes sufficient difference with him. It was observed that the apparatus and organization for extinguishing fires in the city was very primitive, water being conveyed in a barrel-shaped vehicle, and other very simple means adopted. The water-ways of the city, with a proper hose-system, ought certainly to supply sufficient water for any possible exigency. In the several districts of the town lofty watch-towers are erected, from which a strict look-out is kept at all hours for fires; and a system of signals is adopted whereby the locality of any chance blaze can be plainly and promptly indicated. In the daytime this is done by means of black balls, and in the night by colored lights. But in St. Petersburg as in Paris destructive fires are of rare occurrence; for if one breaks out, the houses are so nearly fire-proof that the damage is almost always confined to the apartment where it originates.

In leaving St. Petersburg, it must be admitted that one encounters a great amount of formality relating to passports and other matters seemingly very needless. Though the principal sights of the city are called free, yet one cannot visit them unattended by a well-known local guide or without disbursing liberally of fees. Foreigners are not left alone for a moment, and are not permitted to wander hither and thither in the galleries, as in other countries, or to examine freely for themselves. One is forbidden to make even pencil sketches or to take notes in the various palaces, museums, armories, or hospitals; and if he would afterwards record his impressions, he must trust solely to memory. The author was subjected to constant surveillance in both St. Petersburg and Moscow, which was to say the least of it quite annoying; his correspondence was also withheld from him, — but no serious trouble worth expatiating upon was experienced. In passing from city to city it is absolutely necessary to have one's passport *viséd*, as no railroad agent will sell a ticket to the traveller without this evidence being exhibited to him; and finally, upon preparing to leave the country, one's passport must show the official signature authorizing this purpose. There is a proverb which says, "The gates of Russia are wide to those who enter, but narrow to those who would go out." No native of rank can leave the country without special permission, which is obtainable on the payment of a certain tax, though not unless it meets the Emperor's approval. Under former emperors this has been a source of considerable dissatisfaction to people who desired to travel abroad, and who could not obtain the needed permission of the Tzar, but we were told that under the present government much greater liberty of action is accorded to subjects of all classes in this respect. It is hardly necessary to remind the reader that in an absolute monarchy the will of the ruler is law. In Russia all power is centred in the Emperor. For the purpose of local administration, Poland, Finland, the Baltic provinces, and the Caucasus have each their own form of government, having been permitted to retain their local laws and institutions to a certain extent when they were not at variance with the general principle of the Empire. Though at the imperial headquarters of government the Emperor is aided by four great Councils, he is free to accept or reject their advice as he pleases.

The censorship of the press is still enforced to a certain extent, though as already intimated it is far from being so rigid as heretofore. At the Hôtel d'Angleterre, where the author made his temporary home, it was noticed that a copy of the "New York Herald" was kept on file for the use of the guests; but it was also observed that it was not delivered from the Post-office until the day subsequent to its receipt, which gave the officials ample time to examine and pass upon the contents. On the day following our arrival the Herald was delivered at the hotel minus a leading article, which had been cut out by the Post-office officials, who did not consider the subject, whatever it may have been, wholesome mental food to lay before the Emperor's subjects. On expressing surprise to our host at this mutilation of the newspaper, we were answered only by a very significant shrug of the shoulders. Residents are very careful about expressing any opinion regarding the official acts of the Government. Books, newspapers, or reading matter in any form if found among a traveller's baggage is generally taken possession of by the officers of the customs; but if one is willing to submit to the necessary red tape and expense, they will be returned to him upon his leaving the country.

CHAPTER XV.

On the Road to Moscow. — Russian Peasantry. — Military Station Masters. — Peat Fuel for the War-Ships. — Farm Products. — Scenery. — Wild-Flowers. — City of Tver. — Inland Navigation. — The Great River Volga. — The Ancient Muscovite Capital. — Spires and Minarets. — A Russian Mecca. — Pictorial Signs. — The Kremlin. — The Royal Palace. — King of Bells. — Cathedral of St. Basil. — The Royal Treasury. — Church of Our Saviour. — Chinese City. — Rag Fair. — Manufactures.

THE distance from St. Petersburg to Moscow is a little over four hundred miles, the railroad built by American contractors having been constructed absolutely upon a straight line, without regard to population or the situation of considerable towns lying near the route. The Russians measure distance by versts. The line between the two cities is six hundred and four versts in length, which is equivalent to four hundred and three English miles. At the time when the route for the railroad was surveying there was a great diversity of interest developed as to the exact course it should follow, and bitter disputes grew up between individuals and communities. These varied antagonistic ideas at last culminated in so decided an expression of feeling that the commissioners having the matter in charge were forced to appeal to the Emperor to settle the matter. He listened to the statement of facts, examined the topographical maps laid before him representing the country over which the proposed road was to pass, and settled the matter in true autocratic style. Taking a rule, he laid it upon the map between the two cities and drew with a pencil a perfectly straight line from one to the other, saying to his commissioners, "Build the road exactly upon that line;" and it was done. The cars upon this route carry the traveller directly into the heart of Russia. One is apt to become a little impatient at the moderate speed attained upon the railroads in this country, twenty-five miles per hour being the average rate of progress. Yet the roads are remarkably well built, and the rolling stock, as a rule, is superior to that generally found in Southern Europe. It is a remarkable fact that at the breaking out of the Crimean war there were less than eight hundred miles of railroad in the Tzar's entire dominions, while to-day there are about twenty thousand miles of well-constructed and efficient roads of this character, forming a complete system permeating all populous sections of the country; and to this may be added an annual increase of from six to eight hundred miles. Had Nicholas I. possessed the means of moving large bodies of troops with promptness from one part of his extended domain to another which now exist, England and France would have found their dearly-bought and but partially-achieved victory in the Crimea an impossibility. While her enemies possessed rapid transit from all points, and open communication with their base of supplies both by steamboat and railroad, Russia's soldiers had hundreds of miles to march on foot, over nearly impassable roads, in order to reach the seat of war. Now the Emperor can concentrate troops at any desired point as promptly as any other European power.

On the trip from St. Petersburg to Moscow one proceeds through scenery of the most monotonous and, we must add, of the most melancholy character,— flat and featureless, made up of forests of fir-trees, interspersed with the white birch and long reaches of wide, cheerless, deserted plains. The dense forest forms a prominent feature of Russia north of the line of travel between the two great cities, covering in that region fully a third part of the surface of the country; indeed, the largest forest in Europe is that of Volskoniki, near the source of the Volga. On the contrary, to the south of Moscow the vast plains or steppes are quite free from wood, in fact only too often consisting of mere sandy deserts, unfit for habitation. It seemed as though no country could be more thinly inhabited or more wearisomely tame. Now and again a few sheep were seen cropping the thin brown moss and straggling verdure, tended by a boy clad in a fur cap and skin capote, forming a strong contrast to his bare legs and feet. Few people are seen and no considerable communities, though occasional sections exhibit fair cultivation. This is partly explained by the fact that the road was built simply to connect Moscow and St. Petersburg, as already explained. Though inhabited for centuries by fierce and active races, the appearance here is that of primitiveness; the log-cabins seem like temporary expedients, — wooden tents, as it were. The men and women who are seen at the stations are of the Calmuck type, the ugliest of all humanity, with high cheek-bones, flattened noses, dull gray eyes, copper-colored hair, and bronzed complexions. Their food is not of a character to develop much physical comeliness. The one vegetable which the Russian peasant cultivates is cabbage; this mixed with dried mushrooms, and rarely anything else, makes the soup upon which he lives. Add to this soup a porridge made of maize, and we have about the entire substance of their regular food. If they produce some pork and corn, butter and cheese, these are sold at the nearest market, and are of far too dainty a character for them to indulge in, since a certain amount of money must be raised somehow for the annual visit of the tax-gatherer. We are speaking of the humble masses; of course there are some thrifty peasants, who manage to live on a more liberal scale, and to provide better subsistence for their families, but they form the exception. The railroad is owned and operated by the Government, and it was a little ludicrous to see the station-masters in full uniform wherever the train stopped, with their swords and spurs clanking upon the wooden platforms. A naval officer might with just as much propriety wear spurs upon the quarter-deck as a local railroad agent on shore. But the customs here are unlike those of other lands; Russia resembles herself alone.

With the exception of the provinces which border on the Caucasus, all Russia is prairie-like in surface. The moderate slopes and elevations of the Urals scarcely break this vast plain which covers so large a share of the globe. Two fifths of European Russia are covered with woods, interspersed with morass and arable land; but as regards fuel, the peat beds in the central regions are practically inexhaustible, forming a cheap and ever-present means for the production of heat in the long dreary winters, as well as for steam-producing purposes on railroads and in manufactories. In the general absence of coal mines, the importance of the peat-product can hardly be over-estimated. It is considered by consumers that the same cubic quantity of peat will yield one third more heat in actual use than wood, retaining it longer; besides which it possesses some other minor advantages over the product of the forest. At some points on the line of the railroad immense mounds of peat were observed which had been mined, dried, and stacked for future use by the employees of the Government. The visible amount of the article was often so great as to be quite beyond estimate by a casual observer. The long broad stacks in more than one instance covered several acres of land, closely ranged with narrow road-ways between them. They were twenty feet or more in height, and conical-shaped to shed the rain. Prepared with rock-oil, coal-dust, and some other combustible, we were told that this peat had been successfully used on the Russian war-steamers, proving superior to coal in the ordinary form, besides taking up much less room in the ships' bunks. As to procure fuel for her ships of war has been a problem difficult to solve heretofore, this immense storage of peat looked to us as if designed to meet this special purpose. The peasantry, as we have said, are generally quite poor, though many of them now own their little farms, which the want of pecuniary means compels them to work with the most primitive tools; besides which they are entirely unaided by the light of modern agricultural experience. No other country, however, is so rich in horses, mines of gold, silver, copper, and precious stones, or in the more useful products of iron, lead, and zinc. The fecundity of the Russians is something elsewhere unequalled; still the inhabitants average but about fifteen to the square mile, while Germany has nearly eighty, and England a hundred and fourteen. The average climate is not unfavorable to health, though there are insalubrious districts whose condition is traceable to local causes. The birch forests with their tremulous, silvery aspect, delicate and graceful, increase as one penetrates towards central Russia upon this line; and there is ample evidence of fair fertility of soil, which is by no means made the most of. Rye, barley, oats, and flax seem to constitute the principal crops under cultivation: while it was observed that nearly every cabin, however humble, had its low, sheltered line of rudely-constructed beehives, honey taking the place of sugar among the common people. The villages were of rare occurrence, but when seen presented road-ways as broad as the boulevards of great cities, yet only lined by low, turf-roofed cabins. The winter season is so long and severe that it is difficult for the peasant to wrest from the half-reluctant earth sufficient upon which to subsist. He lives in a log-cabin of his own construction; wife, daughter, and son all join the father in hard field-labor, not a small share of which was observed to be ditching, in order to render the marshy soil available for crops. The brief season must be made the most of, and therefore many hours are given to work and few to sleep. These peasants are surrounded by all sorts of superstitions from their very birth. Each of the many festivals of the year has its strange rites, songs, and legends. The woods are believed to be inhabited by demons and water-sprites, and peopled by invisible dwarfs and genii. They still trust to charms and incantations for the cure of diseases, like the Lapps and other semi-barbarians, while their rude log-cabins are but one degree better than the habitations of these nomads. Nothing could be more simple than the interior arrangements of their cabins, never omitting, however, the picture of some saint, before which a lamp is kept burning day and night. There is always a rude table, some pine benches, and a huge stove. A wooden shelf raised a few feet from the floor is the sleeping-place, and the bedding consists of sheep-skins, the condition of which, long used and seldom if ever washed, may be imagined. A painted frame-house is hardly to be seen outside of the large towns; no peasant would aspire to such a luxury.

Forests of such density of undergrowth as to defy ingress to man frequently line the railway for miles together; but the dull, dreary loneliness of the way is relieved by occasional glimpses of wild-flowers scattered along the road-side in great variety, diffusing indescribable freshness. Among them, now and again, a tall, glutinous, scarlet poppy would rear its gaudy head, nodding lazily in the currents of air, and leading one to wonder how it came in such company. A peculiar little blue-flower was frequently observed with yellow petals, which seemed to look up from the surrounding nakedness and desolation with the appealing expression of human eyes. Snow-white daisies and the delicate little hare-bell came also into view at intervals, struggling for a brief, sad existence, unless the elfin crew consoled them beneath the moon's pale ray. We must not fail to mention that the stations are beautified by floral displays of no mean character. It seems that professional gardeners travel on the line, remaining long enough at each place to organize the skilful culture of garden-plants by the keeper's family during the summer season; but it made one shudder to imagine what must be the aspect of this region during the long frost-locked Russian winter.

On reaching Tver we crossed the Volga by a high iron bridge, — one of the greatest rivers of the world, the Mississippi of Russia. The average traveller does not stop at Tver any longer than is necessary for the purpose of the railroad officials, but it is a considerable and rising place, especially since the railroad between the two great cities chanced to run through its borders. It contains a little over thirty thousand inhabitants; has its Kremlin, cathedral, theatre, library, and public parks. An English-speaking Russian, evidently a man of business and affairs who was bound for Moscow, gave us a very good idea of Tver. Its locality upon the river makes it the recipient of great stores of grain, wool, and hemp for distribution among western manufacturers. Wood-cutting and rafting also engage a large number of the population, the product in the shape of dimension lumber, deals, etc. finally being shipped to western European ports. Our informant also spoke of this being the centre of an intelligent community scarcely exceeded by the best society of St. Petersburg. From this point the river is navigable for over two thousand miles to far off Astrakhan. In a country so extensive, and which possesses so small a portion of seaboard, rivers have a great importance; and until the introduction of the growing system of railroads, they formed nearly the only available means of transportation. The canals, rivers, and lakes are no longer navigated by barges propelled by horse-power. Steam-tugs and small passenger steamboats now tow great numbers of flat-bottomed boats, which are universally of large capacity. Freight by this mode of conveyance is very cheap; we were told at Nijni Novgorod that goods could be transported to that great business centre from the

Ural Mountains, a distance of nearly fourteen hundred miles by river, for twenty-five shillings per ton. The Volga is the largest river in Europe; measured through all its windings, it has a length of twenty-four hundred miles from its rise among the Valdai Hills, five hundred and fifty feet above the sea-level, to its *débouchure* into the Caspian. Many cities and thriving towns are picturesquely situated mostly on its right bank, where available sites upon elevated ground have been found, — as in the case of Kostroma, and also at Nijni-Novgorod, where it is joined by the Oka. In addition to these rivers there are also the Obi, the Yenisei, the Lena, the Don, and the Dnieper, all rivers of the first class, whose entire course from source to mouth is within Russian territory, saying nothing of the several large rivers tributary to these. We must not forget, however, those frontier rivers, the Danube, the Amoor, and the Oxus, all of which are auxiliary to the great system of canals that connect the headwaters of all the important rivers of Russia. The Volga by this system communicates with the White Sea, the Baltic, and the Euxine, — statistics showing that no less than fifteen thousand vessels navigate this great river annually.

While we are placing these interesting facts before the reader relating to the material greatness and facilities of the Empire, we are also approaching its ancient capital, upon which the far-reaching past has laid its consecrating hand. It is found to stand upon a vast plain, through which winds the Moskva River, from which the city derives its name. The villages naturally become more populous as we advance, and gilded domes and cupolas occasionally loom up above the tree-tops on either side of the road, indicating a Greek church here and there amid isolated communities. As in approaching Cairo one sees first the pyramids of Gheezeh and afterwards the graceful minarets and towers of the Egyptian city gleaming through the golden haze, so as we gradually emerge from the thinly-inhabited, half-cultivated Russian plains and draw near the capital, first there comes into view the massive towers of the Kremlin and the Church of Our Saviour with its golden dome, followed by the hundreds of glittering steeples, belfries, towers, and star-gilded domes which characterize the ancient city. We were told that the many-towered sacred edifices of Russia have a religious significance in the steeples, domes, and spires with which they are so profusely decorated. Usually the middle projection is the most lofty, and is surrounded by four others, the forms and positions varying with a significance too subtile for one to understand who is not initiated in the tenets of the Greek Church. Though some of these temples have simply a cupola in the shape of an inverted bowl, terminating in a gilded point capped by a cross and crescent, few of them have less than five or six superstructures, and some have sixteen, of the most whimsical device, — bright, gilded chains depending from them, affixed to the apex of each pinnacle. When one looks for the first time upon the roofs of the Muscovite city as it lies under the glare of the warm summer sun, the scene is both fascinating and confusing. The general aspect is far more picturesque at Moscow than at the capital on the Neva, because the city is here located upon undulating and in some parts even hilly ground; besides which St. Petersburg is decidedly European, while Moscow is Tartar in its very atmosphere. The first is the visible growth of modern ideas; the last is the symbol of the past.

Though Moscow has been three times nearly destroyed, — first, by the Tartars in the fourteenth century; second, by the Poles in the seventeenth century; and again, at the time of the French invasion under Napoleon, in 1812, — still it has sprung from its ashes each time as if by magic power, and has never lost its original character, being a more·splendid and prosperous capital than ever before since its foundation, and is to-day rapidly increasing in the number of its population. The romantic character of its history, so mingled with protracted wars, civil conflicts, sieges, and conflagrations, makes it seem like a fabulous city. The aggregate of the population is not much if any less than that of St. Petersburg, while the territory which it covers will measure over twenty miles in circumference. "In spite of all the ravages and vicissitudes through which Moscow has passed in the thousand years of its existence," said a resident to us, " probably no city in the world is less changed from its earliest years." Descriptions of the place written by travellers nearly three centuries since might pass for a correct exhibit of the ancient capital to-day. The impress of the long Tartar occupation in the fourteenth and fifteenth centuries still remains both in the architecture and the manners and customs of the people, while much of its original barbaric splendor permeates everything. At St. Petersburg the overpowering influence of European civilization is keenly felt; here, that of Oriental mysticism still prevails.

The city is unique taken as a whole. One seems to breathe in a semi-Asiatic barbarism while strolling through its quaint streets and antiquated quarters. There are no avenues long enough to form a perspective, the streets winding like a river through a broad meadow, but undulating so as occasionally to give one a bird's-eye view of the neighborhood. Still there are modern sections which might be taken out of Vienna, London, Dresden, or Paris, for one finds characteristics of them all combined mingled with the gilded domes of an Indian city, and the graceful minarets of Egypt. A certain modern varnish is now and then observable. Gas has been introduced, and tramways are laid in some of the principal thoroughfares. Like the Manzanares at Madrid or the Arno at Florence, the Moskva is not a deep river, though its channel conveys ten times the amount of water that flows in those just named. It winds ribbon-like in and about the city, adding greatly to its picturesqueness as seen from an elevation. True, this city is in a central position as regards the length and breadth of Russia, but that is about all one can say in favor of the location. St. Petersburg reclaimed from the Finland swamps has the commerce of the world at its door, and therein presents a *raison d'être*, which almost excuses the labor and loss of life and treasure which it cost.

Moscow is to the Russian what Mecca is to the pious Moslem, and he calls it by the endearing name of "Mother." Like Kief and the Troitzkoi, it is the object of pious pilgrimage to thousands annually, who come from long distances and always on foot. The ludicrously illustrated signs are as numerous here as they are in the capital, often running into caricature. For instance, a fruit-dealer puts out a gaudily-painted scene representing a basket of fruit and its carrier coming to grief, the basket and contents falling from the carrier's head and the fruit flying in all directions. A milk-shop exhibited a crude sign depicting a struggle between a hungry calf and a dairy-maid as to which should obtain the lacteal deposit from the cow. These signs answer their purpose, and speak a mute language intelligible to the Russian multitude. The city is said to have once contained "forty times forty churches and chapels," but it has not so many to-day, though there must be between six and eight hundred. The ambassadors of Holstein said in 1633 that there were two thousand churches and chapels in the capital. The Kremlin which crowns a hill is the central point of the city, and is enclosed by high walls, battlement rising upon battlement, flanked by massive towers.

The name is Tartar, and signifies a fortress. As such it is unequalled for its vastness, its historical associations, and the wealth of its sanctuaries. It was founded six or seven hundred years ago, and is an enclosure studded with cathedrals covering broad streets and spacious squares. That of Krasnoi exhibits a bronze monument in its centre erected in honor of Mininn and ,Tojarsky, two Muscovite patriots. The Kremlin is a citadel and a city within itself, being the same to Moscow that the Acropolis was to Athens. The buildings are a strange conglomerate of architecture, including Tartarian, Hindu, Chinese, and Gothic, exhibited in cathedrals, chapels, towers, convents, and palaces. We did not count them, but were told that there were thirty-two churches within the walls. The cathedral of the Assumption is perhaps the most noteworthy, teeming as it does with historic interest, and being filled with tombs and pictures from its dark agate floor to the vast cupola. Here, from the time of Ivan the Great to that of the present Emperor, the Tzars have all been crowned; and here Peter placed the royal insignia upon the head of his second wife, the Livonian peasant-girl. One picture of the Virgin in this church is surrounded by diamonds and other precious stones which are valued at half a million of dollars. It is to be presumed that on the occasion of an Emperor's coronation, or that of some great religious festival, the squares, streets, and areas generally of the Kremlin become crowded with ecclesiastics, citizens, strangers, soldiers, and courtiers in gala array; but it seemed a little dreary and lonely to us amid all its antiquity and mildewed splendor. Silence reigned supreme, save for the steady tread of the sentinels; all was loneliness, but for the presence of the sight-seer and his guide. However busy the city close at hand, commerce and trade do not enter within the walls of the Kremlin. One's thoughts were busy enough, over-stimulated in fact, while strolling through the apartments of the Imperial Palace. In imagination, these low-studded apartments, secret divans and closets became repeopled by their former tenants. It was remembered that even to the days of Peter the Great Oriental seclusion was the fate of empresses and princesses, upon whom the highest state officials might not dare to look,— whose faces in short were always hidden. But scandal says that thus unnaturally secluded, their woman wit taught them ways of compensation; for in spite of guards and bolts, they received at times visits from their secret lovers, the great risk encountered but adding zest to such clandestine achievements. To be sure, as a penalty a head was now and then severed from the owner's body, and some gay Lothario was knouted and sent off to Siberia to work out his life in the mines; but that did not change human nature, to which royalty is as amenable as the rest of creation. The grand Palace as it now stands was built by the Emperor Nicholas, or rather it was repaired and enlarged by him, embracing all the ancient portions as originally designed, but the rest of the structure so extended as to afford suites of royal state apartments which are unsurpassed by any palace in the world, either in spaciousness, magnificence of finish or furniture. The Throne Room is beyond comparison the most superb apartment of its character which the author has ever seen. Magnificent as the interior is, the external architectural effect of the Palace is in such decided contrast with that of the surrounding churches, monasteries, towers, and sacred gates as to create a singular incongruity.

The venerable, crenellated walls of the Kremlin, which measure about two miles in circumference, forming nearly a triangle, are pierced by five gates of an imposing character, to each of which is attributed a religious or historical importance. Often have invading hosts battered at these gates, and sometimes gained an entrance; but strange to say, they have always in the end been worsted by the faithful Muscovites. Over the Redeemer's Gate, so called, is affixed a wonder-working picture of the Saviour, which is an object of great and universal veneration. No one, not even the Emperor, passes beneath it without removing his hat and bowing the head. A miracle is supposed to have been wrought in connection with this picture of the Redeemer at the time when the retreating French made a vain attempt to blow up the buildings of the Kremlin; hence the special honor accorded to it. The gate itself was erected in 1491, and is like the main tower of a large cathedral or an isolated campanile. It is painted red, with green spires, and flanked on the sides by small chapels.

The National Armory, also within the walls, is of great interest, quite unsurpassed in its collection of Oriental arms, but those of all nations are also well represented. It will be remembered that Moscow was in the olden time as celebrated for the excellence of its steel weapons, and especially for the temper of its sword blades, as were Toledo and Damascus. In the grand courtyard of the Kremlin, near that pillar-like structure the Tower of Ivan, hundreds of Napoleon's captured cannon lay idly on the earth, recalling the tragic story of the French invasion; but then it was remembered that the French have also at Paris their Column of Vendôme, the encircling bas-reliefs of which contain the metal of many captured Russian cannon. So while scores of battle-torn Muscovite flags hang aloft in the church of the Invalides at the French capital, the tri-color also decks the walls of Peter and Paul in the fortifications of St. Petersburg,—toys in " that mad game the world so loves to play," but, alas! what do they represent but condensed drops of blood?

Opposite the Arsenal stands the Senate House of Moscow, the High Court of Appeals, built by Catherine II. The main hall is of great capacity and magnificence; the whole building underwent complete restoration in 1866. The summit of the Tower of Ivan the Great, erected in 1600, affords a widespread view of the city in every direction; and perhaps it may be said to be the best that can be obtained. It is one of the most conspicuous structures in the

Kremlin, standing partially by itself, and is seen from a long distance as one approaches by rail. The tower consists of five stories, and is three hundred and twenty-five feet in height. The basement and three stories above it are octagonal, the last cylindrical, the whole embracing a wild confusion of design. Half-way up is a gallery from whence the former sovereigns used to harangue the people. The lower story is a chapel dedicated to Saint John, while the other stories contain many bells, the heaviest of which, we were told, weighed over sixty tons. In the upper portion there is a chime of silver bells which daily ring forth the national anthem at meridian. The racket and din produced when *all* the bells in the tower are rung together, as they are on Easter eve, must be deafening.

The famous King of Bells of which we have all heard so much, and which according to the records was tolled at the birth of Peter the Great, stands near the foot of the Tower of Ivan. It is broken, but weighs in its present condition nearly four hundred and fifty thousand pounds. The piece broken from its side, which is seen close at hand, weighs eleven tons. The height of the bell is twenty-one feet. When it was cast in 1730, by order of the Empress Anne, the gold, silver, and copper consumed in the operation weighed ninety-one hundred and twenty tons, valued at the royal sum of half a million dollars. History tells us that the casting took place with religious ceremonies, and royal ladies vied with one another in throwing their golden ornaments into the great caldron which supplied the molten metal. Doubtless this very generosity of contribution only served to impart brittleness to the bell. As to improving the purity of tone, modern experience shows that foreign metals, however pure in themselves, would detract from that. After the great bell fell from the supporting-tower, — which was destroyed by fire, and which is supposed to have stood very nearly over the spot where the bell now rests, — it lay buried in the earth for over a hundred years, until it was dug up and placed on its present foundation by order of the late Emperor Nicholas I. As we stood there beside the monster bell, a shudder passed over us sufficiently visible to attract the observation of the guide. "Is monsieur cold?" he asked. "No, it was only a passing thought that moved us," was the reply. "Ah! something of far-off America?" he suggested. "Nearer than that," was the response. "It was the recollection of that terrible fifty-three thousand pounds of bell-metal which swings in the cupola of St. Isaac's. If that comparatively baby-bell could make one so thoroughly uncomfortable, what might not this giant do under similar circumstances!" It is doubtful, however, if the guide clearly understood to what the author referred.

The most strikingly fantastic and remarkable structure architecturally in all Moscow is the Cathedral of St. Basil, which is absolutely top-heavy with spires, domes, and minarets, ornamented in the most irregular and unprecedented manner. Yet as a whole the structure is not inharmonious with its unique surroundings, the semi-Oriental, semi-barbaric atmosphere in which it stands. It is not within the walls of the Kremlin, but is located just outside and near the Redeemer's Gate, from which point the best view of it may be enjoyed. No two of its towering projections are alike, either in height, shape, or ornamentation. The coloring throughout is as various as the shape, being in yellow, green, blue, golden-gilt, and silver. Each spire and dome has its glittering cross; and when the sun shines upon the group, it is like the bursting of a rocket at night against a background of azure blue. It is of this singular, whimsical, and picturesque structure that the story is told how Ivan the Terrible caused the architect's eyes to be blinded forever when his work was completed and approved, in order that he might never be able to produce another temple like it. The reader need hardly credit the story however, since it has been attributed to so many other structures and individuals as greatly to impair its application in this instance. Space would not suffice us were we to attempt to describe the interior of St. Basil; but it is as peculiar as is the exterior. Each of the domes and towers forms the apex to a separate chapel, so that the cathedral is divided into a dozen and more altars dedicated to as many different saints. The interior is painted throughout in arabesque. Napoleon ordered his soldiers to destroy this cathedral; but fortunately, in the haste and confusion attending the retreat of the French army, the command was not executed. While looking upon St. Basil, with its myriad pinnacles flashing in the rays of the sun, it was natural to recall Hawthorne's quaint idea, that were edifices built to the sound of music some would appear to be constructed under the influence of grave and solemn tones, others, like this unique temple, to have danced forth to light fantastic airs and waltzes. In front of the many-domed cathedral is a circular stone from whence the Tzars of old were accustomed to proclaim their edicts; and it is also known as the Lobnoé Mièsto, that is, "The Place of the Skull," because of the many executions that have taken place upon it. Ivan the Terrible rendered the spot infamous by the series of executions which he ordered to take place here, the victims being mostly innocent and patriotic persons of both sexes. Here Prince Scheviref was impaled by order of this same tyrant, and here several others of royal birth were recklessly sacrificed. In looking upon St. Basil one is almost sure to be reminded of the Alhambra, in Moorish Grenada. Notwithstanding its strangely conglomerate character, no one can say that it is not symmetrical and justly balanced in its various lines; still, so unreal is its whole as to seem like a creation in some magic Arabian tale, an unsubstantial structure of the imagination.

The Treasury of the Kremlin, erected so late as 1851, is a historical museum of crowns, thrones, state costumes, and royal regalia generally, including in the latter department the royal robes of Peter the Great;

also his crown in which there are about nine hundred large diamonds, and that of his widow Catherine I., which contains about three thousand of the same precious stones, besides one grand ruby of extraordinary value. One comes away from the labyrinth of palaces, churches, arsenals, museums, and treasury of the citadel, after viewing their accumulation of riches, absolutely dazed and entirely surfeited. Properly to examine the Treasury alone would require many days. It is a marvel of accumulated riches, the proud spoils of time. Here are to be seen the crowns of many now defunct kingdoms, such as those of Kazan, Georgia, Astrakhan, and Poland,— all heavy with gold and precious stones. The crown-jewels of England and Germany combined would hardly equal in value these treasures. The most venerable of the crowns which were shown us here is that of Monomachus, brought from Byzantium more than eight hundred years ago. This emblem is covered with jewels of the choicest character, among which are steel-white diamonds and rubies of pigeon's-blood hue, such as do not find their way into jewellers' shops in our day. Think of the centuries this vast wealth has lain idle upon these royal crowns, and of the aggregate sum in current money which it represents; then calculate the annual loss of interest, say at three per cent per annum, and the result will reach a sum approximating to the amount of the National debt of Great Britain!

While viewing the varied attractions within the walls of the Kremlin one could not but recall a page from history, and remember the brave, heroic, self-sacrificing means which the people of this Asiatic city adopted to repel the invading and victorious enemy. It was an act of sublime desperation to place the torch within the sanctuary of Russia and to destroy all, sacred and profane, so that the enemy should also be destroyed. It was a deed of undaunted patriotism, and the grandest sacrifice ever made to national honor by any people. " Who would have thought that a nation would burn its own capital ? " said Napoleon.

The Church of our Saviour is perhaps one of the finest as it is also the most modern cathedral in the country, its snow-white walls, capped by five golden domes, being the most prominent object to meet the eye as one looks at the city from the high terrace of the Kremlin. It stands upon a natural rise of ground, a plateau overlooking the Bridge of Moskva Rekoi, quite by itself, covering seventy-three thousand square feet, surrounded by open grounds, which are planted with flowering shrubs, blooming flowers, and thrifty young trees. Begun in 1812 to commemorate the deliverance of Moscow from the French, the edifice has but just been completed. It is in the Græco-Byzantine style; the top of the cross upon the centre cupola is three hundred and forty feet above the ground. The foundation is of granite, but the entire building is faced with white marble. The interior is gorgeously decorated with frescos from Biblical and Russian history, and is dazzling in its vast richness of detail. The interior of St. Isaac's at St. Petersburg has been closely imitated in some important particulars. The entire floor is of marble, and the walls are lined with exquisite varieties of the same. Here on the 25th of December is annually celebrated, with great pomp and ceremony, the retreat of the French invaders from Russian soil. " God with us," is the motto sculptured over the grand entrance of this magnificent temple, the aggregate cost of which was over twelve millions of dollars.

Lying on the east side of the Kremlin and adjoining its walls is a section of the city also enclosed within high walls, known as the Chinese City. It is a queer division of the metropolis, with towers and buttresses like a fortification, called by the Russians "Kitai Gorod." Herein assemble the thieves, pickpockets, and rogues generally, who are to be seen throughout the day crowded together in one of the largest squares, holding a sort of rag fair to exchange their ill-gotten goods with one another. To the stranger they present the aspect of a reckless mob, composed of the very dregs of the population, and ready to engage in any overt act. Unmolested by the police they busy themselves exchanging old boots and shoes, half-worn clothing, stolen trifles, and various articles of domestic use, all amid a deafening hubbub. The entire district is not however given up to this "racket," but contains some fine shops, comfortable dwellings, and two excellent hotels, as Russian hotels are rated. One passes through this section in approaching the Redeemer's Gate from the east side, but will wisely avoid all personal contact with the doubtful denizens of Rag Fair.

It was a source of surprise to the author to find Moscow so great a manufacturing centre, more than fifty thousand of the population being regularly employed in manufacturing establishments. There are over a hundred cotton mills within the limits of the city, and between fifty and sixty woollen mills; also thirty-three silk mills, and a score of kindred establishments in the manufacturing line. It appeared, however, that enterprise in this direction was confined almost entirely to textile fabrics. The city is fast becoming the centre of a grand railroad system, affording the means of rapid and easy distribution for the several products of these mills, and there is reason to anticipate their steady increase.

CHAPTER XVI.

Domestic Life in Moscow. — Oriental Seclusion of Women. — The Foundling Hospital. — A Christian Charity. — A Metropolitan Centre. — City Museum. — The University. — Tea-Drinking. — Pleasure Gardens. — Drosky Drivers. — Riding-School. — Theatres. — Universal Bribery. — Love of Country. — Russians as Linguists. — Sparrow Hill. — Petrofski Park. — Muscovite Gypsies. — Fast Life. — Intemperance. — A Famous Monastery. — City Highways. — Sacred Pigeons. — Beggars.

THE domestic life of the people of Moscow (we speak of the acknowledged upper class) is quite Oriental in its character. The stranger, no matter how well he comes accredited, when he visits a dwelling-house is hospitably entertained, as hospitality is interpreted here; but it is by the master only. The ladies of the household are very rarely presented to him, and are seldom seen under any circumstances, even the opera being tolerated at Moscow half under protest, on account of its bringing ladies into a more intimate relation with the world at large. To the domestic caller scalding tea is served in tumblers, with slices of lemon floating on the top; but no other refreshments are offered. The host is courteous, he invites you to drive with him, and seems glad to show you the monuments and famous localities, and to give any desired information; but his family, harem-like, are kept out of sight. Even a courteous inquiry as to their health is received with a degree of surprise. The ladies of Cairo and Constantinople are scarcely more secluded. This, however, may be termed old Russian style; young Russia is improving upon Eastern customs, and is becoming slowly more Europeanized. These remarks apply less to St. Petersburg than to Moscow. As the Asiatic comes more closely in contact with Europeans he assimilates with their manners and customs, and women assume a different domestic relationship. Thus ladies and their partially grown-up children, accompanied by husband and friends, are not infrequently seen driving in public at the capital; but scarcely ever is this the case at Moscow. Indeed, we saw no instance of it here. Men were seen at the public places of amusement, parks, tea-gardens, and the like, accompanied by women; but they were not ladies, nor were they their wives or daughters.

One of the most interesting and important institutions of the city is its remarkable Foundling Hospital, which is conducted by the Government at an annual expense of five millions of dollars. The royal treasury appropriates a large portion of this sum each year to its support, besides which it is most liberally endowed by private bequests. The building which is occupied by the hospital, or rather the series of buildings, forms a large quadrangular group on the north bank of the Moskva, half a mile east of the Kremlin. The length of the frontage is fully a thousand feet, enclosing finely-kept, spacious gardens which cover several acres of ground, divided between pleasant paths, greensward, and shady groves. Here, on a sunny afternoon at the close of July, the author saw between fifteen and sixteen hundred infants paraded under the branches of the trees, sleeping in their tiny cradles or in the sturdy arms of the country-bred nurses, of whom there were over five hundred. These were all wet-nurses, each hearty, well-fed peasant woman being expected to nurse two infants. These women were all clad in snow-white cotton gowns and muslin caps, appearing scrupulously neat and clean, the muslin about head and face contrasting strongly with their nut-brown complexions. Some of the little ones who seemed to thrive best by such treatment are fed with the bottle, while careful and scientific care is afforded to each and all alike. Besides three or four regular attending physicians, the arrangements are presided over and the detail carefully carried out by a corps of trained matrons, the most thorough order, discipline, and system being observed as existing in every department. Just within the garden gate, at the main entrance, a bevy of thirty or forty children, rosy-cheeked, bright-eyed boys and girls, not over six years of age, were amusing themselves in childish games; but they came instantly to us with smiling, happy faces, extending their little hands as a token of welcome to the stranger. Selecting any one of these promising children, the thought occurred how proud many a rich family would be to have such an one for its rightful heir; and then we wondered what might be the future of these graduating from here under the ban of a clouded parentage. It seems that a few children are retained until about the age of these, though the number is comparatively small. Their contented, vigorous, healthful appearance showed how judicious and well-applied must be the system that could produce such physical results.

"There is no denying the fact that some of these boys have princely blood in their veins," said our intelligent guide, pointing to a merry group who were playing together. "Secrets are well kept in Russia. They will be carefully watched, and their well-being indirectly advanced. By and by they may get into the army, and be gradually promoted if they are deserving, becoming officers by a favor which they cannot analyze, and perhaps finally achieving a name and filling a high station. We have many such instances in the army and civil service, — men filling important positions, of whose birth and early antecedents no questions are asked. Sometimes marked and special resemblances may possibly lead to shrewd surmises, but no one gives such thoughts the form of words."

This institution was founded by Catherine II. in 1762, that at St. Petersburg having been established a few years subsequent; but the latter now equals the parent establishment both in size and in the importance of the work which it accomplishes. The average receipt of infants in each of these hospitals is over a thousand per month at the present time, and perhaps eleven hundred would be even nearer the aggregate. The hospitals are kept open night and day. No infant, whatever its condition, is ever refused shelter, good care, and proper nourishment. The little creatures are not left in secret, as is the case in most similar European institutions, or by unknown parties, but are openly received, no disguise whatever attending the relinquishment. Probably one third of the children born in the two great capitals of this country are illegitimate, while many who are born of married parents are also brought here because of the inability of their natural protectors properly to provide for them. It is this last feature which leavens the whole system in the eyes of the million; that is to say, because a mother is seen giving up her child here it does not follow that it is illegitimate. But be the individual circumstances what they may, the Government cheerfully takes charge of all the infants that are offered. The only question which is asked of those resigning their offspring is whether it has been baptized by a priest, and what name is desired to be given to it. The little one is then registered upon the books of the establishment, and a metallic number placed about its neck, never to be removed until it finally leaves the charge of the institution. As soon as the children become a month or six weeks old and are considered to be in perfect health, they are given in charge of country people who have infants of their own. These peasants are paid a regular weekly stipend for the support of the little strangers, rendering an account monthly of their charge, which must also be exhibited in person. All are under the supervision of a visiting committee, or bureau of matrons, having no other occupation, and who must regularly weigh the children and enter their progress or otherwise upon the books of the hospital, an account being opened for each infant received. One would think that among such large numbers as are accommodated monthly confusion would ensue; but so perfect is the system of accounts, that any child can be promptly traced and its present and past antecedents made known upon reasonable application. A mother, by proving her relationship and producing the receipt given to her for her child, can at any time up to ten years of age reclaim it, first proving her ability properly to support and care for her offspring. If a child is not reclaimed by its parents at ten or twelve years of age, it is apprenticed to some useful occupation or trade, and in the mean time has been regularly sent to school. The neatness, system, and general excellence observed at these Foundling Hospitals is worthy of emulation everywhere, and the whole plan seemed to us to be a great Christian charity, though no sensible person can be blind to the fact that there are two sides to so important a conclusion. There are many political economists who hold that such a system encourages illegitimacy and vice. A late writer upon the subject, whose means of observation may have been much more extended than those of the author of these pages, has spoken so decidedly that it is but proper to present his convictions in this connection. He says: "Unfortunately this famous refuge [the establishment in Moscow] has corrupted all the villages round the city. Peasant girls who have forgotten to get married send their babies to the institution, and then offer themselves in person as wet-nurses. Having tattooed their offspring, each mother contrives to find her own, and takes charge of it by a private arrangement with the nurse to whom it has been officially assigned. As babies are much alike, the authorities cannot detect these interchanges, and do not attempt to do so. In due time the mother returns to her village with her own baby, whose board will be well paid for by the State at the rate of eight shillings per month; and perhaps next year and the year after she will begin the same game over again."

We were informed that a large proportion of the boys who survive become farm-laborers, and that many of the girls are trained to be hospital nurses; others are apprenticed to factory work. If any of the latter become married at or before the age of eighteen, the State furnishes them with a modest trousseau. Up to the period of eighteen years, both sexes are considered to be "on the books of the institution," as it is termed, and to be amenable to its direction. When the young men arrive at this age, they are furnished with a good serviceable working-suit of clothes, and also a better suit for holiday wear, together with thirty roubles in money. These gratuities serve as a premium upon good behavior and obedience to authority. One sad feature of the system was admitted by the officials, and that is the large percentage of the mortality which seems inevitable among the infants. Notwithstanding every effort to reduce the aggregate of deaths, still it is estimated as high as seventy per cent; or in other words, not more than thirty out of each hundred admitted to the Foundling Hospitals live to the age of twenty-one years. This heavy loss of life is traceable in a large degree to hereditary disease, not to the want of suitable treatment after the children come into the charge of the institution.

Moscow is isolated in a degree, having no populous neighborhood or suburb. The forest and the plain creep up to its very walls; outlying villages and increasing population generally announce the approach to large cities; but both St. Petersburg and Moscow are peculiar in this respect. This city, however, as we have before remarked, is gradually becoming the centre of a great net-work of railways, like Chicago; and therefore the characteristic referred to must gradually disappear. It is built like Rome upon seven hills, and is the culminating point of Russian as that capital is of Italian history. While St. Petersburg is European, and annually growing to be more so, Moscow is and must continue to be Asiatic. As one gazes about him, the grandeur, sadness, and vicissitudes of its past, not exceeded by that of any other capital in the world, crowd upon the memory. In portions the confusion evinced in its composition of squares, streets, avenues, and narrow lanes is almost ludicrous and quite bewildering. There are no long uniform lines of architecture, like those of the capital on the Neva. Miserable hovels, dirty court-yards, and vile-smelling stables break the lines everywhere after one leaves the principal thoroughfares, and not infrequently even upon them. The barbarous as well as the semi-civilized aspect is ever present. Mosque, temple, triumphal-arch, cabins, campaniles, convents, and churches mingle heterogeneously together, as though they had dropped down indiscriminately upon the banks of the Moskva without selection of site. After the great conflagration of 1812 the object must have been to build, and to do so quickly. This was evidently done without any properly concerted plan, since there is not a straight street in all Moscow. Around the barriers of the city however there extends a boulevard, which occupies the site of the old line of fortifications; which is decked with grassy slopes, limes, maples, and elms, forming an attractive drive.

The Moscow Museum is a modern establishment, but is rapidly growing in importance. Here one can study comprehensively the progress of art and science in Russia during the past century, the chronological arrangement being excellent, and copied after the system inaugurated for a similar purpose at Copenhagen. The Museum occupies a fine building near the new Cathedral of Our Saviour, formerly the palatial residence of the Pashkof family. Its library already exceeds two hundred thousand bound volumes, and is especially rich in rare and ancient manuscripts. The excellent and scientific arrangement of this entire establishment was a source of agreeable surprise. The fine-arts department presents some choice paintings and admirable statuary, both ancient and modern; while the zoölogical collection contains much of interest. The favorite seat of learning is the Moscow University, founded by the Empress Elizabeth, daughter of Peter the Great, in 1755; its four principal faculties being those of History, Physics, Jurisprudence, and Medicine. It is a State institution, under the immediate control of the Minister of Public Instruction. At this writing, the University has some two thousand students. The terms of admission, as regards cost to the pupils, are merely nominal, the advantages being open to all youth above seventeen, who can pass a satisfactory examination. Here also is another large and valu. able library open to the public, aggregating over two hundred thousand bound volumes. This liberal multiplication of educational advantages in the very heart of Oriental Russia is an evidence of gradual progress, which tells its own story.

It seemed especially odd that a people who drink so profusely of fermented liquors, should also drink so much tea. It may be doubted if even the Japanese exceed them in the consumption of this beverage, and it is certain that the latter people use more tea in proportion to the number of inhabitants than do the Chinese. At Moscow tea-drinking is carried to the extreme. The *traktirs*, or tea-houses, can be found on every street, and are crowded day and evening by people who in summer sit and perspire over the steaming decoction, while they talk and chatter like monkeys. The stranger drops in to see native life, manners, and customs, while he sips scalding tea like the rest, and listens to the music of the large organ which generally forms a part of the furniture, and which when wound up will discourse a score or more of popular waltzes, airs, and mazurkas. These remarkable musical instruments are manufactured especially for this region, and frequently cost, as we were told, a thousand pounds sterling each. The habitués are from all classes of the populace, soldiers, civilians, priests, and peasants,—these last, slow, slouching, and shabby, with no coverings to their heads, except such an abundant growth of coarse sun-bleached hair as to suggest a weather-beaten hay-stack, "redundant locks, robustious to no purpose." These peasants, mechanics, and common laborers, though they drink tumbler after tumbler of nearly boiling hot tea, are only too apt to wind up their idle occupation by getting disgracefully tipsy on that fiery liquor corn-brandy, as colorless as water, but as pungent as *aqua-fortis*. To the tea-gardens in the immediate environs both sexes resort, and here one sees a very pleasant phase of Russian life,—tea-drinking *en famille* among the middle classes. The article itself is of a superior quality, much more delicate in flavor than that which is used in England or America; but it is never made so strong as we are accustomed to take it.

Happy family groups may be seen gathered about the burnished urns in retired nooks, and even love-episodes are now and then to be witnessed, occurring over the steaming beverage. These gardens are decorated in the summer evenings with the gayest of colored paper lanterns,—the flickering, airy lamps festooned among the tall trees and the low shrubbery, as they sway hither and thither, resembling clouds of huge fire-flies, floating at evening over a tropical plantation. There are also exhibitions nightly of fancy fire-works, minor theatricals, and comic song-singing. Tramways lead from the centre of the town to these popular resorts, or a drosky will take one thither at a mere trifling charge. The drosky drivers of Moscow appear to be one degree more stupid than those of St. Petersburg, impossible as that may seem. Like the cocher of Paris they all expect and ask for a *pourboire*. In the capital on the Neva the driver suggests "Na tchai" (tea), as you hand him his fare,— that is, he desires a few pennies to procure a drink of tea; but in Moscow the driver says more honestly, "Na vodka" (brandy). And yet there are many who are satisfied with the milder decoction, and will sit and sip it as long as any one will pay for it,—recalling the jinrikisha men of Yokohama, who seemed to have no desire for any stimulant but boiling hot tea, and plenty of it. The drosky drivers of Moscow dress all alike, and precisely like their brethren in the capital, in long blue padded pelisses, summer and winter, with a low bell-crowned hat, from beneath which protrudes an abundance of carrot-colored hair, of the consistency of dried meadow-grass.

It will interest the traveller to visit briefly the great National Riding-School of Moscow, a building embracing an area of five hundred and sixty feet long by one hundred and fifty-eight feet wide. It is covered with what appears to be a flat roof, but is without supporting pillars of any sort on the inside. A full regiment of cavalry can be exercised here with perfect convenience. This was the largest building in the world unsupported by prop of any kind, until the St. Pancras railway station was built in London. The interior is ornamented with bas-reliefs of men in armor and with ancient trophies. By ascending a winding staircase one can see the net-work of massive beams which sustain the roof, a perfect forest of stays and rafters. In a climate such as prevails here at least two thirds of the year, it is impossible to manœuvre troops in the open air with any degree of comfort, not to say safety; hence this structure was raised and supplied with huge stoves to afford the means of exercising the troops even in mid-winter.

Moscow has four theatres, two only of which are worthy of the traveller's notice. These are the Botshoi and the Italian Opera, where only entertainments of a high order of merit are permitted to be given. In many of the gay cafés young girls of free manners and lax morals dance in national costumes, among whom one easily recognizes those coming from Circassia, Poland, Lithuania, and the country of the Cossacks.

In their dances and grouping they present scenes that do not lack for picturesqueness of effect. Most of the melodies one hears at these places are quaint and of local origin, quite new to the ear; though now and again a familiar strain will occur, indicating from whence Chopin and others have borrowed. Some of the performers were so strikingly handsome as to show that their personal charms had been the fatal cause which had brought them into so exposed a connection as these public resorts of evil repute. The Bohemian or gypsy girls were the most attractive, — poor creatures coming from no one knows where, wanderers from their birth, and with lives ever enveloped in mystery. One could not but recall the Latin Quarter of Paris and the gay, dissipated night-resorts of London and Vienna. None of the European capitals are without these dark spots upon the escutcheon of civilization.

The author's observation in Cuba and continental Spain had led him to believe the dishonesty of Spanish officials to be quite unequalled; but the Russians far exceed the Spaniards in the matter of venality. The last war between Russia and Turkey brought to light official fraud and briberies, connected especially with the commissary department of the army, which disgraced the whole nation in the eyes of the world. Experiences of so outrageous and startling a character were related to us, illustrative of these facts, as to almost challenge belief, had they not been sustained by reliable authority. So extensive and universal is the system of bribery in Russia, that the question of right in ordinary matters, even when brought before the courts for decision, scarcely enters into the consideration. It is first and last purely a question of roubles. Counterfeit justice is as plentifully disbursed as counterfeit money, and that does much abound. To prove that this system of official bribery is no new thing here, and that it is perfectly well known at headquarters, we have only to relate a well-authenticated anecdote. A chief officer of police, who was one day dashing along the Nevsky Prospect in a handsome drosky drawn by a fine pair of horses, was met by the Emperor Nicholas. His Majesty by a sign stopped the officer, and inquired of him what salary he received from the government treasury. "Two thousand roubles, your Majesty," was the reply. Whereupon the Tzar asked how he contrived to own and keep such a smart equipage upon that sum. "By presents, your Majesty, that I receive from the people of my district," was the frank rejoinder. The Emperor laughed at so straightforward an answer, adding: "I believe that I live in your quarter, and have neglected sending you my present," at the same time handing him his purse. The existence of a system of bribery among the officials of the various departments was only too well known to the Tzar; but such plain speaking was a novelty.

A love, not to say pride, of country seems to be universal among the people at large, in spite of all that may be said or inferred to the contrary. No matter how poor the land may seem to the stranger, to the native-born it is beautiful, or at all events it is well beloved; no disparagement will be permitted for a moment. It was amusing to observe the local rivalry existing between the citizens of Moscow and St. Petersburg. The latter are regarded by the former as parvenus, lacking the odor of sanctity that adheres to the citizens of "holy Moscow." The more ancient metropolis has ever had a quasi official recognition as the capital, though it is not so politically. It will be remembered that in 1724, but a few months before his death, even Peter the Great celebrated the coronation of his wife Catherine at Moscow, not at St. Petersburg; and to this day it has been the crowning place of all his successors. So far as the hearts of the people are concerned, Moscow is their capital.

We often hear surprise expressed that Russians who visit other countries are generally such accomplished linguists; but this is very easily accounted for when we remember that in every noble or wealthy family of St. Petersburg or Moscow there is a German nurse for the young children, an English governess for the young ladies, and a French tutor for them all. Emulating those of more pretension and wealth, the same custom extends to the class of successful merchants' families; so that the average Russian grows up speaking two or three languages besides his native tongue. Life is much less cosmopolitan here than in St. Petersburg. Few emigrants from the far East stop in Moscow; they press on to the more European and commercial city, where Tartars from Kazan,

Adighes from the Caucasus, Swedes and Norwegians from Scandinavia, Finlanders from the North, and Germans from the South mingle together. In polite society French is the language of St. Petersburg, while German is much in use among the mercantile community; but in Moscow it is the native tongue which prevails, as well as Oriental manners and customs.

A drive of about three miles from the city over a wretchedly kept road, where the ruts are positively terrible, brings one to Sparrow Hill, the point from whence Napoleon first looked upon the devoted city. "There is the famous city at last, and it is high time," said Napoleon. He had left the battlefield of Borodino covered with corpses forty miles behind. But what cared the ravaging warrior for the eighty thousand lives there sacrificed? It was this terrible encounter which caused him to say emphatically, " One more such victory would be utter ruin!" From this elevation the invading host pressed forward and entered the Muscovite capital, to find the streets deserted, the public buildings stripped of all valuables, and the national archives removed. There were no officials with whom to treat; it was like a city of the dead. This unnatural solitude gave birth to gloomy forebodings in the hearts of the invaders, — forebodings which were more than justified by the final result of that wholly unwarranted campaign. Soon at various points the conflagration of the city began. If subdued here and there by the French it broke out elsewhere, and at last became uncontrollable. Napoleon entered Moscow on the fifteenth of September and left it in ashes on the nineteenth of October, when there began a retreat which was undoubtedly one of the greatest tragedies of modern times. Half a million men in the flower of their youth had in a brief six months been sacrificed to the mad ambition of one individual.

At Sparrow Hill are many cafés where the native population come to drink tea, and where foreigners partake of cheap, flat Moscow beer and other simple refreshments. From here a notable view is to be enjoyed, embracing the ancient capital in the distance; and it is this charming picture which most attracts strangers to the spot. The broad river forms the foreground, flowing through fertile meadows and highly cultivated fields. When we saw it vegetation was at its prime, a soft bright green carpeting the banks of the Moskva, while the plain was wooded with thriving groves up to the convent walls and outlying buildings of the town. Just back of the tea-houses, crowning the hill, is an ancient birch forest which was planted by Peter the Great, the practical old man having occupied many days in consummating this purpose, during which he worked laboriously among his people, setting out and arranging the birches. The local guides never fail to take all travellers who visit the Muscovite city to Sparrow Hill, where it is quite the thing to drink a tumbler of steaming hot Russian tea, with the universal slice of lemon floating thereon. This tasteless decoction has not even the virtue of strength, but is merely hot water barely colored with an infusion of leaves. However, as it is quite the thing to do, one swallows the mixture heroically. A more pleasant drive of about four or five miles from the centre of the city, over a far better road than that which leads to Sparrow Hill, will take the stranger to a most delightful place of resort known as the Petrofski Park, ornamented with noble old elms in great variety, flower-beds, blooming shrubbery, fountains, and delightfully smooth roads. The lime, the elm, the sycamore, and the oak all flourish here, mingled with which were some tall specimens of the pine and birch. The place is the very embodiment of sylvan beauty, and has been devoted to its present purpose for a century and more, having first been laid out in 1775. Within these grounds is the interesting old Palace of Petrofski, a Gothic structure which, though seldom inhabited, is kept always prepared for noble guests by a corps of retainers belonging to the Government. It is frequently the resort of the Emperor when he comes to Moscow, and always the place from whence a new emperor proceeds to the Kremlin to be officially crowned. It was to this palace that Napoleon fled from his quarters in the city when Moscow was being destroyed by the flames. The *cafés chantants* are many, within the precincts of the Park, — gay resorts of dissipation, whither the people come ostensibly to drink tea, but really to consume beer, wine, and corn-brandy, as well as to assist at the oftentimes very coarse entertainments which are here presented, characterized by the most reckless sort of can-can dancing and bacchanalian songs. Bands of music perform in different parts of the extensive grounds, and gaudily-dressed gypsy girls sing and dance after their peculiar and fantastic style. One detects fine vocal ability now and then exhibited by these wayward creatures, which by patient culture might be developed into great excellence. The singing of these girls is quite unlike such performances generally, — not particularly harmonious, but bearing the impress of wild feeling and passionate emotion. Many of the performers are of a marked and weird style of beauty, and such are pretty sure to wear jewelry of an intrinsic value far beyond the reach of honest industry, — which forms a glaring tell-tale of their immodesty.

The gypsy race of Russia, to whom these itinerants belong, are of the same Asiatic origin as those met with in southern Europe; no country has power to change their nature, no association can refine them. They will not try to live by honest labor; everywhere they are acknowledged outcasts, and it is their nature to grovel like animals. The cunning instinct of theft is born in them; adroitness in stealing they consider to be a commendable accomplishment, — parents teach it to their children. They are wanderers wherever found, begging at one country-house and stealing at the next; in summer sleeping on the grass, in winter digging holes and burrowing in the ground. They are called in central Russia "Tsiganie," and they group together in largest numbers in and about the Eastern Steppe, just as those of Spain do at Grenada and near to the Alhambra. All kindly efforts of the Russian government to civilize these land-rovers has utterly failed; not infrequently it becomes necessary to invade their quarters, and to visit condign punishment upon the tribe by sabre and bullet, to keep them within reasonable bounds. Quite a colony of gypsies inhabit a certain portion of Moscow, having adopted the local dress, and also conformed ostensibly to the conventionalities about them; but they never in reality amalgamate with other races, — they are far more clannish than the Jews. Both the men and women ply trades which will not bear investigation or the light of day. The former make an open business of horse-trading, and the latter of public-dancing, singing, and fortune-telling. Belonging to this community is a small body of singers who practise together, and who are employed at all public festivals in the city, — which would, indeed, be considered quite incomplete without them. This choir consists of six or eight female voices and four male, capable of affording a very original if not quite harmonious performance.

As regards the Petrofski Park, the truth is it is a famous resort for reckless pleasure-seekers, and largely made up of the demi-monde, where scenes anything but decorous are presented to the eyes of strangers during the afternoons and the long summer twilight. But those who wish to see and study "life," fast life, have only to visit the Châteaux des Fleurs, or Marina-Rostcha, which are also in the environs of the town. As in Vienna, Berlin, and Paris, the police, who cannot suppress these resorts, strive to control them so far that they shall not outrage openly the conventionalities of society. Human nature is much the same all over the world, though its coarsest features are more obtruded upon observation in some lands than in others. In extensive travel and experience, the author has learned that it is not always in semi-barbarous countries that grossness and indecency will be found most to prevail. It must be admitted that there are temples of vice in Moscow which for ingenuity of temptation, and lavish and gilded display, are not equalled elsewhere in Europe.

Under the shadow of the spacious and lofty tower which forms a reservoir for the distribution of water for the domestic use of the citizens, there is held in the open square each Sabbath day what is called "The Market," but which might better be designated a weekly fair, a sort of Nijni-Novgorod upon a small scale. Here Jew and Gentile, Asiatic and European, exchange their goods or sell to the citizens. There are confectioners, jewellers, clothiers, hard-ware merchants, dried-fruit venders, fancy-dry-good dealers, tea-booths, tin and earthenware tables,—in short, every domestic article that can be named is here offered for sale. The crowd is great, the Babel of voices deafening, the hustling incessant, occasional quarrels being inevitable. Now one meets a group of courteous, well-dressed people, now an itinerant in rags, now a bevy of boisterous girls and boys, now a long-haired and bearded priest; some are sober, many are drunk. Alas! Sunday is here a day of drunkenness. Speaking plainly upon this subject, there are more intoxicated persons to be seen in the streets of Moscow on the Sabbath than the author has ever encountered upon any day of the week in any other capital. At this Sunday-fair articles are offered at popular prices, presumed to be much lower than is charged by regular merchants who have rent to pay and large establishments to keep up. Upon this conviction the poorer classes especially throng hither to purchase such articles as they require, making the scene one of great activity and general interest. The tall tower of the water-supply was not originally intended for the use to which it has at last been appropriated. It was first erected by the Tzar Peter to mark the northeastern gate of the town, which was held by one faithful regiment when the rest revolted. This same regiment escorted him and his mother for safety to the Troitzkoi Monastery, situated thirty miles from the city, and which is considered to-day as the holy of holies so far as monasteries are concerned in Russia. Hither the Empress Catherine II. made the pilgrimage on foot to fulfil some conditional vow, accompanied by all her court, only advancing, however, five miles each day, and not forgetting to have every possible luxury conveyed in her train wherewith to refresh herself. It will be remembered that Napoleon in his usual rashness had planned to destroy this monastery, and had issued orders to that effect, just as he had done in the instance of St. Basil already referred to; but he was defeated in his purpose by the haste with which the demoralized army retreated from the country.

The Troitzkoi is not merely a monastery, it is also a semi-fortress, a palace, and a town containing eight churches, a bazaar, a hospital, and many stately residences, altogether forming a confused though picturesque group of towers, spires, belfries, and domes. It is dominated by a famous bell-tower two hundred and fifty feet high, containing one of the finest chimes of bells in all Russia, thirty-five in number. In the Church of the Trinity is the shrine of Saint Sergius, an elaborate piece of work of solid silver, weighing nearly a thousand pounds; it is so constructed that the relics of the saint are exposed. The whole of the monastery grounds are enclosed in a high wall twenty feet in thickness, with heavy octagon towers guarding the four principal corners. A deep moat surrounds the wall, and against the attack of a hostile force in former times it was thought to be remarkably protected, and is undoubtedly the strongest fortified monastery in the East. The large prison within the walls has been the scene of as great cruelty during the last two centuries as any similar establishment in Europe or Asia. The name Troitzkoi signifies the Trinity. The treasury of this monastery is famous among all who are specially interested in such matters for its priceless robes and jewels, to say nothing in detail of the aggregated value of its gold and silver plate. It is asserted that there are more and richer pearls collected here than are contained in all the other treasuries in Europe combined. Among other precious gems there are several mitres which contain rubies worth fifty thousand roubles each, being set with other jewels of appropriate richness. The Troitzkoi was pillaged by the Tartars about 1403, and was besieged by the Poles in 1608, at which time the walls were seriously injured; but all is now restored to its original strength and completeness. This ancient monastery stands at the opening of the valley of the Kliasma, a region fruitful with the smouldering ruins of by-gone cities so much older than Moscow that their names even are forgotten. The country between the stream just named and the Volga was the grand centre of early Tartar history. As in the environs of Delhi, India, where city after city has risen and crumbled into dust, so here large capitals have mouldered away leaving no recorded story, and only enforcing the sad moral of mutability.

The idea of comfortable road-beds for the passage of vehicles and good foot-ways does not seem to have entered the minds of the people of Moscow. The cobble-stone pavements are universal, both in the middle of the streets and on that portion designed for pedestrians. These stones, without any uniformity of size, are miserably laid in the first place, added to which they are thrown out of level by the severity of the annual frosts, so that it is a punishment to walk or to drive upon them. The natives are perhaps accustomed to this needless discomfort, and do not heed it; but it is a severe tax upon the endurance of strangers who remember the smooth roadways of Paris, Boston, and New York. A few short reaches of the square granite-stone pavements were observed, probably laid down as an experiment; but great was the relief experienced when the drosky rolled upon them after a struggle with the cobble-stone style of pavement. Many otherwise fine streets both here and in St. Petersburg are rendered nearly impassable by wretched paving.

One is struck by the multitude of pigeons in and about the city. They are held in great reverence by the common people, and no Russian will harm them. Indeed, they are as sacred here as monkeys in Benares or doves in Venice, being considered emblems of the Holy Ghost, and under protection of the Church. They wheel about in large blue flocks through the air so dense as to cast shadows, like swift-moving clouds between the sun and the earth, alighting fearlessly where they choose, to share the beggar's crumbs or the bounty of the affluent. It is a notable fact that this domestic bird was also considered sacred by the old Scandinavians, who believed that for a certain period after death the soul of the deceased under such form was accustomed to come to eat and drink with as well as to watch the behavior of the mourners. Beggary is sadly prevalent in the streets of the Muscovite capital,— the number of maimed and wretched-looking human beings forcibly recalling the same class in Spanish and Italian cities. This condition of poverty was the more remarkable when contrasted with its absence in St. Petersburg, where a person seen soliciting alms upon the streets or in tattered garments is very rare.

CHAPTER XVII.

Nijni-Novgorod. — Hot Weather. — The River Volga. — Hundreds of Steamers. — Great Annual Fair. — Peculiar Character of the Trade. — Motley Collection of Humanity. — An Army of Beggars. — Rare and Precious Stones. — The Famous Brick Tea. — A Costly Beverage. — Sanitary Measures. — Disgraceful Dance Halls. — Fatal Beauty. — A Sad History. — Light-Fingered Gentry. — Convicts. — Facts About Siberia. — Local Customs. — Russian Punishment.

A JOURNEY of about three hundred miles (or as the Russians state it, four hundred and ten versts) in a northeasterly direction from Moscow, by way of the historic town of Vladimir, famous for its battles with the Tartars, brings us to Nijni-Novgorod, — that is, Lower Novgorod, being so called to distinguish it from the famous place of the same name located on the Volkhov, and known as Novgorod the Great. It is older than Moscow, antedating it a century or more, and is the capital of a province bearing the same name. The residence of the governor of the district, the courts of law, and the citadel are within the Kremlin, where there is also a fine monument in the form of an obelisk eighty feet high, erected to the memory of Mininn and Pojarski, the two patriots who liberated their country from the Poles in 1612. This Kremlin, like that at Moscow, is situated on an elevation overlooking the town and the broad valley of the

Volga. The site of the upper town, as the older portion of the place situated about the Kremlin is called, is quite remarkable, being a sort of overhanging bluff, commanding a level view as far as the eye can reach over an undulating country, through which winds the noblest river of Russia. The climate here is subject to great extremes of heat and cold, — the mercury freezing, it is said, in winter, and sometimes bursting in the heat of the summer sun. As we stood upon this bluff enjoying the comprehensive view, the heat of the mid-day hour and the power of the sun were quite tropical. Indeed, without the partial shelter of an umbrella it would have been as insufferable as mid-day exposure in Ceylon or Singapore. All animal life, so far as possible, sought the shade; and the fine black horses attached to the vehicle which had transported us from the plain below, though driven at a quiet pace, were flecked with foam and panted with distended nostrils. The thermometer on the shady side of the governor's palace close at hand indicated 89° Fahrenheit. To the great extremes of overpowering cold and enervating heat some of the apparent incongruities of the native character may doubtless be attributed. For more than half the year the people are as it were hermetically sealed up by the frost, and in the brief but intense heat of the summer they are rendered inert and slothful by the effect of tropical heat.

We were told that there was here six hundred years ago a very large city, but that to-day the place cannot boast over forty-five thousand fixed population. Thus the story of faded grandeur is written all over the plains of northern Europe and Asia. By ascending what is called Mininn's Tower, one of the finest panoramic views is obtained which can well be conceived of. A vast alluvial plain is spread out before the eye covered with fertile fields and thrifty woods, through which from northwest to southeast flows the Volga like a silver thread upon a verdant ground, extending from horizon to horizon. On this river, which is the main artery of central Russia, are seen scores of swift-moving steamers bound to Saratoff, Astrakhan, and the Caspian Sea, fourteen hundred miles away, while a forest of shipping is gathered about the shore of the lower town and covering the Oka River, which here joins the Volga. From this outlook the author counted over two hundred steamboats in sight at the same time, — all side-wheelers and clipper-built, drawn hither by the exigencies of the local trade contingent upon the period of the great annual fair. The first of these steamers was built in the United States and transported at great trouble and expense to these Russian waters, and has served as the model of the hundreds now employed on the river. The flat-boats which the steamers had towed from various distant points, having been unloaded, were anchored in a shallow bend of the river, where they covered an area fully a mile square. On many of these boats entire families lived, it being their only home; and wherever freight was to be transported thither they went: whether it was towards the Ural Mountains or the Caspian Sea, it was all the same to them.

The Volga has a course of over twenty-four hundred, and the Oka of eight hundred and fifty miles. As the Missouri and Mississippi rivers have together made St. Louis, so these Russian rivers have made Nijni. This great mart lies at the very centre of the water communication which joins the Caspian and the Black seas to the Baltic and White seas, besides which it has direct railroad connection with Moscow and thence with the entire east of Europe. The Volga and its tributaries pour into its lap the wealth of the Ural Mountains and that of the vast region of Siberia and Central Asia. It thus becomes very apparent why and how this ancient city of Nijni-Novgorod is the point of business contact between European industry and Asiatic wealth.

The attraction which draws the traveller so far into the centre of European Russia, lies in the novelty of the great annual fair held at Nijni for a period of about eight weeks, and which gathers for the time being some two hundred thousand people,— traders and spectators,— who come from the most distant provinces and countries, as well as from the region round about. A smaller and briefer fair is held upon the ice of the rivers Volga and Oka in January, but is comparatively of little account; it is called a horse-fair, being chiefly devoted to trade in that animal. The merchandise accumulated and offered

GRAND FAIR AT NIJNI-NOVGOROD. 337

for sale at the grand fair in August and September is gathered principally from the two richest quarters of the globe. It is of limitless variety, and in quality varying from the finest to the coarsest. As an example of this, jewelry was observed of such texture and fashion as would have graced a store on the Rue de la Paix, offered for sale close beside the cheapest ornaments of tinsel manufactured by the bushel-basketful at Birmingham and Manchester. Choice old silverware was exposed side by side with iron saucepans, tin-dippers, and cheap crockery utensils, — variety and incongruity, gold and Brummagem everywhere in juxtaposition. There is an abundance of iron and copper from the Urals, dried fish in tall piles from the Caspian Sea, tea from China, cotton from India, silks and rugs from Persia, heavy furs and sables from Siberia, wool in the raw state from Cashmere, together with the varied products of the trans-Caucasian provinces, even including wild horses in droves. Fancy-goods from England as well as from Paris and Vienna, toys from Nuremberg, ornaments of jade and lapis-lazuli from Kashgar, precious stones from Ceylon, and gems from pearl-producing Penang. Variety, indeed! Then what a conglomerate of odors permeated everything, dominated by the all-pervading musk, boiled cabbage, coffee, tea, and tanned leather! Everything seemed to loom up through an Oriental haze, a mirage of fabulous merchandise. In the midst of the booths and lanes there rose the tall, pointed spire of a mosque, which we were told was the most northerly Mahome-

tan temple extant. If any business purpose actuates
the visitor, let him keep his wits about him, and above
all remain cool; for it will require an effort not to be
confused by the ceaseless buzzing of this hive of
human beings. Sharpers are not wanting, but are
here in force to take advantage of every opportunity
that offers. Many who come hither thrive solely by
dishonesty. It is a sort of thieves' paradise, — and
Asiatic thieves are by far the most expert operators
known in either hemisphere. Most of them are itinerants, having no booth, table, or fixed location, but
yet carrying conspicuously about them evidences of
some special line of trade, and evincing a desire to
sell at remarkably low prices, — all of which is a spe-
cious disguise under which to prosecute their dishonest
purposes.

The period of great differences in prices in localities
wide apart has, generally speaking, passed away, and
everywhere the true value of things is known. Circumstances may favor sellers and buyers by turns,
but intrinsic values are nearly fixed all over the
world. Nothing is especially cheap at this great
Russo-Asiatic fair except such articles as no one
cares to purchase, though occasionally a dealer who
is particularly anxious to realize cash will make a
special sacrifice in the price demanded. The Tartar
merchant from the central provinces of Asia knows
the true value of his goods, though in exchange he
pays large prices for Parisian and English luxuries.
Gems so abundant here can only be bought at a just

approximation to their value in the markets of the world; and unless one is willing to encounter the risk of being grossly deceived in quality, and to lose much time in bargaining, they had far better be purchased elsewhere. All the tricks of trade are known and resorted to at such a gathering. The merchant begins by demanding a price ridiculously above the amount for which he is willing eventually to sell, — a true and never wanting characteristic of Oriental trade. No dealer has a fixed price at Nijni. The Asiatic enjoys dickering; it is to him the life of his occupation, and adds zest if not profit to his business transactions, and by long practice he acquires great adroitness in its exercise.

The principal attraction to the traveller, far above that of any articles which form the varied collection of goods displayed for sale, is to observe the remarkable distinction of races and nationalities that are here mingled together. Tartars, Persians, Cossacks, Poles, Egyptians, Finns, Georgians, with many others, crowd and jostle one another upon the narrow lanes and streets. Many of these are in neat national costumes. We recall as we write a group of Greeks in their picturesque attire, who formed a theatrical picture by themselves; while others were in such a mass of filthy rags as to cause one to step aside to avoid personal contact and its possible consequences. Though familiar with the Spanish and Italian cities where they much abound, the author has never before seen so many beggars — professional beggars — congregated together. The variety of features, of physical development, of dress, manners, customs, and languages was infinite. It would be impossible to convey an idea of the ceaseless Babel of noise which prevailed, — the cries designating certain goods, the bartering going on all about one in shrill voices, laughter mingled with sportive exclamations, and frequent trivial disputes which filled the air. But there was no actual quarrelling, — the Russian police are too vigilant, too much feared, too summary for that; open violence is instantly suppressed, and woe betide the culprit! Such is this unique fair, which presents one of the rude and ancient forms of trade that is rapidly disappearing by the introduction of railroads. The glory of Nijni-Novgorod is, we suspect, already beginning to wane; but it would seem that the fair still represents all the gayest features of the olden time, having been held here annually since 1366, tradition pointing to even an earlier date.

The site of the fair-grounds is triangular in shape, and lies between the two rivers Volga and Oka, forming yearly a large and populous temporary town, with numerous streets of booths, restaurants, small shops, bazaars, tents, and even minor theatres, while the wharves of the rivers are crowded with bales of rags, grain, hides, skins, casks of wine, madder, and cotton. The aggregate value of the goods disposed of at these yearly gatherings of traders is enormous, being estimated as high as eighty millions of dollars! Centuries since, the two extremes of western Europe and

THE ALEXANDRITE GEM.

China used also to meet at Kazan to exchange merchandise; but long ago this trade was transferred to Nijni, which is now the only notable gathering-place of the sort in Russia. We were told that the united length of the streets, lanes, and alleys of the fair often reached a distance of thirty miles, and this seemed to be rather an under than an over estimate. Some idea may be formed of the great distances which traders pass over to meet here, from the fact that there were seen Bucharians from the borders of China as well as merchants from the north part of the Celestial Empire. The former brought with them, in connection with other goods, precious stones for sale. Some choice turquoises were observed in their possession, such as one can purchase nowhere else in first hands. Speaking of gems, there were also fine specimens of the native product offered by those who dealt in jewelry,— among them some very fine Alexandrites, a comparatively modern discovery from the Ural mines, which were named after the Emperor Alexander I. The Alexandrite is opaline, being dark green by daylight and ruby red by artificial light at night, though strong artificial light will bring out its peculiar properties at any time. In hardness it seems to be of about the same texture as the emerald, and when a clear, flawless specimen is obtained, it is valued almost as highly as that rare and beautiful gem. The story told about the Alexandrite, and which we are inclined to believe is true, is that only one "pocket," as it is technically designated, was ever discovered, and that has long since been exhausted, all subsequent search having utterly failed to produce a single specimen. At first the value of this remarkable stone was not realized, and it remained neglected upon the spot where it was found, until a European geologist chanced to see and explain its gem-like qualities, after which it became much sought for and properly valued. Very few are to be found for sale in Europe, and fewer in America. The author saw one of these stones at St. Petersburg which was exquisitely cut and clear as a crystal, though green in color, for which the sum of three thousand roubles was demanded. As it weighed fifteen carats, this was at about the rate of one hundred dollars per carat. At Nijni or St. Petersburg one must pay nearly Paris and New York prices for real gems.

Specimens of other gems from the Urals though not abundant were still in considerable variety,— not offered at the booths, but by itinerants who came to our hotel, and displayed them in a somewhat secret manner, being very particular to keep quite out of sight of the crowd. One of these dealers took from his bosom a small flat leather receptacle wherein he showed some fine emeralds, colored diamonds, rubies, and topazes. Of the latter gem there were specimens in green, blue, yellow, and white, most of them too poorly cut to show their fine beauty and brilliancy to advantage. The Armenian who exhibited this collection had also garnets of several distinct colors, the finest of which was of a light cinnamon hue. He had also tourmalines black as jet, and pink rubellites with sapphires as fine as those from Ceylon. All these precious stones, he said, were from the Ural mines. The same region furnishes also gold, silver, copper, and platinum, the latter valuable product in larger quantities than comes from any other part of the world. An emerald mine was accidentally discovered in the Ural range near Ekaterinburg so late as 1830. A peasant who was passing through a wood chanced to see an emerald gleaming among the upturned roots of a fallen pine; and further research showed that many precious gems of the same sort were mingled with the surrounding soil. Such discoveries soon become known. The peasant was enriched for life, but Government as usual in such cases claimed the mine.

Thibet and North China merchants who come to Nijni occupy nearly six months in travelling to and from their native districts. They bring their famous brands of "brick tea," said to be the finest produced, and of which the Russians partake so liberally, paying more than double the price per pound that is usually charged for the best brands that reach the American market. One who has travelled in Japan is impressed with the idea that its people draw one half their sustenance from tea-drinking, of which they partake many times each day; but neither these Russians nor the Asiatics take the decoction one quarter as strong as it is used with us. An idea prevails here that the tea from China which comes by the overland route is much superior to that which reaches Southern Europe and America by sea, and the price is gauged accordingly; but even brick tea comes to Nijni half the distance and more by water carriage, and if there is any deteriorating effect traceable to that cause, it cannot be exempt. There is a brand known as "yellow tea" in great favor here,— a grade which we do not see in this country at all. It is of a pale color when steeped and of delicate flavor, being used as an after-dinner beverage in Russia, as we employ coffee. It is sold at the fair in small fancy packages as put up in China, each containing one pound of the leaves. Price six dollars for a package!

Where there is so large and promiscuous an assemblage of human beings, sickness of an epidemic character would be sure to break out were it not that a most rigid sanitary system is established and enforced. This precaution is especially important, as personal cleanliness is a virtue little known and less practised among Russians and Asiatics. In the large cities the Russian takes his weekly bath of steaming water, nearly parboiling his body; and that must last him for seven days. The average citizen sleeps in his clothes during the interim without change, satisfied with bathing his face and hands in a pint or less of water daily. The Nijni fair-grounds have open canals in various parts to afford immediate access to water in case of fire, and also ample underground sewerage formed by stone-lined drains which extend all over the place. These drains are flushed several times daily during the season of the fair by water pumped from the Volga.

The dance-halls, music-rooms, and places of general amusement are of such a character as might naturally be anticipated, presenting disgraceful features of frailty and vice scarcely surpassed in the large European capitals. One spacious square of the grounds is occupied by four large three-story houses, which are nothing less than acknowledged dens of vice. From these houses, which are on the four sides of the square, flags and streamers are all day gayly flaunting, and fancy lanterns are grouped at night. Bands of instrumental performers pour forth from their several piazzas noisy refrains, while parading hither and thither upon the broad verandas, or looking out from the windows, many a prematurely aged and saddened face appears, — faces, alas! which assumed smiles and gayety of tone cannot effectually disguise. The unfortunate girls who are attached to these establishments are of varied nationalities. Many are Russian, some are Poles, others are from far-off Cashmere and Nepaul; even the Latin Quarter of Paris has its representatives here, as well as the demi-monde of Vienna.

One dark-eyed, handsome, even refined appearing girl, who kept quite by herself, was detected as being a quadroon. Observing that the author was American, she acknowledged that she came from New Orleans. The brief truthful history of this girl, who possessed all the fatal beauty of her race, may be found instructive. She had been the travelling companion of a heartless titled Englishman, who had induced her to run away from her respectable Louisiana home, and had finally deserted her at St. Petersburg after a year of travel in various parts of the world and a considerable sojourn in India. Without a guinea in her purse or the means of honestly earning money, her fate seemed to be inevitable; and so she had drifted she hardly knew how or where, until she was here in this maelström of vice, Nijni-Novgorod. One must have possessed a heart of stone to be able to look unmoved into the tearful eyes of this poor unhappy girl, who had bought her bitter experience at such terrible cost. Quietly closing her hand upon the gold that was offered her with some earnest, well-meant advice, she said: "This shall be the nucleus of a sum wherewith to return to my mother and my Louisiana home, or it shall purchase that which will end for me all earthly misery!" Poor Marie Fleur! We shall probably never know what fate has befallen her.

Interspersed about the lanes and streets were many gay eating and drinking booths, cafés where gypsy dancers and singing girls appeared in the evening. With the close of the day the business of the fair is mostly laid aside, and each nationality amuses itself after its native fashion. Rude musical instruments are brought forth, strange and not inharmonious airs fall upon the ear, supplemented here and there by songs the words of which are utterly unintelligible except to a small circle of participants. The whole

scene forms a motley picture, as party-colored as
Harlequin's costume, while the whole is shadowed by
the ever-present, vigilant Russian police. Smoking
is not permitted in the streets or among the booths;
to light a match even subjects one to a fine, such
is the great fear of fire; but still the unmistakable
fumes of tobacco which permeated the atmosphere
showed that within the walls of their own apartments
smokers were freely indulging in their wonted habit.
The governor's business residence during the fair is
very near its centre. The lower portion for the time
being is transferred into a grand bazaar, for the sale
of the lighter and more choice fancy articles, including
European manufactured goods. There is here
also a large restaurant where a good dinner may be
had at a reasonable price, the bill of fare embracing
the peculiar dishes of many different nationalities, —
and though others did, the author did not partake of
Tartar horse-flesh. A boulevard extends from behind
the governor's house towards the cathedral and an
Armenian church. The shops along this thoroughfare
are principally occupied by goldsmiths and dealers in
silver-ware. Some apparently very ancient examples
of the latter would have delighted the eye of a curio
hunter; they were in the form of clasps, mugs, drinking-horns,
and spoons of quaint designs, no two alike,
affording an endless variety from which to choose.

We were told of some curious doings of the light-fingered
gentry who are naturally attracted to the
fair, and who drive a very successful business during

the few weeks of its continuance, provided they be not detected and locked up. These rogues are not confined to any one nationality, but are composed of immigrants from far and near. They seem equally adroit however, whether Asiatics or Europeans. One was arrested during the late season at Nijni upon whose person eleven purses and porte-monnaies were found as the product of a single day's operation. The rascal was a Polish Jew, "childlike and bland." He was apparently a pedler, dealing in tapes and shoe-strings. Some London thieves the year before the last, having heard of the great Russian fair which continued so many weeks, drawing together purchasers from many lands, who came with well-lined pocket-books, accordingly resolved to invade Nijni. They came, they saw, they conquered; but it was a very brief triumph. The Asiatic thieves "spotted" the English rogues at sight, but let them operate until they had possessed themselves of ample booty, while the local rogues remained quiescent and watched the fun. Then the Eastern experts picked their pockets of every farthing they had stolen; having done which they adroitly drew the attention of the police to them. The cockneys were compelled to leave the place instantly, and to beg their way to an English port where they sadly embarked for home, wiser if not richer than when they resolved to "raid" the great Oriental fair.

The numbers of persons arriving during the fair is so great as to exhaust all reasonable means of comfortable lodgement, and where the great mass sleep is generally considered to be a mystery; yet a stroll about the town at day-break will solve it. Rolled up in their rags, thousands drop down to rest like dogs upon the ground wherever fatigue overtakes them. Other thousands sleep behind their stalls and booths upon the softest place they can find. Open sheds are utilized by hundreds, who lie there upon the floor packed like herring under a temporary roof. It may be safely stated that not one person in fifty who attends the fair removes his clothing from his body while he is there. Even the weekly bath must be given up here, unless it consists of a brief plunge into the Volga.

On the route to Nijni from Moscow, at a station on the railway line, a bevy of convicts was seen on their way to Siberia. They represented all ages, from the lad of fifteen to the decrepit and gray-haired old man of sixty or seventy. Condemned people are now conveyed as far on their way as possible by rail, and then begin their long journey upon foot towards the region which according to popular belief rarely fails to become their grave in a few brief years. Some of these men — there were no women among them — appeared to us as though society were fortunate to be rid of them, and as if they very likely deserved the fate which awaited them, be it never so severe. There were others, however, if the human countenance may be trusted, who seemed to merit a better fate. Some of them had grossly outraged the laws, and some few were political prisoners. But be their condemnation upon what ground it may, when once started upon this journey they left all hope behind. The prisoners whom we saw did not appear to be guarded with much strictness. They were permitted to walk about freely within certain lines; still, military espionage is so thorough and complete that any attempt to escape would surely cost the prisoner his life. None of these prisoners were manacled or confined by bonds of any sort; and though we watched them specially, no harshness was exhibited by either soldiers or officers towards them. The prisoners seemed to accept the position, and the soldiers to be only performing routine duty. Feeling more than ordinary interest in the subject, we were led to seek for information touching this penal servitude.

We were told by unprejudiced persons that many of the current stories about Siberia were pure fiction, and that not a few of the attributed terrors relating to that district were without truth. To sober, honest, industrious enterprise it was not only a very habitable but even desirable locality, undoubtedly with some drawbacks; but there is no limit to its mineral wealth and other possibilities. In spite of its climate, the soil under proper culture is represented to be prodigiously fertile. Our principal informant had been there several times, and had mercantile interests in the country: he was not of Russian but German birth. It seems that many persons go to Siberia voluntarily every year, some following closely in the track of each lot of prisoners despatched thither. If what we heard and have reason to believe is really true, Siberia will eventually prove to Russia what Australia and Van Diemen's Land have to England.

The Russian travels with all his toilet and sleeping necessaries with him. Towels, soap, pillow, and blanket form a part of his regular outfit when he travels by rail or otherwise at night. Though one pays for sleeping-car accommodations, only reclining seats are furnished, and not even a pitcher of water or a towel can be found inside of the cars. This seemed to be the more surprising because of the excellence of the road-bed, the remarkable perfection of the rolling stock, and the manifest desire upon all hands, so far as the officials were concerned, to render the passengers as comfortable as possible. Anything like refreshing slumber was out of the question in a half upright position, and after a night passed in coquetting with sleep, at six or seven o'clock in the morning the cars stopped at a way-station for twenty-five minutes, both in coming from Moscow to Nijni and in returning, the journey both ways being made by the night-express. On the platform of this station a line of peasant women stand behind a series of basins placed temporarily upon a long bench. One of these women pours a small stream of water from a pitcher upon the traveller's hands, and he is thus enabled to make a partial toilet, wiping his face upon a very suspicious-looking towel, also furnished by the woman who supplies the water. For this service she expects ten kopecks, the smallest current silver coin. However, water upon the face and temples even in limited quantity, after a long dusty night-ride in the cars, is grateful and refreshing, incomplete though the ablution may seem, and one felt duly thankful. It was quite as ample accommodation in that line as the average Russian citizen required.

Before closing this chapter, and apropos of the subject of Siberia, let us say a few words more. It should be remembered as regards the severity of punishment for crime in Russia, and particularly as to banishment to Siberia, that the sentence of death is now rarely inflicted in this country. Persons who are condemned to expiate their crimes by deportation to this penal resort, would in other European countries be publicly executed. Nearly all other nations punish undoubted treason with death. Russia inflicts only banishment, where the convicted party has at least air and light, his punishment being also mitigated by obedience and good behavior. This is paradise compared to Austrian, Spanish, German, and Italian prisons, where the wretched dungeon existence is only a living death. It is a fact that of late years, and especially since the accession of Alexander III. to the throne, so mild has the punishment of banishment to Siberia come to be considered that it has lost its terror to the average culprit. We were assured that not one third of the convicts sent thither for a limited term elect to return to their former homes, but end by becoming free settlers in the country, and responsible citizens.

CHAPTER XVIII.

On the Road to Poland. — Extensive Grain-Fields. — Polish Peasantry. — A Russian General. — No Evidence of Oppression. — Warsaw and its Surroundings. — Mingled Squalor and Elegance. — Monuments of the City. — Polish Nobility. — Circassian Troops. — Polish Language. — The Jews of Warsaw. — Political Condition of Poland. — Public Parks. — The Famous Saxony Gardens. — Present Commercial Prosperity. — Local Sentiment. — Concerning Polish Ladies and Jewish Beauties.

FROM Moscow to Warsaw one travels a long and rather dreary seven hundred miles, the first half of which is characterized by such sameness, verst after verst, as to render the journey extremely monotonous. The country through which we passed is heavily wooded, and affords some attractive sport to foreign hunters who resort hither for wolf-shooting. In the summer season these repulsive creatures are seldom dangerous to man, except when they go mad (which in fact they are rather liable to do), in which condition they rush through field and forest heedless of hunters, dogs, or aught else, biting every creature they meet; and such animals, man or beast, surely die of hydrophobia. The wolves are at all seasons more or less destructive to small domestic stock, and sometimes in the severity of a hard winter they will gather in large numbers and attack human beings under the craze of ravenous hunger. But as a rule they are timid, and keep out of the way of man. There are also some desirable game-birds in these forests which are sought for by sportsmen, but the wolves are all that the foreign hunter seeks. The wild bison still exist here, though it is forbidden to shoot them, as they are considered to belong to the Crown, but the gradual diminution of their numbers from natural causes threatens their extinction. If they were not fed by man during the long winters they would starve. The Emperor sometimes presents a specimen to foreign zoölogical gardens.

As we advanced, the country put on a different aspect. The beautiful lavender color of the flax-fields interspersed with the peach-bloom of broad, level acres of buckwheat produced a cheerful aspect. These fields were alternated by miles of intensely green oats, rye, and other cereals; indeed, we have seen no finer display of grain-fields except in western America. The hay-makers in picturesque groups were busy along the line of the railroad, nine tenths of them being women. The borders of Poland exhibited a scene of great fertility and successful agricultural enterprise. As we crossed the frontier a difference in the dress of the common people was at once obvious. Men no longer wore red shirts outside of their pantaloons, and the scarlet disappeared from the dress of the women, giving place to more subdued hues. The stolid square faces of the Russian peasantry were replaced by a more intelligent cast of features, while many representatives of the Jewish race began to appear, especially about the railroad stations, where they were sure to be offering something for sale. At the frontier town of Brest the extensive fortifications attracted notice, where considerable bodies of infantry and artillery were also observed. These elaborate fortifications are said to embrace a line of twenty miles, and are kept fully up to a war standard. As to the defensive condition of Russian forts, Alexander III. considers prevention better than cure, and is at all times prepared for an emergency. The dwelling-houses which began to come into view were of a much superior class to those left behind us in Russia proper. Log-cabins entirely disappeared and thatched roofs were rarely seen, while good substantial frame-houses appropriately painted became numerous. Neat little flower-plats were seen fenced in adjoining the dwellings, containing pretty shrubbery, flowers, and fruit-trees. Lines of bee-hives found place near the dwellings, and everything was suggestive of thrift and industry.

On the same train in which we had travelled from Moscow was Prince Gurkon, commander-in-chief of all the armies of Russia. He was a man past the middle age, with a countenance of pleasing expression, not wanting in firmness, but still quite genial. The Prince was almost covered on the left breast with the insignia of various orders. He was in full military uniform, attended by a staff of a dozen officers, and being on an official tour of inspection was received with a salvo of guns at Brest. He was inclined to conversation, and was not a little curious about America, concerning whose political and military status he had many questions to ask. Like all of his countrymen he expressed hearty sympathy with our Republic, and spoke intelligently of American history and progress. He had special respect for General Grant as a soldier, and remarked that fortunately Russia had disposed of the terrible incubus of serfdom at a less bitter and bloody cost than America incurred in the suppression of negro slavery.

After crossing the borders of Poland, the thoughtful stranger cannot divest himself of an earnest even though silent sympathy with the people who are so thoroughly disfranchised in a political sense; and yet truth compels us to say, that few if any outward signs of oppression met the eye. We must confess that a decided effort to discover something of the sort proved quite a failure. The masses of the people are cheerful and talkative in the extreme, exhibiting a strong contrast in this respect to those of Russia, who have a chronic expression of dreariness and inanity, and who, as a rule, are essentially silent and sad. With their national existence annihilated, so to speak, we had been led to anticipate discontent and grumbling among the Poles, neither of which we encountered. Warsaw is seemingly as thoughtless over these matters and as gay as any capital in Europe. As regards the nationality of Poland, her fate is certainly decided for many years to come, if indeed it be not settled for all time. And without prejudice or any false sentiment, one is forced to think perhaps this is best for Poland. Dismembered as she is, every new generation must amalgamate her more and more completely with the three powers who have appropriated her territory and divided the control of her people among them. We continue to speak of Poland as a distinct country, though the name is all that remains of its ancient independence. The map of Europe has long since been reconstructed in this region, — Austria, Germany, and Russia coolly absorbing the six millions of Poles, and Warsaw being the capital of Russian Poland.

It was at the close of the second day's journey since leaving Moscow that we approached Warsaw in a course nearly due west, witnessing one of those fiery sunsets which are only seen in their intensity towards the close of summer in the north. The gorgeous light escorted us into the capital across the long and lofty iron bridge which stretches from the Praga suburb over the broad, sandy bed of the Vistula. This remarkable bridge is one thousand nine hundred feet in length, and was designed by the same architect that superintended the construction of the Nicholas Bridge at St. Petersburg. The curtain of night fell in sombre folds as we drove through the streets of the old city amid a blaze of artificial light, the town being gayly illumined on account of its being the birthday of Alexander III. It was observed that this illumination was in some respects peculiar, long rows of gas-jets, extending by means of temporary pipes along the gutters by the sidewalks, supplementing the blaze in the windows of stores and dwelling-houses, so that one seemed to be passing between two narrow streams of liquid fire. It is a long drive from the railroad station to the Hotel Victoria, but when it is once reached, the traveller finds himself located in the centre of Warsaw and in very comfortable quarters.

The city extends about six miles along the left bank of the Vistula and upon high land. The river — which is navigable, though at the time of our visit it was very low — extends the whole length of Poland from north to south, its source being in the Carpathians and its mouth at Dantzic. The city, which covers a great surface in proportion to the number of its inhabitants, is enclosed by ramparts pierced by ten gates, and is defended by a castle of modern construction. The fortification is well kept up to a war-standard, especially in the department of modern artillery. The garrison was drilling at the time of our visit in the management of some new and heavy guns. Warsaw has nearly half a million of inhabitants, one third of whom are Jews, who monopolize the main branches of trade, and who appear in an exaggerated aspect of their repulsive peculiarities. There is but one synagogue worthy of mention belonging to this people, who certainly would require more were they composed of a race adhering strictly to their religious professions. The temple referred to is an extremely plain, unpretentious one, which is capable of accommodating twelve or fifteen hundred persons, and is generally visited by strangers in the city. The prevailing religion in Poland is Roman Catholic, and doubtless much of the bitterness of feeling which exists between this people and the Russians is caused by religious differences, fomented by the Catholic priests.

On arriving in a new city, an experienced traveller will instinctively seek some suitable point from which to obtain a clear and comprehensive view of the entire locality, which will thus become mapped upon the brain, so that all after movements are prosecuted with a degree of intelligence otherwise impossible. Here the St. Petersburg railway station in the Praga district affords the desired view. From hence a vast panorama spreads out before the eye in every direction. On the banks of the Vistula opposite may be seen the citadel, the older portions of the town, with its narrow streets and lofty houses, the castle and its beautiful gardens, as well as the newer sections of the city, including the public promenades and groves about the royal villa of Lazienki. Viewed from Praga as it slopes upward, the effect of the city is very pleasing, and a closer examination of its churches, former palaces, and fine public buildings confirms the favorable impression of its architectural grandeur. This view should be supplemented by one of a bird's-eye character to be obtained from the cupola of the Lutheran Church, which will more clearly reveal the several large squares and main arteries, bordered by graceful lime-trees, thus completing a knowledge of its topography.

In spite of its misfortunes, Warsaw ranks to-day as the third city in importance as well as in population in the Russian empire. It was not made the capital of Poland until 1566, when it succeeded to Cracow. It is now but the residence of a viceroy representing the Emperor of Russia. The town is heavily garrisoned by the soldiers of the Tzar; indeed, they are seen in goodly numbers in every town and village of any importance, and are represented even at the small railroad stations on the line from Moscow. War and devastation have deprived the city of many of its national and patriotic monuments, but its squares are still ornamented with numerous admirable statues, and with a grand array of fine public buildings. In the square of the Royal Castle there was observed a colossal bronze statue of Sigismund III.; in another quarter a bronze statue of Copernicus was found. It will be remembered that he was a Pole by birth and was educated at Cracow, his name being Latinized from Kopernik. There is a thirteenth-century cathedral close by, whose pure Gothic contrasts strongly with the Tartar style so lately left behind in middle Russia. This old church was very gray and crumbling, very dirty, and very offensive to the sense of smell,— partly accounted for by obvious causes, since about the doors, both inside and out, swarmed a vile-smelling horde of ragged men, women, and children, sad and pitiful to look upon.

The square close at hand has more than once been the scene of popular demonstrations which have baptized it in the life-blood of the citizens. The finest public buildings and elegant residences were found strangely mingled with wooden hovels; magnificence and squalor are located side by side, inexorably jumbled together. We remember no other city in all Europe which has so many private palaces and patrician mansions as may be seen in an hour's stroll about Warsaw; but it must be admitted that the architecture is often gaudy and meretricious. Here for centuries there were but two grades of society; namely, the nobles and the peasants. Intermediate class there was none. A Polish noble was by law a person who possessed a freehold estate, and who could prove his descent from ancestors formerly possessing a freehold, who followed no trade or commerce, and who was at liberty to choose his own habitation. This description, therefore, included all persons who were above the rank of burghers or peasants. The despised Jews were never considered in the social scale at all, and were looked upon by both nobles and peasants as a necessary evil contingent upon trade. They were not even subject to military service until the Russians assumed power. Now the Jews enter in large numbers into the service of the Tzar, especially as musicians forming the military bands. Being intelligent and to a certain degree educated, they are also employed in places where recruits only fit for service in the lower ranks would not be trusted, and we were told that they make excellent common soldiers.

Where the great iron bridge which spans the Vistula joins the shore on the right bank, one comes upon the barracks of the Circassian troops who form a portion of the local garrison. Here we chanced to witness some of their peculiar cavalry drill, where, among other manœuvres, the exercise of dashing towards an object placed upon the ground and catching it up on the point of the sword or lance while the rider is at full speed, was practised. These soldiers are most efficient as cavalry, being what is termed born horsemen. Russians, Circassians, and other Eastern troops garrison Warsaw, while Polish soldiers are sent elsewhere for good and sufficient political reasons. The support of the entire scheme of power in Russia, as in Germany and Austria, turns upon military organization and efficiency; hence this element crops out everywhere, and its ramifications permeate all classes in Warsaw, as at St. Petersburg or Berlin.

In passing through Poland the country presents to the eye of the traveller almost one unbroken plain, admirably adapted to agriculture, so much so that it has long been called the granary of Europe. The Polish peasants are extremely ignorant, if possible even more so than the same class in Russia proper; but they are a fine-looking race, strongly built, tall, active, and well-formed. There are schools in the various districts, but the Polish language is forbidden to be taught in them; only the Russian tongue is permitted. The peasantry have pride enough to resist this in the only way which is open to them; namely, by keeping their children from attending the schools. Therefore, education not being compulsory, as it is in Norway and Sweden, little benefit is derived from the common-school system as here sustained. With a view utterly to abolish the Polish language, it is even made a penal offence to use it in commercial transactions.

The Polish peasantry as a whole are by no means a prepossessing race. Naturally dull, they are still more demoralized and degraded by an unconquerable love of intoxicants, the dram being unfortunately both cheap and potent. In every village and settlement, no matter how small, there are always Jews who are ready and eager to administer to this base appetite, and to rob the poor ignorant people of both health and money. It is unpleasant to speak harshly of the Jewish race, especially as we know personally some highly cultured, responsible, and eminently respectable men who form a decided exception to the general rule; but the despised and wandering children of Israel, wherever we have met them, certainly appear to exercise an evil influence upon the people among whom they dwell. We record the fact with some hesitation, but with a strong sense of conviction. Poland appears to be after Palestine a sort of Land of Promise to the Jews; but they are certainly here, if nowhere else, a terrible scourge upon the native race. Their special part of the town — the Jews' Quarter — is a mass of filth, so disgusting, so ill-smelling, that one would think it must surely breed all sorts of contagious diseases; but here they live on in unwholesome dens, amid undrained, narrow streets and lanes, often in almost roofless tenements. Bayard Taylor wrote of the Polish Jews: "A more vile and filthy race, except the Chinese, cannot disgust the traveller." Here, as in other parts of the world, the Hebrew people have a history full of vicissitudes, and are composed of various tribes, Galician, Moldavian, Hungarian, and native Polish; but in their general characteristics they are identical, being universally wedded to filth and greed. While they are strangely interesting as a study they are never attractive, with their cringing, servile manners and dirty gabardines, their cadaverous faces, piercing black eyes, their hooked noses and ringleted locks. Wherever met they are keen-witted, avaricious, patient, frugal, long-suffering. The race is now banished from what is known as Great Russia, and so far as Government is concerned is barely tolerated in Russian Poland; but to drive them hence would be to decimate the country in population.

The present political condition of Poland is the more impressive, as we remember that she was a great civil power when Russia was little better than semi-barbarous. Now neither books nor papers are permitted to be published in the native tongue, and all volumes printed in the Polish language are confiscated wherever found, even in private libraries. The public library of Warsaw, which contained some hundred and sixty thousand bound volumes, was conveyed to St. Petersburg long ago, and Polish literature may virtually be said to be suppressed. While becoming conversant with these facts, it was natural as an American that we should speak plainly of the outrageous character of such arbitrary rule. The intelligent and courteous Russian with whom we were conversing could not see why it was any worse for his Government to claim possession and direction of Poland than it was for England to do the same in the instance of Ireland. This was a style of arguing which it was not very easy to meet. "It became a political necessity for us to take our portion of Poland and to govern it," said the gentleman to whom we refer, " but she is far more of a burden than an advantage to Russia. Only the common people of this country — the masses — have been really benefited by the present state of affairs."

The "Avenues" is the popular drive and promenade of the citizens of Warsaw, bordered by long lines of trees and surrounded on all sides by elegant private residences. Here also are located inviting public gardens where popular entertainments are presented, and where cafés dispense ices, favorite drinks, and refreshments of all sorts. The well-arranged Botanical Gardens are not far away, affording a very pleasing resort for all lovers of floral beauty. Just beyond these gardens comes the Lazienki

Park, containing the suburban palace built by King Stanislaus Poniatowski in the middle of the last century, and which is now the temporary residence of the Emperor of Russia when he visits Warsaw. The grounds occupied by the Park are very spacious, affording great seclusion and deep shady drives; for though it so closely adjoins the city, it has the effect of a wild forest composed of ancient trees. The royal villa stands in the midst of a stately grove, surrounded by graceful fountains, tiny lakes, and delightful flower gardens. There is a fine array in summer of tropical plants in tubs and many groups of marble statuary, more remarkable for extravagance of design than for artistic excellence, if we except the statue of King John Sobieski. Adjoining the Park is that of the Belvidere Palace, formerly the residence of the Grand Duke Constantine; but the place is now quite deserted, though everything is kept in exquisite order.

Most of the city houses are built of brick or stone, the former being stuccoed so as to give the general effect of the latter. The churches are numerous and fine. It may be said, indeed, that the public buildings throughout the city are on a grand scale. The two principal streets are Honey Street and that of the New World, so called. There are a plenty of hotels, but mostly of a very inferior character, several being kept in what were once palaces, generally by Germans or some other foreigners, never by Poles. The people whom one meets upon the streets seem to be more Asiatic in their features and general aspect than the residents of St. Petersburg, showing clearly their Tartar descent; but in manners, customs, and dress they are much more European than the Russians.

There are several large open squares in Warsaw where provision markets are held daily by the country people, but especially in the early morning and forenoon. The principal one is located near the Saxony Gardens, the trade of which is entirely conducted by women; and so varied is the business here that it partakes of the character of a public fair rather than that of a provision market. Vegetables, flowers, fruit, fish, poultry, tools, clothing, toys, domestic utensils, boots, shoes, and articles of female attire, all enter into the objects collected and offered for sale. The women are mostly of Jewish extraction, a large number of the middle-aged wearing wigs, under which their natural hair was cut short. On inquiry it was found that this is an old Jewish custom with women of that race in Poland,—that is, as soon as they are married to shave their heads and wear false hair, a practice which we have never observed elsewhere, and which is not followed here by the more pretentious families of the Hebrew population. The market square adjoining the Saxony Gardens affords a highly picturesque sight, where the mingling of colors, races, and costumes is curious to study. In the gardens we have one of the most attractive and oldest city parks in Europe, where the trees are very large and of great variety, while the flowers which adorn the grounds on all sides, mingled with artificial ponds and fountains, delight the eye and regale the senses. We have all heard of the Saxony Gardens of Warsaw, but we have never heard them overpraised. A military band performs here night and morning during the summer season, while mineral waters — a specialty here — are freely drunk by the promenaders, recalling familiar scenes at Saratoga.

The city to the practical eye of an American seemed to be commercially in a state of more rapid growth and prosperity than any capital which has been treated of in these pages. In matters of current business and industrial affairs it appeared far in advance of St. Petersburg. The large number of distilleries and breweries was unpleasantly suggestive of the intemperate habits of the people. The political division of Poland which we have incidentally spoken of was undoubtedly a great outrage on the part of the three powers who confiscated her territory, but the author is satisfied, while writing here upon the spot, and after careful consideration, that this radical change was a good thing for the people at large. With what has seemed to be the bitter fortune of Poland we have all of us in America been taught from childhood to sympathize to such an extent that romance and sentiment have in a degree prevailed over fact, blinding cooler judgment. There are those who see in the fate of Poland that retributive justice which Heaven accords to nations as well as to individuals. In past ages she has been a country always savagely aggressive upon her neighbors, and it was not until she was sadly torn and weakened by internal dissensions that Catherine II. first invaded her territory. Nine tenths of the population were no better than slaves. They were in much the same condition as the serfs of Russia before the late emancipation took place. They were acknowledged retainers, owing their service to and holding their farms at the option of the upper class; namely, the so-called nobility of the country. This overmastering class prided itself upon neither promoting nor being engaged in any kind of business; indeed, this uselessness was one of the conditions attached to its patent of nobility. These autocratic rulers knew no other interest or occupation than that of the sword. War and devastation constituted their profession, while the common people for ages reaped the fruit of famine and slaughter. Even in what were called days of peace, the court and the nobles spent their time in vile intrigues and bloody quarrels. However hard these reflections may seem, they are fully sustained by the history of the country, and are frankly admitted to be true by intelligent natives of Warsaw to-day.

There is no denying the fact, leaving the question of right and justice quite out of the discussion, that the breaking up of Poland politically has brought about a degree of peace, wealth, prosperity, and comparative liberty such as the masses of the people of this so long distracted land have not known for centuries.

That there is shameful despotism exercised by the ruling powers all must admit; but there is also peace, individual liberty, and great commercial prosperity. In the days which are popularly denominated those of Polish independence, the nobility were always divided into bitter factions. Revolutions were as frequent as they are in Spain, Mexico, or South America to-day, the strongest party for the time being disposing of the crown and ruling the country amid tumult and bloodshed.

"The class who so long misruled Poland are now powerless," said a native resident of Warsaw to us. "The sacrifice of our political nationality has been indeed a bitter experience; but it has at least given the country a breathing spell, and the rank and file of the people a chance to recuperate their fallen fortunes. We had become impoverished by internal dissensions and endless conflicts abroad; now we enjoy peace and material prosperity. If the matter depended upon a popular vote as exercised in America," he added, "there would be found only a designing few who would vote for a restoration of the old régime." The gentleman whom we have quoted belonged to thé mercantile class, and was native born; therefore we think his words may be taken as reflecting the average sentiment of the citizens of Warsaw.

Let us not forget in these closing pages to speak of the Polish ladies. They are almost universally handsome, with large expressive eyes, dark and deep as the Norwegian fjords, lighting up faces full of tenderness and sympathy. They are generally more accomplished in what is considered womanly culture among the better classes than are the ladies of Southern Europe, being almost universally good musicians and fine vocalists, as well as possessing a natural gift of languages. In secret these daughters of Poland are extremely patriotic, though the public expression of such sentiments is hardly admissible under the circumstances. It is not surprising that they should regret the loss of a condition of society which made them all princesses, so to speak. The representatives of this class are little seen in public, very many having removed to Paris, where they constitute a large and permanent colony. When encountered here, they are vehemently earnest as to patriotism, and ready to encourage any extravagant measure looking towards a possible restitution of Polish nationality.

A fellow traveller between Warsaw and Vienna, in responding to a casual remark touching the extraordinary beauty of the Polish ladies, — "ladies whose bright eyes rain influence," — told the author of a gallant friend's experience with the gentler sex of several nationalities. It seems that the person referred to lost his heart in Germany, his soul in France, his understanding in Italy, and was made bankrupt of his senses in Poland. When his affections were thus reduced to a complete wreck, the gentleman settled down to matrimonial felicity in Russia! Some of the

Jewish women of Warsaw, of the wealthier class, are extremely handsome, so marked in this respect that it was a pleasure to look at them. Many of the race are blondes of the most decided stamp. Unlike Parisian, London, or Vienna beauties, their charms are all quite natural. They require no rouge to heighten the color of their glowing complexions, no shading of the eyes, no dyeing of the hair, no falsifying of the figure, no padding. These Jewesses are beholden to Nature alone for their charms of person.

The Polish language as spoken by the people of Warsaw is indeed a puzzle to a stranger, being a sort of Slavic-Indo-European tongue. When Poland enjoyed a distinctive nationality, no less than six different dialects were spoken in the several provinces of the kingdom. There is so much similarity, however, between the Polish language proper and the Russian tongue that the people of the two nationalities easily understand each other, and on the borders there is a singular conglomerate of the two tongues spoken by the peasantry. Until towards the close of the eighteenth century, the Polish historians wrote almost exclusively in the Latin language, and her poets also expressed themselves in that classic medium; hence the paucity of Polish literature. As already intimated, the German and Russian languages are spreading over the country, and will eventually obliterate the native tongue without the enforcement of arbitrary measures on the part of the dominant powers.

Commercially, Warsaw seems destined to a steady growth and prosperity; but in the higher paths of civilization as evinced by mental culture, the growth and dissemination of scientific knowledge, and the general education of the masses, it is and must remain for a long time to come far behind the much more inviting and interesting capitals of Scandinavia.